LEADERS OF RUSSIA
AND THE SOVIET UNION

LEADERS OF RUSSIA AND THE SOVIET UNION

From the Romanov Dynasty to Vladimir Putin

JOHN PAXTON

Fitzroy Dearborn

An Imprint of the Taylor & Francis Group
New York • London

Cover photo: Josef Stalin (right) and Vladimir Lenin (left), 1922. Library of Congress, Prints and Photographs Division, LC-USZ62-111092.

The photograph is widely held to be a fake from two different sources, crudely joined in an effort to bolster Stalin's position during Lenin's illness in 1922.

Published in 2004 by

Fitzroy Dearborn
An imprint of the Taylor & Francis Group
29 West 35th Street
New York, NY 10001-2299
www.routledge-ny.com

Published in Great Britain by
Fitzroy Dearborn
An imprint of the Taylor & Francis Group
11 New Fetter Lane
London EC4P 4EE
www.routledge.co.uk

10 9 8 7 6 5 4 3 2 1

Typeset by: Compset, Inc.
Printed by: Edwards Brothers
Cover design by: Elise Weinger.

Library of Congress Cataloging-in-Publication Data

Paxton, John.
    Leaders of Russia and the Soviet Union: from the Romanov dynasty to
Vladimir Putin / John Paxton.
        p. cm.
Includes bibliographical references and index.
    ISBN 1-57958-132-3 (alk. paper)
    1. Russia—History.   2. Soviet Union—History.   3. Russia (Federation)—History.
    4. Russia—Kings and rulers—Biography.   5. Heads of State—Soviet Union—
Biography.   6. Presidents—Russia (Federation)—Biography.   I. Title.
DK40.P36 2004
947'.009'9—dc22   2003025361

This, my last book, is dedicated to all those who have helped me for over fifty years—typists, researchers, co-authors, copy editors, proofreaders and indexers, but above all to Joan for constant encouragement.

CONTENTS

PREFACE

Leaders of Russia and the Soviet Union: From the Romanov Dynasty to Vladimir Putin provides succinct biographies of leaders from the election of the first Romanov, Michael, in 1613 to President Vladimir Putin. It highlights how their influence was great, disastrous, or purely negative. It does not aim to be a history of Russia. There are some leaders who ruled for long periods such as Peter I (the Great) and Catherine II (the Great) who engineered enormous changes and some such as Lenin and Stalin who changed Russia completely. Some tsars only lasted a very short time and achieved little but have been included to show historical continuity; Ivan V is an example.

The aim is to give a useful reference tool for students, researchers, historians, as well as Russian history enthusiasts. A glossary of terms and a general chronology are aimed to help the reader, as is a select list of further reading.

As readers and writers know, transliteration problems arise in any book on Russia. I used the Library of Congress transliteration system, but it was necessary to break the rules from time to time. Certain forms, such as "Alexei Sergeyevich," do not belong to the Library of Congress or to the British Standard schemes. Instead, they usually trace back to the idiosyncratic schemes of early translators who mixed equivalents, such as "Alexis," with transliterations. I have used English forms for such people as "Catherine II (the Great)," and such places as "Moscow."

Dates also present confusion because until 1918, the Julian rather than the Gregorian calendar was used in Russia. Consequently, dates determined by the Julian calendar are twelve days behind the Gregorian calendar in the nineteenth century and thirteen days behind in the twentieth century. When Russia adopted the Gregorian system, the Julian date January 31 became Gregorian date February 14. In this book I have used the Old Style, except for external events, where I have used New Style throughout.

I have to thank the London Library, as usual, for much help and for their vast range of Russian titles, and the British Embassy in Moscow for help on particular questions. I also thank Penny White for her usual meticulous typing and Dione Daffin who tackled the computer with courage to the shame of the author who lives in the world of the quill.

Every effort has been made to trace all copyright holders but if any has been inadvertently overlooked, the author and publishers will be pleased to make the necessary arrangement at the first opportunity.

If errors are found they are my own and I shall be pleased, although sad at the time, to be alerted so that they can be corrected for future editions.

John Paxton
Bruton, Somerset, England
September 2003

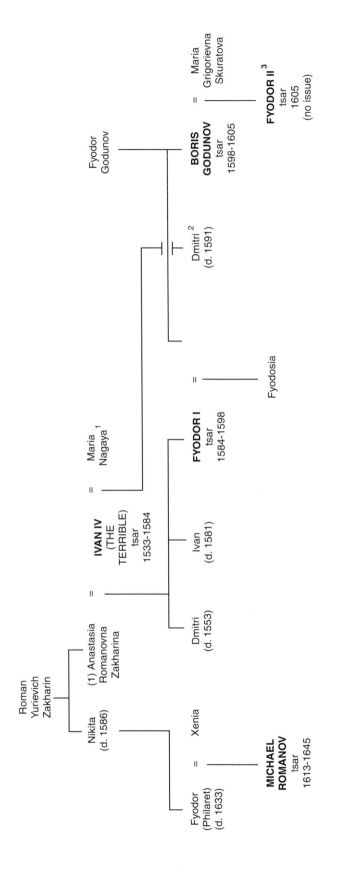

Roman
Yurievich
Zakharin

Nikita
(d. 1586)

(1) Anastasia
Romanovna
Zakharina

=

IVAN IV
(THE
TERRIBLE)
tsar
1533-1584

=

Maria
Nagaya [1]

Fyodor
Godunov

Fyodor
(Philaret)
(d. 1633)

=

Xenia

Dmitri
(d. 1553)

Ivan
(d. 1581)

FYODOR I
tsar
1584-1598

=

Dmitri [2]
(d. 1591)

BORIS
GODUNOV
tsar
1598-1605

=

Maria
Grigorievna
Skuratova

MICHAEL
ROMANOV
tsar
1613-1645

Fyodosia

FYODOR II [3]
tsar
1605
(no issue)

[1] Seventh wife of Ivan IV.
[2] Murdered at Uglich on May 15, 1591.
[3] Murdered at Moscow on June 1, 1605.

Succession from Ivan IV (1533) to Michael (1613).

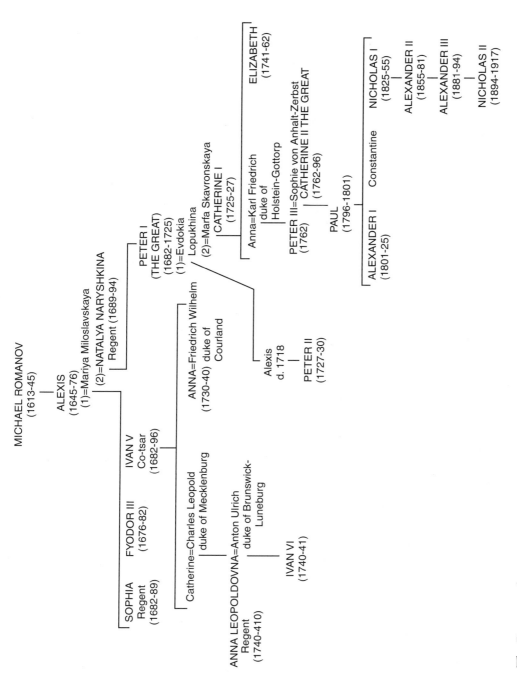

The Romanov dynasty.

INTRODUCTION

Leaders of Russia and the Soviet Union: From the Romanov Dynasty to Vladimir Putin is a reference book covering the period from the seventeenth century to the present day. The year 1613 is one of the many watersheds in Russian history and marks the end of the Time of Troubles. It also is the beginning of the reign of the Romanovs with the election of Michael as tsar.

The Time of Troubles was a period in Russian history between the extinction of the Rurik dynasty in 1598 and the establishment of the house of Romanov in 1613. During this time there were five tsars in Moscow whose claims were dubious (including an imposter and a Polish prince), Polish and Swedish invasions, and widespread popular and Cossack unrest. It ended with the expulsion of the Poles from Moscow by patriotic volunteers and the election of Tsar Michael Romanov, the dynasty who would rule Russia for the next three hundred years.

Michael's father, Patriarch Philaret (1553?–1633), known in secular circles as Fyodor Nikitich Romanov, was a successful soldier and diplomat. Compelled to take monastic vows by Boris Godunov, he was released by the first False Dmitri and made metropolitan of Rostov in 1606. In 1609 the second False Dmitri made him Patriarch of All Russia. He was arrested and sent to Poland in 1611. After his son Michael was elected tsar, he returned to Moscow, where he became one of the leaders in the national revival of 1612–1613, and was enthroned as patriarch in 1619.

So from 1613 until the abdication of Nicholas II in 1917, there were three hundred years of Romanovs on the Russian throne. The contrast in the personalities and abilities of these autocrats is the most astonishing aspect of this reference book. It has been said that successful absolutism depends upon the intelligence, energy, and charisma of the monarch himself. The length of the reigns is also varied and includes a number of assassinations. Succession was part of the problem and was only solved in 1797 when Tsar Paul issued a new law that provided for the succession to the throne according to primogeniture in the male line and also ruled that the successor should be of the Orthodox faith.

The stars of the Romanov era were Peter I (the Great), Catherine II (the Great), and Alexander II for his emancipation of the serfs.

Obviously, Lenin and Stalin dominate the political, economic, and social changes that took place when we move into the Soviet period. If Lenin had lived a little longer, it is possible that Stalin would not have been his successor.

In the latter part of the twentieth century the architects of change were Khrushchev, Gorbachev, and Yeltsin. Few would have predicted the end of the Soviet Union twenty years ago but it is too early to judge what contribution Vladimir Putin will make to the Russian Federation.

I

MICHAEL

Mikhail Fedorovich Romanov, July 12, 1596–July 13, 1645.

Tsar of Russia 1613–1645.

Michael's father, Fyodor Nikitich Romanov, was banished, together with his family, by Boris Godunov, and he was forced to become a monk under the name of Philaret (*see* p. xiii). Later he was to become patriarch of Moscow and also co-tsar with Michael (1618–1633).

By the time the election of a new tsar took place, most of the leading boyar families had discredited themselves in the struggle for power that had been in progress since 1584: in that struggle the Romanovs had figured as martyrs, owing to their persecution by Boris Godunov. Before his accession to the throne Michael lived with his mother on the family estate of the Romanovs in the village of Domnina. In his seventeenth year he was pale, nervous, and pious and the boyars who supported his candidature are said to have imposed limitations on the tsar's power. Michael was elected Sovereign of All Russia by a *zemsky sobor* (Assembly of the Land) in Red Square, Moscow on February 21, 1613, and consecrated Tsar on July 11, in the Dormition Cathedral of the Kremlin. His freedom of action was restricted from the outset by the fact that he owed his position on the throne to election, and the frequency with which he consulted the zemsky sobor (sixteen times in his reign) on major questions of policy shows that he felt the need of national support. The fact that in 1625 he adopted the title of autocrat could have had no great significance. In 1624 Michael married Maria Vladimirovna Dolgorukaya, member of another prominent boyar family, and on her early death he took as his second wife Evdokia Lukianovna Streshneva, daughter of a small landowner, who became the mother of his heir Alexis.

With limited ability, Michael at first leaned on favorites, but in 1618 his father, Patriarch Philaret, became his principal adviser, with the titles of co-tsar and of "Great Sovereign." The new régime was faced with formidable tasks.

In 1613 the treasury coffers were empty, and measures for restoring the financial position of the state played an important part in Michael's legislation. They included a reassessment of the basis of taxation that, by tending to tie the peasants to the land, powerfully reinforced the development of serfdom.

Michael resumed relations with foreign states and carried on diplomatic relations with the courts of central and eastern Europe. A plan he formed for marrying his daughter to Prince Valdemar of Denmark broke down because of Valdemar's refusal to join the Orthodox Church—although he had been given reassurance that this was not necessary. Great attention was paid to the development of Siberia and of the trade routes down the Volga to the Caspian Sea and Persia. He produced other reforms particularly in the Russian army. The southern borders were steadily pushed out over the steppe by the foundation of new towns, joined by defensive lines.

Russia was exceedingly weak after the "Time of Troubles," and both Sweden and Poland claimed Russian territories; Sweden claimed land to the northwest, and Poland claimed Smolensk and large stretches of land to the west. Towards the end of the reign a force of Don Cossacks seized and offered to the tsar the fortress of Azov, a Turkish possession. The Cossacks had withstood a siege of four months but felt that they could not hold on. Michael referred the offer to a zemsky sobor, which refused it on the ground that there was no money for a war with Turkey, and the acceptance of Azov would have involved a war.

Michael died on July 13, 1645, having named Alexis as his heir, and was buried in the Archangel Cathedral of the Kremlin in Moscow.

CHRONOLOGY

1613   The *zemsky sobor* elect Michael Romanov as tsar and he is crowned by Metropolitan Cyril in Moscow (February 21). Philaret, father of the tsar, is taken prisoner.

1618   Philaret Romanov, father of the tsar, is freed by the Poles and is elected patriarch and shares power with his son. Under Philaret's influence, from 1622 to 1633, the role of the *zemsky sobor* is gradually reduced.

1624   Marriage of Michael to the princess Maria Vladimirovna Dolgorukaya, who died in 1625.

1625   Michael marries Evdoxia Lukianovna Streshneva, who dies in 1645.

1633   Philaret dies. Michael Romanov restores power to the *zemsky sobor* convoking it during crises.

1645   Michael dies, and his eldest son, Alexis, succeeds him. The accession to the throne is confirmed by a vote of the *zemsky sobor* (July 13).

BIBLIOGRAPHY

Dukes, P. *The Making of Russian Absolutism 1613–1801.* 1990.

2

ALEXIS

Alexis Mikhailovich Romanov, March 9, 1629–January 30, 1676.

Tsar of Muscovy 1645–1676.

Son of Michael, first tsar of the house of Romanov, and father of Peter I (the Great). Alexis Mikhailovich was consecrated tsar on July 16, 1645, after the death of his father. He was one of the most educated men of his time and wrote and edited many important decrees and documents. Called "Tishaishii" (the Quietist), because of his piousness and good nature, he delighted in field sports, particularly falconry, and wrote a technical manual on the subject. He also enjoyed practical jokes and also often lost his temper. Alexis was married twice: from 1648 to 1669 to Maria Ilinishna Miloslavskaya (1626–1669), and from 1671 to 1676 to Natalia Kirillovna Naryshkina (1651–1694). There was a total of twenty-one children from both marriages.

This was a period of change for Russia in the seventeenth century when the medieval period was beginning to fade. A group of Russians at the tsar's court became the first "Westernizers" and Alexis chose his advisers, Morozov, Afanasy Lavrentievich Ordin-Nashchokin (1605?–1680) and Artamon Sergeyevich Matveyev (1625–1682) from this group. Boris Ivanovich Morozov (1590–1662) was tutor and, after 1648, brother-in-law of Tsar Alexis of Russia. Alexis was dependent on advisers in the early part of his reign and Morozov directed the affairs of state at the beginning of Alexis's reign in 1645. He was keen on Western culture and encouraged Alexis to wear Western clothing. Morozov was hated by the populace, having cut government salaries, and this reached a peak when he increased the salt tax in 1646, which caused severe unrest in Moscow in 1648 and further disturbances in Novgorod and Pskov in 1650. Morozov was temporarily sent into protective exile and never regained his former power.

Following the "salt rebellion," Alexis called a meeting of the Assembly of the Land and they elected a commission that drew up a new legal code, the *Ulozhenie* of 1649. Measures included severe punishments for anyone challenging the political or religious order. It finalized the process of serfdom including the period in which fugitive peasants could be returned to their masters, which became indefinite. Merchants and craftsmen were bound to their towns. Traveling abroad was not permitted except with permission of the tsar. Some restrictions were placed on the church; it could not acquire additional land and a Monastery Department was formed to oversee church estates.

The movement toward change met with strong disapproval from many people, particularly when it seemed to be spreading to the sphere of religion and undermining the foundations of the true Orthodox faith. The development of printing meant that it was essential to have authoritative versions of texts and saw the introduction in 1653–1654 of a revised version of the church service books, and of certain small reforms in ritual observance, which merely corrected distortions that had crept in during the Middle Ages. This was the signal for a mass protest that led to the great schism in the Russian church. All non-Orthodox foreigners had to live outside the walls of Moscow; this area became known as the German quarter.

In 1652 Alexis was responsible for the appointment of Metropolitan Nikon of Novgorod to the patriarchate. Nikon was a known supporter of reform but was opposed to some of the measures affecting the church in the Ulozhenie. He was, however, insistent that the Russian church should conform to Greek Orthodox rituals. This brought him into conflict with many, including Archpriest Avvakum. Some of the issues included the correct spelling of the name Jesus and whether the sign of the cross should be made with two or three fingers. This dispute led to a schism and a separate church was formed in defiance of the patriarch and the tsar. These "Old Believers" or

Schismatics were vigorously persecuted and suffered exile, long imprisonment, or death.

Nikon surrounded himself with much pomp. He assumed the title of "Great Sovereign" creating the impression that Moscow had two tsars. In 1658 Alexis forbade Nikon to use this title. Nikon refused to perform his official duties and withdrew to a nearby monastery. Eventually, in 1666, he was brought to trial—Alexis having persuaded the patriarchs of Antioch and Alexandria to be present—and Nikon lost his office and was reduced to the rank of an ordinary monk. This ended a trial of strength between church and state.

External affairs saw the acquisition of the Ukraine. The people of the Ukraine had revolted against Polish rule and in 1653 offered their allegiance to Tsar Alexis. War was the result because the king of Poland could not accept the loss of this important possession. The war from 1654 to 1667 ended with Moscow, under the Treaty of Andrusovo, gaining all the territory east of the river Dnieper and the city of Kiev on its right bank; it also regained Smolensk, which had been held by Poland after "The Time of Troubles."

To finance the wars Alexis debased the currency by using copper instead of silver for coins. This caused an uprising, known as the "copper rebellion" in Moscow in 1662. Many died as a result and in 1663 a decree reestablished the silver currency and copper coins were melted down.

The war with Poland brought Muscovy into conflict with Sweden but under the Treaty of Cardis of June 1661, Muscovy surrendered all the land that it had conquered from Sweden.

Soon after the signing of the Treaty of Andrusovo in 1667 the most serious of many revolts took place in southeastern Russia led by the cossack leader Stenka Timofeyevich Razin (?–1671) in 1670–1671. Stenka Razin captured the whole of the central and lower courses of the river Volga. Many members of the upper classes were massacred, however, the soldiers and peasants welcomed him. By the time Stenka Razin reached Simbirsk his army was 200,000 strong. It was, however, defeated by Muscovite troops. Stenka Razin escaped but in 1671 was captured and executed.

Samuel Collins, who was physician to Alexis in Moscow in the early 1660s, wrote in his *The Present State of Russia* published in London in 1671, "without doubt this present Emperour of Russia is as pious, conscientious, clement, merciful and good a Prince as any in the world. As for his People and Ministers of State, they are like other Nations, ready to act anything for Bribes or Money, and to deceive as many as they can."

Without doubt this present Emperour of Russia is as pious, conscientious, clement, merciful and good a Prince as any in the world.

Alexis died in 1676 and was buried in the Archangel Cathedral of the Kremlin in Moscow.

CHRONOLOGY

1629	Alexis born (March 9).
1645	Morozov, Alexis's former tutor, exercises a *de facto* regency.
1648	Alexis marries Maria Ilinishna Miloslavskaya (dies 1669).
1670–1671	Uprising of Stenka Razin who together with fugitive serfs and others savages Ukraine and Southern Russia.
1671	Alexis marries Natalia Kirillovna Naryshkina. Stenka Razin executed.
1676	Alexis dies (January 30) and is buried in the Archangel Cathedral of the Kremlin, Moscow.

BIBLIOGRAPHY

Avrich, P. *Russian Rebels 1600–1800.* 1972.

Baron, S. H. *Muscovite Russia.* 1980.

Collins, S. *The Present State of Russia.* 1671.

Field, C. *The Great Cossack. The Rebellion of Stenk'ka Razin against Alexis Michaelovitch.* 1947.

Longworth, P. *Alexis: Tsar of All the Russias.* 1984.

Palmer, W. *The Patriarch and the Tsar.* 1871–76.

3
FYODOR III

Fyodor Alexeyevich Romanov, May 30, 1661–April 27, 1682.

Tsar of Russia 1676–1682.

Fyodor was the son of Alexis's first wife, Maria Miloslavskaya, and the throne was dominated by his mother's relatives. He came to the throne at the age of fourteen and a struggle began between the rival Naryshkins, relatives of Alexis's second wife, and Miloslavsky families. The Naryshkins were exiled but when Fyodor died, at the age of twenty, the Naryshkins wanted to place Peter, his half-brother on the throne instead of Fyodor's full brother, Ivan. The *streltsy*, a hereditary military caste, revolted and installed Ivan's sister Sophia as regent.

Fyodor endeavored to modernize the government of the country and this included the abolition of *mestnichestvo*, the system by which appointment of court officials, ambassadors, and army officials depended upon inherited rank and status. Records of genealogical tables were burned in 1682, thus abolishing mestnichestvo. The abolition was inspired by Vasily Golitsyn (1643–1714) who was appointed by Fyodor. Fyodor was instrumental in gaining freedom for the ex-patriarch Nikon in 1680 who died on the homeward journey from the northern monastery where he had been in exile.

When Fyodor acceded to the throne, his chief adviser was Artamon Sergeyevich Matveyev (1625–1682) who was, in 1654, chief of the streltsy, and head of the foreign department in 1671. Fyodor fell victim to intrigue and in 1674 he was exiled to Siberia but recalled to Moscow and pardoned in 1682 by Peter I (the Great).

Later in the reign Vasily Golitsyn became the most important member of the government.

During Fyodor's reign an attempt by the Ukraine to break away from Russia (1677–1681), with the help of Turkey, was foiled. The Treaty of Bakhchisarai (1681) brought the war with Turkey to an end. Muscovy retained Kiev and the Turks retained Podolia.

Fyodor and his brother Ivan were both invalids. In 1680 Fyodor married Agafia Grushevskaya who died the following year. In 1682 he married Marfa Apraxina (d. 1716). There was a child (Ilya) by the first wife, who was born and died in 1681. Fyodor died without designating an heir.

CHRONOLOGY

1661 Fyodor born (May 30).

1676 Fyodor III accedes to the throne.

1682 Fyodor III abolishes the *mestnichestvo.*

1682 Fyodor III dies (April 27).

BIBLIOGRAPHY

Grey, I. *The Romanovs: The Rise and Fall of a Russian Dynasty.* 1971.
Lincoln, W. B. *The Romanovs: Auctocrats of All the Russias.* 1981.

4

IVAN V

Ivan Alexeyevich Romanov, August 27, 1666–January 29, 1696.

Joint tsar with Peter I (the Great) 1682–1696.

Ivan was the son of Tsar Alexis and Alexis's first wife Maria Miloslavskaya. He was not expected to be heir to the throne, because of ill health and blindness. After the death of Fyodor III, he was, as eldest remaining son, considered by his mother's family, the Miloslavskys, the rightful heir. However, the Boyars' Duma voted for Ivan's half-brother, the ten-year-old Peter Alexeyevich, the future Peter I (the Great). Following a revolt by the *streltsy* (a hereditary military caste) which was encouraged by Sophia, the sister of Ivan, against the Naryshkin clan, Ivan was named as First Tsar and Peter as Second Tsar under the regency of Sophia. Both Ivan and Peter were consecrated tsar on June 25, 1682, at a joint coronation, believed to be unique in the history of European monarchies.

Because of ill health, Ivan V played no role in political affairs of state and devoted much of his time to prayer, fasting, and pilgrimages. He married Praskovia Feodorovna Saltykova, who died in 1723, and had five children, including the future Empress Anna Ivanovna. He died on January 29, 1696, and was buried in the Archangel Cathedral of the Kremlin in Moscow.

CHRONOLOGY

1666   Ivan V born (August 27).

1682   Consecrated tsar, jointly with Peter (June 25).

1696   Ivan V dies (January 29).

BIBLIOGRAPHY

O'Brien, C. B. *Russia under Two Tsars.* 1952.

5

SOPHIA

Sophia Alekseyevna, September 17, 1657–July 14, 1704.

Ruler of Russia 1682–1689.

Sophia was the daughter of Tsar Alexis and Maria Miloslavskaya. After the death of her brother Tsar Fyodor III in 1682, the successors to the throne were her feeble-minded and partially blind brother Ivan and her half-brother Peter, son of Alexis's second wife, Natalia Naryshkina (1651–1694). Initially Peter was declared Tsar, but after rioting on the part of the *streltsy* and much bloodshed, Peter and Ivan were declared joint tsars and Sophia was declared regent and thus was effectively the autocratic ruler of Russia. Her chief adviser and lover was Prince Vasily Golitsyn (1643–1714), who became foreign minister. She was extremely active in foreign and internal affairs.

In 1686 Russia concluded the "Eternal Peace" with Poland, confirming the truce of 1667, by which Russia gained Kiev and the territory east of the Dnieper River in exchange for a promise to join a European coalition against the Turks. Russia concluded the favorable Nerchinsk Treaty with China in 1689. This was a political and commercial agreement between Russia and China that also established boundaries between the two countries. The agreement gave Russia Transbaikalia (east of Lake Baikal) and gave China the Amur valley, and it permitted Russian trade caravans to enter Peking (modern day Beijing). The agreement was later enlarged in 1727 and remained the basis of Russo-Chinese relations until the mid-nineteenth century. There were two unsuccessful Crimean campaigns, led by Golitsyn, and these tended to undermine Sophia's authority.

At home Sophia was instrumental in the establishment of the Academy of Slavic, Greek, and Latin Studies. She encouraged foreigners to settle and gave permission for Dutch and Germans to establish a textile industry in Russia. She continued the harsh treatment meted out to Old Believers.

In 1689 Sophia plotted to depose Peter, aiming to become sole ruler. Peter was warned and fled to the fortified Troisky Monastery, contacting the commanders of the army to inform them of the situation. Peter was supported by the Moscow patriarch, by the majority of the nobles, and part of the streltsy. Golitsyn was deported and Sophia was kept in a convent and from that date until 1694 Peter's mother, Natalia Naryshkina, acted as regent. Ivan V died in 1696.

During Peter's Grand Embassy abroad in 1698 another attempt was made by Sophia's supporters to cause a rebellion.was suspected of knowing about the plot and, assuming the name Susanna, was imprisoned in the Cloister of Intercession in Suzdal where she died.

CHRONOLOGY

1657 Sophia born (September 17).

1682 Becomes regent (May 29).

1689 Overthrown by supporters of Peter I (the Great) and exiled to Novodevichy Monastery.

1698 Sophia forced to take the veil under the name of Susanna.

1704 Sophia dies (July 14).

BIBLIOGRAPHY

Hughes, L. *Sophia, Regent of Russia 1657–1704.* 1990.
O'Brien, C. B. *Russia under Two Tsars 1682–1689.* 1952.

6

PETER I (The Great)

Peter Alexeyevich Romanov, May 30, 1672–January 28, 1725.

Tsar of Russia 1682–1721 (sole ruler from 1696) and
Emperor of Russia 1721–1725.

Peter was the first emperor of Russia and youngest son of Tsar Alexis Mikhailovich. When Peter's half-brother Fyodor III died in 1682 without issue, the patriarch of Moscow and the leading boyars decided that Peter should be the tsar rather than his older, but handicapped, half-brother Ivan. Ivan's older sister Sophia, however, organized a coup by the palace guards which resulted in the coronation of Ivan and Peter as joint tsars, with the appointment of Sophia as regent. The next seven years Peter spent in a village near Moscow with his mother. Physically and mentally far in advance of his years, and receiving no systematic education, Peter picked up a mass of knowledge and technical skills, mainly from foreigners in Russian service who lived in a suburb nearby—particularly the Swiss Lefort, the Scotsman Patrick Gordon, and the Dutchman Franz Timmerman.

François Jacob Lefort (1653–1699) was a Swiss soldier who fought for the Russian army. He was a close friend of Peter I and had a considerable influence over him. It is thought that he suggested to Peter that he undertake foreign travels. He assisted in the reorganization of the army and the navy and was appointed a general and an admiral. In 1697 he headed the Grand Embassy.

Peter left nominal precedence to Ivan but in fact ruled the country himself following the resignation of Sophia as regent. Peter's first care on assuming the government was to form an army disciplined according to European tactics, in which task he was greatly aided by Gordon and Lefort. He also strove to create a navy and a merchant fleet. Peter, thinking the possession of a portion of the Black Sea would

Peter I. Portrait by Jean-Marc Nattier, 1717. The State Hermitage Museum, St Petersburg.

best supply the required facilities of accessible seaboard and port, declared war against Turkey and took the city of Azov after a long siege in 1696.

In 1697 Peter organized an embassy of 250 to visit Western Europe. He was, in fact, the first tsar to travel west except on a military campaign. J. Bouvet in *The Present Condition of the Muscovite Empire* (1699) wrote: "the motive which could induce so great a prince to leave for some time his native country cannot be attributed to any other cause than his most ardent desire of improving his own knowledge and that of his subjects, quite contrary to what has been practiced by his predecessors, who looked upon the ignorance of their subjects as the main foundation stone of their absolute power."

The Grand Embassy consisted of three ambassadors headed by François Lefort. It left Moscow on March 9, 1697, and over a period of eighteen months traveled through Sweden, Holland, and England at the invitation of King William III, and in the Hapsburg Empire. There were three main aims of the embassy: the first was to bring concerted action against Turkey by European states, the second was to obtain greater knowledge of shipbuilding, and the third was to recruit craftsmen and sailors. By 1698 Peter had recruited over 750 foreigners to work in Russia. Peter traveled with the embassy incognito as Pëtr Mikhailov and spent many months working as a craftsman in the docks of Amsterdam and then London, where he arrived in January 1698 with a squadron of the Royal Navy. He stayed in England for three and a half months. Although he travelled incognito, Peter dropped the disguise when it suited him.

John Evelyn (1620–1706), the English diarist, wrote in 1698, "The Tsar of Muscovy being come to England, and having a mind to see the building of ships, hir'd my house at Sayes Court, and made it his Court and Palace, new furnished for him by the King." While Peter was in his house Mr. Evelyn's servant wrote to him: "There is a house full of people, and right nasty. The Tsar lies next your Library, and dines in the parlour next your study. He dines at 10 o'clock and 6 at night, is very seldom at home a whole day, very often in the King's Yard, or by water, dressed in several dresses. The King is expected there this day, the best parlour is pretty clean for him to be entertained in. The King pays for all he has."

During his stay he did so much damage that Mr. Evelyn had an allowance of £150 for it. He particularly regretted the mischief done to his famous holly hedge, which might have been thought beyond the reach of damage. It is said that one of Peter's favorite recreations was to demolish the hedges by riding through them in a wheelbarrow.

Later the tsar went on to Vienna and met Emperor Leopold I but was unable to continue his journey to Venice and France because of the revolt of the *streltsy*. He was forced to return to Russia, but before he arrived General Gordon had already crushed the revolt. Peter's wife, Evdokia Feodorovna Lopukhina, was suspected of complicity in the plot. The marriage was repudiated and she was exiled to the Cloister of the Intercession in Suzdal.

In 1712 he married his mistress Catherine, who became Empress Catherine I. In 1717 Peter I made a second visit to Western Europe with the tsarina, visiting the Dutch Republic and France. In Paris Peter had meetings with the regent and with Louis XV in the Tuileries. Visits were also made to the Sorbonne, the Observatory, and the Opera. During this visit to Paris he recruited over sixty skilled technicians to work in Russia.

In the guise of an inferior official of the embassy he visited the three Baltic provinces, Prussia, and Hanover, reaching Amsterdam, where he worked for some time as a shipwright. To his other studies he added the study of astronomy, natural philosophy, geography, and even anatomy and surgery.

In 1700 Peter entered into an alliance with the kings of Poland and Denmark to make a combined attack on Sweden. Taking advantage of the Swedes being employed elsewhere he quietly appropriated a portion of Ingria. In 1703 Peter founded St. Petersburg, having captured the Swedish fortress of Nöteborg, situated where the river Neva flows out of Lake Ladoga and enters the Gulf of Finland. It became known as the "Window on the West." He established a church dedicated to the Apostles Peter and Paul, situated on the island of Saiatschie; the Neva divides at this point into the main streams of the delta. The strategic delta had been contested by German and Swedish forces since the thirteenth century. Thousands of workers joined in the task of building, including prisoners of war and criminals released from prison. Masons had no alternative but to work in St Petersburg because of a decree that allowed only wooden buildings to be built elsewhere in Russia. Every nobleman who owned thirty families of serfs was compelled to build a house, at his own expense, in the new city.

The Admiralty and shipyards were the first constructions but there were elaborate plans for such roads as Nevsky Prospekt, which was cut through the forests from the river Neva to the newly built monastery of St. Alexander Nevsky. (Alexander Nevsky defeated Sweden in 1240 and his bones are buried in the monastery.) Government buildings were built and continuous expansion was achieved by bridging the many channels of the river Neva and building on the islands. Members of the government as well as trading and skilled classes were obliged to live there. The city was proclaimed the capital of Russia in 1712.

In the long contest with Sweden, the Russians suffered a series of defeats, until Peter totally routed the Swedish king at the Battle of Poltava. It was fought on July 8, 1709, between Russian forces under Peter and Swedish forces under Charles XII during the Great Northern War for control of the Baltic. The Swedes had besieged the town of Poltava. The Russians set up a countersiege, which successfully drew the Swedish off and engaged them in conditions favorable to Russia. The Russian commander under Peter was General Prince Aleksandr Menshikov (1673–1729). A friend of Peter I whose reforms he influenced and helped, Menshikov later ruled

Russia during the reign of Catherine I and the minority of Peter II. The battle was immortalized by Pushkin in his epic poem *Poltava*. Charles XII escaped to Turkey, where he remained until 1714. Peter next prepared for war with the Turks, who at the instigation of Sweden had declared war against him. In this contest Peter lost his previous conquest, the port of Azov and the territory belonging to it.

The Treaty of Nystad was signed on September 10, 1721, concluding the Great Northern War (1720–1721) and the period of Sweden's military greatness. Sweden ceded to Russia Ingria, part of Karelia, Livonia (including Estonia), and several islands in the Baltic. Russia retained Vyborg but returned the rest of Finland to Sweden and paid Sweden an indemnity. In 1722 Peter commenced a war with Persia and compelled the shah to hand over the three Caspian provinces along with the towns of Derbent and Baku.

Peter introduced many reforms, the most important of which were the abolition of the Moscow patriarchy. When Patriarch Adrian died in 1700 he was not replaced and in 1721 Peter abolished the patriarchate and replaced it with a Holy Synod subordinated to the tsar. He reformed the central government, with the setting up of specialized government departments; he reformed provincial administration, with the appointment of provincial governors; he introduced a properly organized military and civil service open to any suitable person irrespective of origin; and he made financial reforms, including the introduction of a soul (poll or head) tax, which was a capitation tax paid by every male peasant and by urban artisans and burghers, in 1723. It became an important element of state revenue; in the meantime, the household tax and tax on cultivated land were abolished. Although this placed a considerable burden on the peasants it resulted in an increase in the area of land cultivated, since it was in a peasant's interest to cultivate as much as possible in order to pay the tax. The accumulation of arrears of the tax forced the government to lower the rate of tax in 1725, in 1742, and again in 1750–1758. Later it was increased again, reaching one ruble in 1794. It was finally abolished in 1887.

Peter I (the Great) had a great influence on education in the eighteenth century. A modernized Russian alphabet replaced church Slavonic. The School of Mathematics and Navigation was founded in Moscow (1699) and was soon followed by schools of engineering, artillery, and surgery. The Naval Academy of St. Petersburg was created in 1715 and the Academy of Sciences was founded in 1725. Education for the sons of the nobility was provided through the Corps of Pages, Cadets, and Midshipmen.

Other controversial reforms included the beard tax. In Muscovy beards were "essential to personal salvation" but the shaving of beards was begun by Peter after his return from the Grand Embassy.

Wishing to modernize Russia, Peter ordered that beards be shaven and Western dress adopted. For Peter the beard represented all that was backward and uncivilized in Russia.

Wishing to modernize Russia, Peter ordered that beards be shaven and Western dress adopted. For Peter the beard represented all that was backward and uncivilized in Russia. For the majority of Orthodox believers, however, the beard had a special religious significance, and they considered it shameful to shave their beards. At first all Russians except the clergy were ordered to shave. An article by N. Sokolov in *Raskol V Saratorskom Kraie* published in St. Petersburg 1888 reported that:

In 1700 a boyar was sent to Kamyshin, a town on the Volga, to instruct the governor and town officials to shave off their beards and dress in the new style. They obeyed and the boyar returned to the capital. Their compliance enraged a nearby settlement of cossack Old Believers who promptly attacked the town and sacked it. The governor escaped and hid on a nearby island while the cossacks cut the heads off anyone who had been so imprudent as to shave. Persons found wearing Western dress had their pockets filled with stones and were dropped into the Volga. Others were tied to tree trunks and similarly cast into the river to be used for target practice. The cossacks stayed on the rampage for six weeks—until the governor was eventually handed over.

Despite the fact that his beard had grown the cossacks still expressed a desire to kill him. They only spared his life when the entire population of Kamyshin interceded on his behalf. They finally withdrew under the threat of an advancing punitive force, having extracted from the townspeople an oath never to shave again.

After the end of the Northern War in 1721, Peter was proclaimed emperor. Tsar as a title comes from the Latin *Caesar* used by the rulers of Muscovy from the fifteenth century to Peter I (the Great), who adopted the title Emperor of all the Russias in 1721. However the title Tsar remained in popular usage during the imperial period. In 1722 Peter promulgated a new law of succession, which enjoined that each monarch should nominate his own successor, and also established the Table of Ranks that formed a hierarchy of fourteen ranks of civil, military, and court services.

Table of Ranks (1722):

	Civil	Navy	Army
1	Chancellor	General-Admiral	Generalissimo Field Marshal
2	Actual Privy Councillor	Admiral	General of Artillery General of Cavalry General of Infantry
3	Privy Councillor	Vice-Admiral	Lieutenant General
4	Actual State Councillor	Rear-Admiral	Major General
5	State Councillor	Captain-Commander	Brigadier
6	Collegiate Councillor	First Captain	Colonel
7	Court Councillor	Second Captain	Lieutenant Colonel

8	Collegiate Assessor	Lieutenant-Captain of the Fleet Third Captain of Artillery	Major
9	Titular Councillor	Lieutenant of the Fleet	Captain or Cavalry Captain
10	Collegiate Secretary	Lieutenant-Captain of Artillery	
11	Ship's Secretary	Lieutenant of Artillery	Staff Captain or Staff Cavalry Captain
12	Secretary in Superior Courts and in *guberniya* administration	Midshipman	Lieutenant
13	Provincial Secretary	Artillery Constable	Sublieutenant
14	Collegiate Registrar		Guidon Bearer

The Table of Ranks was used until 1917 although adaptations were made from time to time. Classes 1 and 2 were addressed as "Your Supreme Excellency," 3, 4 and 5 as "Your Excellency," and 6 to 14 as "Your Honor."

Peter added rules to the Table of Ranks to show how they should be interpreted. Important ones included:

Those princes who are related to Us by blood or those who are married to our princesses always take precedence and rank over all other princes and high servants of the Russian state.

Naval and land commanding officers are to be determined in the following manner: if they both are of the same rank, the naval officer is superior at sea to the land officer; and on land, the land officer is superior to the naval officer, regardless of the length of service each may have in his respective rank.

Whoever shall demand respect higher than is due his rank, or shall illegally assume a higher rank, shall lose two months of his salary; if he serves without salary then he shall pay a fine equal to the salary of his rank; one third of that fine shall be given to a hospital fund. The observance of this rank procedure does not apply on such occasions as meetings among friends or neighbors or at social gatherings, but only to churches, the Mass, Court ceremonies, ambassadorial audiences, official banquets, official meetings, christenings, marriages, funerals, and similar public gatherings. An individual will also be fined if he should make room for a person of lower rank. Tax collectors should watch carefully [for any signs of violations of these procedures] in order to encourage service [to the state] and to honor those already in service, and [at the same time] to collect fines from impudent individuals and parasites. The above prescribed fines are applicable to male and female transgressors.

An identical penalty will be given to anyone who will demand a rank without having an appropriate patent for his grade.

Equally, no one may assume a rank that has been acquired in the service of a foreign state until We approve it, an action which We shall do gladly in accordance with his service.

No one may be given a new rank without a release patent, unless We personally have signed that release.

All married women advance in ranks with their husbands, and if they should violate the order of procedure they must pay the same fines as would their husbands if they had violated it.

Although We allow free entry to public assemblies, wherever the Court is present, to the sons of princes, counts, barons, distinguished nobles, and high servants of the Russian state, either because of their births or because of the positions of their fathers, and although We wish to see that they are distinguished in every way from other [people], We nevertheless do not grant any rank to anyone until he performs a useful service to Us or to the state . . ..

Peter I (the Great) had eleven children many of whom died in infancy. Alexis Petrovich (1690–1718) was the eldest son and was brought up by his mother, Evdokia Lopukhina, and her relatives, supporters of the traditional order, and he resisted his father's efforts to win him over to his own views. In 1716 he fled abroad. Lured back to Russia two years later by promises that were not kept, he was forced publicly to renounce his right to the throne and was later tried and sentenced to death as a traitor. The exact circumstances in which he died have not been established but it is known that in his last days he was severely tortured. He had married Princess Charlotte of Brunswick and left a son, who became the Emperor Peter II.

Peter did much to develop Russia's trade and industry and encouraged scholarship. Though personally cruel and barbaric in many of his habits, he was a great monarch, who transformed Russia and brought her into the concert of the great European powers.

Peter I (the Great) died in 1725 without nominating an heir. The day before he died he wrote "Leave all to . . . .," and the rest of the sentence was indecipherable scrawl. He is buried in the Cathedral of the St. Peter and St. Paul Fortress in St. Petersburg.

CHRONOLOGY

1672	Peter I (the Great) born (May 30).
1682	After *streltsy* attack on the Kremlin Ivan V and Peter I are established as co-tsars at a double coronation.
	Beginning of the regency of Sophia with Prince Vasily Golitsyn as foreign minister.
1688	Peter I (the Great) marries Evdokia Lopukhina.
1689	Sophia's regency overthrown, with Ivan's consent.
	Natalia Naryshkina, Peter's mother, becomes regent.
1694	Natalia Naryshkina, the regent, dies.

1696	Death of Ivan V. Peter I (the Great) becomes sole tsar.
1697–1698	Great Embassy to Western Europe.
1698	Streltsy revolt breaks out and is savagely suppressed. Peter returns to Moscow. More than 200 are condemned to death.
	Sophia, the ex-regent, is sent into exile to the Cloister of the Intercession in Suzdal.
1703	St. Petersburg is founded.
1704	Sophia, the ex-regent, dies and is buried in the Novodevichy Convent.
1709	Decisive Russian victory over Sweden at Poltava, forcing Charles XII to take refuge in Turkey.
1716	Flight of Tsarevich Alexis to Vienna and Naples.
1718	Death of Alexis.
1721	Peter I (the Great) acquires the right to nominate his own successor and assumes title of "Emperor of all the Russias."
1724	Catherine, the second wife of Peter I (the Great), whom he married privately in 1707, is crowned as empress.
1724	Death of Peter I (the Great) without having designated a successor. Accession of Catherine I.

BIBLIOGRAPHY

Anderson, M. S. *Peter the Great.* 1978.

Gordon, A. *The History of Peter the Great, Emperor of Russia.* 1755.

Hughes, L. *Peter the Great: A Biography.* 2002.

de Jonge, A. *Fire and Water: A Life of Peter the Great.* 1979.

Massie, R. K. *Peter the Great. His Life and World.* 1981.

Troyat, H. *Peter the Great.* 1988.

7

CATHERINE I

Marfa Skavronskaya (Ekaterina Alexeyevna), April 5, 1684–May 6, 1727.

Empress of Russia 1725–1727.

Catherine I was the first empress of Russia and was the second wife of Peter I (the Great). She was the daughter of a Lithuanian peasant, and before converting to the Orthodox faith her name was Marfa Skavronskaya. Employed as a servant she married a Swedish dragoon. When Marienberg fell to Russian forces Marfa was captured and put to work in the regimental laundry. From there she passed on to Prince Aleksandr Danilovich Menshikov (1673–1729). He was a favorite of Peter I (the Great) whose reforms he influenced and helped. Menshikov ruled Russia during the reign of Catherine I and the minority of Peter II. Eventually, because of intrigue at court, he was banished to Siberia. In 1703 Peter saw Marfa at Menshikov's house and took her as his mistress. In 1705 she converted to the Orthodox faith and on February 19, 1712, publicly married Peter, having secretly married him in 1707.

After the death of Peter, Catherine was placed on the throne by the guards regiments. There was no constitutional provision for appointing a new monarch. The other candidate was Peter I's grandson, Peter Alexeyevich, but the two guards regiments favored Catherine I, partly because she paid off their arrears of pay. She lacked the ability to rule, and real power, however, remained in the hands of the Supreme Privy Council established in 1726 and dominated by Prince Menshikov. Throughout her reign she contented herself with the pleasures of court life, spending enormous sums.

She died on May 6, 1727, and was buried in the Cathedral of the St. Peter and St. Paul Fortress in St. Petersburg.

Catherine I. Portrait by Jean-Marc Nattier, 1717. The State Hermitage Museum, St Petersburg.

CHRONOLOGY

1684 Catherine I born (April 5).

1725 Accession to the throne (January 28).

Succession supported by Imperial Guards and most ministers.

1726 Establishment of a seven-member Supreme Privy Council, presided over by the empress.

1727 Death of Catherine and accession of Peter II, grandson of Peter I (the Great) and son of Tsarevich Alexis (May 6).

BIBLIOGRAPHY

Longworth, P. *Three Empresses*. 1972.

8

PETER II

Peter Alexeyevich Romanov, October 12, 1715–January 19, 1730.

Emperor of Russia 1727–1730.

Peter II was the grandson of Peter I (the Great) and only son of the ill-fated tsarevich Alexis and his wife Princess Charlotte of Brunswick. After the death of his father, in 1718, he was regarded as the heir to the throne, but he lost his rights to it in 1722, when Peter I (the Great) decreed that the sovereign should have power to nominate his own successor. Peter I died in 1725 without having exercised this power and the succession was thus left open. The senate proclaimed the late tsar's widow, Catherine I, empress. On her death Peter II succeeded her without open dispute. By order of Catherine I, until he reached his majority, the state should be ruled by the Supreme Privy Council but in the first year of the reign actual power was in the hands of Prince Aleksandr Danilovich Menshikov (1673–1729). His education was supervised by Menshikov who was disliked by Peter II. Menshikov planned to maintain his influence by marrying his daughter to Peter II but was overthrown, his property confiscated, and exiled to Siberia.

On January 9, 1728, Peter II moved to Moscow with his court and the Supreme Privy Council. Here his coronation took place on February 25, 1728, in the Dormition Cathedral of the Kremlin.

On November 30, 1729, he became engaged to the eighteen-year-old Ekaterina Alexeyevna Dolgorukova. But on January 6, 1730, he caught a chill during a military review and subsequently contracted smallpox, dying on January 19, 1730. He was buried in the

Archangel Cathedral of the Kremlin. The male line of the Romanov dynasty ends with Peter II.

Peter II. Anonymous artist. The State Hermitage Museum, St Petersburg.

CHRONOLOGY

1715 Peter II born (October 12).

1727 Accession to the throne (May 6).

1730 Death of Peter II from smallpox (January 19).

BIBLIOGRAPHY

Grey, I. *The Romanovs: The Rise and Fall of a Russian Dynasty.* 1971.
Lincoln, W. B. *The Romanovs: Autocrats of All the Russias.* 1981.

9

ANNA

Anna Ivanovna Romanova, January 28, 1693–October 17, 1740.

Empress of Russia 1730–1740.

Anna was the daughter of Ivan V and niece of Peter I (the Great). She married Friedrich Wilhelm, the duke of Kurland in 1710, who died 1711. After the death of Peter II the Supreme Privy Council offered the throne to Anna, conditional on her accepting less than autocratic power and that she remain subject to the council. On ascending the throne, exploiting the divisions in the nobility, she declined to have her power curtailed and became an autocrat and abolished the council in 1730, replacing it with a senate with its former power. On April 28, 1730, she crowned herself in the Dormition Cathedral of the Kremlin in Mosow.

The conditions that the Supreme Privy Council aimed to place on Anna, sometimes known as the "Conditions of Mitau," were:

1. that she did not marry;
2. that she did not appoint a successor;
3. that the Supreme Council controlled state affairs;
4. that the council's membership should remain eight;
5. that the empress could not declare war;
6. that the empress could not make peace;
7. that she could not levy taxes;
8. that she could not commit state funds;
9. that she could not confiscate estates, neither could she grant estates;
10. that she could not appoint anyone to a rank higher than that of a colonel;
11. all armed forces, including the guards, to be under the control of the Supreme Council.

Thus, for a very short period, constitutional rule was established in Russia. Anna had exchanged an absolute monarchy for an absolute oligarchy in the form of the council. Although the agreement suited the Dolgorukys and Golitsyns, it was not welcomed generally by the gentry. On February 25, 1730, Anna destroyed the agreement and on March 4 she dissolved the council by a manifesto when the lower nobility and guards regiments supported her assumption of absolute power. In 1732 the imperial court and administration moved back to St. Petersburg.

Anna appears to have spent little time on affairs of state, and power lay with her favorite, Ernst Johann Biron (Bühren) (1690–1772), who during her reign was the virtual ruler of Russia; this period was known as the *Bironovshchina* (Biron era). He held no official administrative position in Russia but with other Germans treated Russians with contempt and the country as a private estate. In 1727 he became her lover and was made grand chamberlain and count. He was extremely unpopular owing to his vindictive and corrupt character. Regent for three weeks after Anna's death, he was deposed and banished to Siberia. Peter III, however, permitted him to return to St. Petersburg.

The period of Anna's reign was one of internal stability and of successful foreign policy. Anna designated the infant Ivan to be her successor the day before she died and appointed Biron as regent. All this was arranged by Biron without reference to the senate, the Holy Synod or representatives of the Russian people. She died in St. Petersburg on October 17, 1740, of kidney disease, leaving no heirs. Anna was buried in the Cathedral of St. Peter and St. Paul Fortress in St. Petersburg.

CHRONOLOGY

1693 Anna born (January 28).

1730 Anna elected to the throne by the Supreme Privy Council. Unsuccessful attempt by Supreme Privy Council to impose conditions on Anna. Supreme Privy Council abolished and Senate restored (April 28).

1740 Death of Empress Anna (October 17).

BIBLIOGRAPHY

Longwoth, P. *Three Empresses*. 1972.

10

IVAN VI

Ivan Antonovich of Brunswick–Wolfenbüttel, August 12, 1740–July 5, 1764.

Emperor of Russia 1740–1741.

Ivan was the son of Anna Leopoldovna and Anton Ulrich, duke of Brunswick-Lüneburg. He was nominated by his great-aunt, Empress Anna, as her heir. He succeeded to the throne at the age of two months. Ernest Johann Biron remained regent. However, on November 9, Biron was overthrown and sent to Siberia, after only twenty-two days as regent, by the vice chancellors Andrey Osterman and Field Marshal Burkhard Christoph, Graf von Münnich. The child emperor's mother was declared regent.

On November 25, 1741, the emperor was overthrown by the Imperial Guard led by Elizabeth Petrovna Romanova, daughter of Peter I (the Great). The child and his family were exiled first to Riga, then to Rannenborg Castle, and finally, in 1744, to Kholmogory, where, on March 7, 1746, Anna Leopoldovna died. At the beginning of 1756, Ivan Antonovich was taken to Schlisselborg Fortress, where he was kept in solitary confinement and under strict guard. On the night of July 5, 1764, the twenty-four-year old Ivan was stabbed to death by his guards when a second lieutenant of the Schlisselborg garrison, Vasily Yakovlevich Mirovich, attempted to free him. He was secretly buried in a hidden place near the walls of the fortress. The grave was later destroyed.

CHRONOLOGY

1740 Ivan VI born (August 12).

1741 Ivan VI and his family deposed and imprisoned (November 25).

1764 Ivan VI stabbed to death by his jailers (July 5).

BIBLIOGRAPHY

Grey, I. *The Romanovs: The Rise and Fall of a Russian Dynasty.* 1971.

Lincoln, W. B. *The Romanovs: Autocrats of All the Russias.* 1981.

II

ELIZABETH

Elizaveta Petrovna Romanova, December 18, 1709–December 25, 1761

O.S., January 5, 1762 N.S.

Empress of Russia 1741–1761.

Elizabeth was the daughter of Peter I (the Great) and his second wife Catherine (Empress Catherine I). Any claim she may have had to the throne was passed over four times before finally she attained it. During the reign of Anna and the regency of Ernst Johann Biron (1690–1772) she was kept in the background and closely watched. However she had many friends, especially among the regiments, who in November 1741 supported her in a court revolution that drove out the infant Ivan VI and the regent Anna Leopoldovna. She was crowned in the Dormition Cathedral of the Moscow Kremlin on April 25, 1742.

Elizabeth's accession was welcomed because it brought to an end the period of German domination. She admired her father's work and ideas but was poorly educated and had little interest in practical or state affairs. One of her most important acts was made in 1744 when she abolished the death penalty; during her reign no person was executed. Her main preoccupations were dancing, music, theater, and costume. She also incurred heavy expenditure on elaborating St. Petersburg, where the Italian architect Count Bartolomeo Francesco Rastrelli (1700–1771) built for her, at a cost of ten million rubles, the Winter Palace (1754–1762). Russian architecture was dominated by the rococo style, and Rastrelli reconstructed the palaces of Peterhof and Tsarskoye Selo (1783).

Elizabeth chose as ministers patriotic and, on the whole, enlightened Russians, including Count Aleksey Petrovich Bestuzhev-Ryumin (1693–1766), entrusted with the conduct of foreign affairs; Peter Shuvalov, author of schemes for the improvement of state finances;

and Ivan Ivanovich Shuvalov (1727–1797), patron of learning, literature, and the arts; and with the scientist and poet Mikhail Vasilyevich Lomonosov (1711–1765), founder of Moscow University (1755), the first in Russia, with faculties of law, medicine, and philosophy. From the reign of Elizabeth dates also the history of the Russian theater as a regular institution. The first permanent theater opened in 1756. Under Elizabeth the French language and French culture reached the Russian court life and society.

In 1756 Russia joined, for the first time, an all-European coalition, the object of which was to dismember the Prussia of Frederick the Great. Prussia was saved from destruction in the end by the lack of cooperation between the members of the coalition and by the death of Elizabeth, who was succeeded by her nephew Peter III, an ardent admirer of Frederick and of everything Prussian.

Elizabeth died in 1761 leaving no heir and was buried in the Cathedral of the St. Peter and St. Paul Fortress in St. Petersburg.

CHRONOLOGY

1709 Elizabeth born (December 18).

1741 Accession to the throne (November 25).

1742 Elizabeth issues manifesto designating her nephew, the duke of Holstein, as her successor.

1745 Marriage of Peter, duke of Holstein, nephew of Empress Elizabeth and heir to the Russian throne, to Princess Sophia Augusta (later Catherine II (the Great)) of Anhalt-Zerbst.

1761 Death of Empress Elizabeth (December 25 O.S.,/January 5, 1762 N.S.).

BIBLIOGRAPHY

Bain, R. N., *The Daughter of Peter the Great: A History of Russian Diplomacy and of the Russian Court under the Empress Elizabeth Petrovna 1741–1762*. 1899.

Longworth, P. *Three Empresses*. 1972.

Talbot Rice, T. *Elizabeth, Empress of Russia*. 1970.

12

PETER III

Karl Peter Ulrich of Holstein-Gottorp, February 21, 1728–July 6, 1762.

Emperor of Russia 1761–1762.

Peter III was the son of Karl Friedrich, duke of Holstein-Gottorp, and Anna Petrovna, Peter the Great's daughter. Peter III was born in 1728 in Kiel. Until the age of fourteen he lived and was educated at the court of Holstein. He was proclaimed official heir to the Russian throne on November 7, 1742, by his aunt, Elizabeth Petrovna. He was grand-nephew, through his father, Karl Friedrich of Holstein-Gottorp, of Charles XII of Sweden.

On August 21, 1745, Peter married Princess Sophia Augusta Frederica of Anhalt-Zerbst, who was christened into the Orthodox faith as Ekaterina Alexeyevna; the future Catherine II (the Great).

His first act upon ascending the throne in 1761 was to grant amnesty for and return from exile of state figures arrested by Elizabeth after her accession. During his short reign, he introduced various reforms, banned the persecution of dissenters, dissolved the Privy Council and by special decree released the gentry from compulsory state service. Peter was an ardent admirer of Frederick (the Great), and interested himself in drilling and dressing his army on Prussian models.

On June 28, 1762, he was overthrown by a court coup led by his wife, who became Catherine II (the Great). After his deposition, he was imprisoned at Ropsha, south of St. Petersburg, where on July 6, 1762, he was killed by Count Alexei Orlov, Catherine's favorite and one of the organizers of the coup.

On June 28, 1762, he was overthrown by a court coup led by his wife, who became Catherine II (the Great).

He had two children from his marriage with Catherine; a son, later Emperor Paul, and a daughter, who died in infancy.

Peter III was buried in the Annunciation Church of the Alexander Nevsky Monastery but in December 1796, by order of his son Paul, his remains were reburied with full honors in the Cathedral of the St. Peter and St. Paul fortress in St. Petersburg.

CHRONOLOGY

1728 Peter III born (February 21).

1761 Peter III becomes tsar (January 5, 1762 N.S.).

1762 Peter III abdicates (June 28). Peter III murdered in mysterious circumstances (July 6).

BIBLIOGRAPHY

Leonard, C. S. *Reform and Regicide: The Reign of Peter III of Russia.* 1993.

13

CATHERINE II (The Great)

Sophia Augusta Frederica of Anhalt-Zerbst, baptized into the Orthodox church as Ekaterina (Catherine) Alexeyevna, May 2, 1729–November 6, 1796.

Empress of Russia 1762–1796.

Catherine II (the Great) was born and brought up in Stettin and at the invitation of Empress Elizabeth she went, with her mother, to Russia to be married to Elizabeth's nephew, Grand Duke Peter Feodorovich, the heir to the Russian throne. They married on August 21, 1745, but they were an ill-matched pair; Catherine was well-educated, industrious, highly intelligent, and strong-willed. Peter III was disfigured by an attack of smallpox, debauched in habit and, at best, of limited intellect. His main interest was in drilling soldiers and imitating Frederick (the Great), of whom he was a profound admirer. Stories of his cruelty to Catherine may be to some extent discounted, since they emanated from Catherine herself or from her supporters, when later they found it necessary to justify their conduct in getting rid of him. Catherine consoled herself for the failure of her marriage by taking a number of lovers; the first, Sergei Saltykov, a courtier, may have been the father of Emperor Paul, although he was officially recognized as fathered by Peter. Paul was taken away from her by Empress Elizabeth to be brought up under her supervision and trained as her ultimate heir.

Twelve, or more, lovers followed during the course of the reign and they included a future king of Poland, Stanislaus Poniatowski by whom she probably had a daughter, Anna Petrovna, who died in infancy, and Grigory Orlov who helped to bring Catherine to the throne and by whom she had a son, Alexi Grigorievich Bobrinskoy. However, by far the most important was Grigory Alexandrovich Potemkin (1739–1791) who was born near Smolensk of a small gentry

*Catherine II.
Portrait by
Richard Brompton,
1782. The State
Hermitage
Museum,
St Petersburg.*

family. After attending Moscow University he joined the army and participated in 1762 in the coup that led to the deposition of Peter III and the elevation of Catherine II to the throne. In reward for his services he was given a small estate. In 1768 he became a gentleman of the household and, after some military service, in the following year reappeared at court, where he soon became Catherine's favorite and lover.

There is a view held that Potemkin was married to Catherine in 1774. Nevertheless, they ceased to be lovers in 1776, but to the end of his life he retained a strong ascendancy over her and she continued to rely on him as her principal adviser. Potemkin, a man of huge build and strong personality, had all the gifts of the courtier. He was witty and talented, fond of music and art. He took part in Catherine's wars against Turkey, although he did not distinguish himself as a general. On the other hand he had undoubted talents as an administrator, which he was able to employ when Catherine appointed him to organize and colonize the newly conquered lands in the extreme south, known as New Russia. On his initiative the naval ports of Sevastopol, in the Crimea, and Kherson, on the lower Dniester, were founded, and the construction of a Black Sea fleet was begun. His other services included important army reforms. He also founded the city of Ekaterinoslav as the capital of the new lands that, with the Ukraine, were absorbed as an integral part of the Russian Empire.

The story of the tour Potemkin persuaded Catherine to take through her new territories in 1787, in the course of which he is said to have erected cardboard villages and taken other similar measures of deception to produce an appearance of prosperity, has been greatly exaggerated. Potemkin, it is true, amassed enormous wealth and lived on a luxurious scale. The empress showered on him rewards and honors without end. After the conquest of the Crimea in the early 1780s she made him prince of Tauris and built for him in St. Petersburg the magnificent Tauris palace. He kept up a pompous court of his own and in his turn bestowed awards and offices.

When Elizabeth died in January 1761, the grand duke ascended the throne as Peter III, and Catherine became empress consort. However, Peter's reign would last only six months. His personal relations with his wife became even worse than they had been, and before long it became apparent that a conspiracy to remove Peter was brewing. A strong party favored the elevation of Catherine to the throne. Catherine was proclaimed empress in 1762, with the support of the guards regiment, of the court and higher society, and of the mass of the people. Peter was relegated to a small estate at Topsha, near St. Petersburg, where a few weeks later he met his death under circumstances that have never been properly established.

In taking the throne Catherine ousted not only her husband, but also her seven-year-old son Paul, who did not come to the throne until thirty-four years later. There was also another potential claimant in the person of the ex-emperor Ivan VI, who had languished in the fortress of Schlüsselburg since Elizabeth deposed him in 1741. In

In taking the throne Catherine ousted not only her husband, but also her seven-year-old son Paul, who did not come to the throne until 34 years later.

keeping with Russian tradition, a long succession of pretenders appeared. The most important was Don Cossack Yemelyan Ivanovich Pugachev (1726–1775) who, by claiming to be her late husband Peter III, championing the wrongs of the peasant masses, stirred up an upheaval that really threatened the foundations of her throne. Pugachev served in the Seven Years' War against Prussia, the Polish campaign of 1764, and the Russo-Turkish War in 1768–74. Declaring himself Emperor Peter III in 1773, his rebellion started in the Urals and it soon spread over a vast area. His troops captured Kazan, Penza, Saratov, and other cities. On July 31, 1774, Pugachev issued his emancipation decree:

> We, Peter III, by the Grace of God Emperor and Autocrat of All-Russia etc.
>
> This is given for nationwide information.
>
> By this personal decree, with our monarchial and fatherly love, we grant freedom to everyone who formerly was in serfdom or in any other obligation to the nobility; and we transfer these to be faithful personal subjects of our crown; to the Old Believers we grant the right to use the ancient sign of the Cross, and to pray, and to wear beards; while to the Cossacks we restore for eternity their freedoms and liberties; we hereby terminate the recruiting system, cancel personal and other monetary taxes, abolish without compensation the ownership of land, forest, pastures, fisheries and salt deposits; and finally we free everyone from all taxes and obligations which the thievish nobles and extortionist city judges have imposed on the peasantry and the rest of the population. We pray for the salvation of your souls and wish you a happy and peaceful life here on earth where we have suffered and experienced much from the above-mentioned thievish nobles. Now since our name, thanks to the hand of Providence, flourishes throughout Russia, we make hereby known by this personal decree the following: all nobles who have owned either estates granted by the state or inherited estates, who have opposed our rule, who have rebelled against the empire, and who have ruined the peasantry, should be seized, arrested, and hanged; that is, treated in the same manner as these unchristians have treated you, the peasantry. After the extermination of these opponents and thievish nobles, everyone will live in a peace and happiness that shall continue to eternity.

The insurrection finally collapsed, but it caused Catherine II (the Great) to consider seriously problems of law and order in the countryside and the role of the gentry.

Pugachev was captured in September 1774 and brought to trial in Moscow in December and executed there in January the following year.

Catherine was a patron of the arts. Her own literary output was quite great and she encouraged the translation of foreign works. Censorship was slight, that is, until the French Revolution. She founded the Russian Academy of Language, which was responsible for the publication of the first Russian dictionary. She encouraged the public performance of plays and engaged foreign architects. Catherine employed Étienne Maurice Falconet (1716–1791), the French sculptor, to work in St. Petersburg, where he executed the bronze equestrian statue of Peter I (the Great) situated in Decembrists' Square. Known as "The Bronze Horseman," it was the subject of a poem by Pushkin in 1832 and shows Peter reining in his horse on the brink of a rock. The plaster cast was completed in 1779 and the finished statue weighed sixteen tons. The 1,600-ton block of granite on which the statue stands came from Lasht, a village seven miles from St. Petersburg and was maneuvered by five hundred men taking five weeks. The statue was unveiled in August 1782. The pedestal bears the Latin inscription PETRO PRIMO CATHARINA SECUNDA MDCCLXXXII on one side and the same in Russian on the opposite side.

Catherine's reign was one of the most prosperous periods of the Russian Empire. She undertook a considerable number of internal political reforms and they included the creation of Marshals of the Nobility who were elected by assemblies of deputies every three years as well as the Legislative Commission and the Empress's *Bolshoi Nakaz* (Great Instruction). The commission was established by Catherine in order to introduce fundamental changes of policy based on the ideas of the Enlightenment.

The Enlightenment describes the great eighteenth-century movement toward secular, rational, and humane views of man and society and was a reaction against theological observation, the political influence of the church, religious intolerance, harsh legal punishments, and the use of torture by the state. Two important people who influenced Catherine II were Diderot and Voltaire.

Denis Diderot (1713–1784) was coeditor of the French *Encyclopédie*. The first three volumes of this monumental work were translated into Russian very quickly after publication and the work was supervised by the director of Moscow University. The completion in 1772 left Diderot without any source of income; on learning of this, Catherine II (the Great) bought his library and appointed him librarian on an annual salary for the duration of his life, asking him to keep the books until she needed them. In 1773 Diderot went to St. Petersburg to thank her, staying five months and being received with honor and warmth. He wrote *Plan d'une université pour le gouvernement de Russie* (published 1813–1814) for Catherine. However, he soon became disillusioned with Russia's enlightened despotism.

François Marie Arouet Voltaire (1694–1778) was a French philosopher and writer whose influence extended to Russia. During Elizabeth's reign he was elected an honorary member of the Academy of Sciences and was commissioned by the government to serve as a historian to Peter I (the Great). Catherine II (the Great), desirous of strengthening ties with France, corresponded with Voltaire (1768–1778). French ideas, particularly educational theory, came to inform part of Russian life among the upper echelons of society.

Catherine prepared "The Instruction" (*Nakaz*) for the commission, which was to undertake the codification of laws and work toward the modernization of Russian law and life. The *Nakaz* together with its two supplements consisted of 655 articles and was the most important writing of Catherine II. It represented Catherine's ideas on how Russia's laws could be remodeled on Western lines.

Some of her ideas incorporated in the *Nakaz* were: Russia is a European power and the Sovereign is absolute. Because of the size of the State absolute power must be vested in the autocrat. The use of torture is repugnant. Military Service leads to the attainment of honor. Justice should be dispensed in times of peace and war. Discrimination against those of different faiths would greatly endanger the peace and security of its citizens.

At its first session in 1767, the commission consisted of 564 deputies; 28 had been appointed and 536 elected; 30 percent were nobles, 39 percent city dwellers, 14 percent state peasants, 12 percent national minorities, 5 percent representatives of state administration, and 1 representative an ecclesiastic. Serfs were not represented. The commission received 1,441 registers of grievances and despite its 203 sessions, the commission bore little fruit and divided into different factions. It did, however, provide Catherine with a large source of information about Russia, which influenced her later reforms. She disbanded the commission in 1768.

Catherine's account of the Legislative Commission, 1765–1768, reads:

I decided in my own mind [ca. 1765] that the general attitude and the civil law could only be improved by the adoption of useful rules, which would have to be written and ratified by me, for all the inhabitants of the Empire and for all circumstances.

And to this end I began to read and then to write the Instruction for the law-making Commission.

I read and wrote two years and said not a word for a year and a half, but followed my own judgment and feelings, with a sincere striving for the service, the honor, and the happiness of the empire, and with the desire to bring about in all respects the highest welfare of people and of things, of all in general and each individual in particular. When in my opinion I had pretty well arrived at my goal, I began to show parts of the subjects I had worked out to different persons, laying before each that which would be of interest to him, among others Prince Orlov and Count Nikita Panin. The latter said to me: "Those are principles to cast down walls." Prince Orlov thought very highly of my work and often wished to show it to this person or that; but I never showed more than one or two pages at a time. At last I composed the manifesto concerning the calling of delegates from the whole empire, in order to learn more about the conditions of each district. The delegates then assembled in Moscow in the year 1767. I summoned several persons of quite different ways of thinking to the Kolomensky Palace, where I was living at the time, in order to have them listen to the finished Instruction for the Commission on Laws. At every section there was a difference of opinion. I permitted them to cross out and efface whatever they liked. They crossed out more than a half of what I had written, and the Instruction remained as it was printed . . . .

The Commission on Laws assembled and brought me light and knowledge from the whole empire, with which we had to deal and which we had to care for.

Later in Catherine's reign her domestic policy became increasingly repressive. It is thought that her views about the Enlightenment changed; this was probably brought about by the Pugachev rebellion and the French Revolution and because she also recognized the limitations of her own power.

The Charter to the Nobility (or *Dvoryanstvo* Charter) was issued in 1785 and reaffirmed and consolidated the status of the nobility. In the seventeenth century, military service for the Russian nobility, or *dvoryanstvo*, was hereditary. In 1642 and 1649 it was established that only the *dvoryanstvo* could own land worked by serfs. Peter I (the Great) extensively reformed the rights and position of the *dvoryanstvo*; although from then on the *dvoryanstvo* was virtually forced to serve either in the army, navy, or bureaucracy. Catherine recognized the privileged position of the nobility as the ruling class and implicitly recognized the peasants' status as chattel slaves. Her charter also provided for the creation of autonomous corporations of the nobility, with legal powers. The *dvoryanstvo* enjoyed such privileges as exemption from poll tax and the fact that they could not be stripped of estates, title, or status without trial by their peers.

Extracts from the Charter include:

The title of the nobility is hereditary and stems from the quality and virtue of leading men of antiquity who distinguished themselves by their service—which they turned into merit and acquired for their posterity the title of the nobility.

It is to the advantage of both the Empire and the Crown, as it is also just, that the respectful title of the nobility be maintained and approved firmly and inviolably; and therefore, as formerly, now and in the future the title of the nobility is irrevocable, hereditary, and belongs to those honorable families who use it; and accordingly:

A nobleman transmits his noble title to his wife;

A nobleman transmits his noble title to his children hereditarily.

The following acts are contrary to the standards of noble dignity and can deprive one of the title: (i) violation of an oath; (ii) treason; (iii) robbery; (iv) thefts of all sorts; (v) deceitful acts; (vi) violations which call for either corporal punishment or a deprivation of honor; (vii) incitement of others to commit violations—if this be established.

A nobleman cannot be deprived of his title without due process of law.

A nobleman cannot be deprived of his life without due process of law.

A nobleman cannot be deprived of his property without due process of law.

A nobleman can be judged by his peers only.

All criminal acts of a nobleman which for ten years went either unnoticed or had no action taken on them we decree be henceforth forgotten forever.

A nobleman cannot be subjected to corporal punishment.

Noblemen who serve as junior officers in Our armed forces should be punished according to regulations applicable to senior officers.

A nobleman has the power and the authority to give away to whomever he wishes the property which he acquired legally as first owner, to bequeath this property in his will, to confer it as dowry, or to sell or give it away for his livelihood. He may, however, dispose of inherited property only in conformity with the provisions of the law.

The inheritable property of a nobleman who may be convicted of a serious crime should pass on to his legal heirs.

The nobles have the right to purchase villages.

The nobles may have factories and mills in their villages.

The homes of the nobility in villages are to be free from quartering of soldiers.

A nobleman is personally freed from the poll tax.

Under the terms of the Charter to the Towns, issued by Catherine in 1785, residents of cities were divided into six classes:

1. Land proprietors
2. Merchants (divided into three guilds)
3. Artisans [organized into occupational associations (*tekhi*)]
4. Independent artisans
5. Eminent citizens of the liberal professions
6. Foreign and temporary residents

City dwellers were allowed to elect a city *duma*, composed of six municipal councillors, one for each class, and a mayor. According to the terms of the charter the burghers were still liable for soul tax and were unable to own peasants or estates.

The outstanding events of Catherine's reign in foreign affairs were two successful wars with the Ottoman Empire, a war with Sweden, and three partitions of Poland, in which Russia made huge territorial gains. The first partition in 1772 divided Poland between Russia, Prussia, and Austria; the second in 1793 was mainly to Russia's advantage; and under the third in 1795 Poland lost her independence. Later in the fourth partition under the Treaty of Vienna (1815) the kingdom of Poland was established under the suzerainty of the Russian tsars. Altogether in her reign Catherine added 200,000 square miles to Russian territory.

Count Nikita Ivanovich Panin (1718–1783) was Catherine's chief diplomatic adviser (1763–1780) and as Russian minister in Stockholm adopted an anti-French policy favoring close cooperation between England, Prussia, Sweden, and Denmark.

The League of Armed Neutrality was based on a doctrine of armed neutrality at sea; it was advanced by Russia in 1780 in order to protect the trade of neutral states against the British. A number of European countries accepted Catherine's proposals, which became part of international maritime law. Neutral ships were not to be interfered with, even when trading with combatants; combatants' goods in neutral ships were not to be seized; and blockades were not to be legal until they were enforced.

Catherine II (the Great) could use considerable brutal force to defend her throne and combined this with supreme ability to portray to the world that she was an enlightened ruler with very high ideals.

She died on November 6, 1796, and was buried in the Cathedral of the St. Peter and St. Paul Fortress in St. Petersburg.

CHRONOLOGY

1729   Catherine born in Stettin (now Szczecin) Poland (April 21).

1745   Marries Peter Feodorovich, heir to the Russian throne (August 21).

1762   Catherine, wife of Peter III, gains throne by coup d'etat (June 28).

Peter III abdicates (June 28).

Peter III murdered in mysterious circumstances (July 6).

Senate ratifies coup d'etat (August).

Catherine II (the Great) crowned in Moscow (September 13).

1794   Catherine II (the Great) declares her intention to prevent Grand Duke Paul from succeeding to the throne.

1796   Catherine II (the Great) dies (November 6).

BIBLIOGRAPHY

Alexander, J. T. *Catherine the Great: Life and Legend.* 1989.
Cronin, V. *Catherine: Empress of All the Russias.* 1978.
Gooch, G. P. *Catherine the Great and Other Studies.* 1954.
Grey, I. *Catherine the Great.* 1961.

14
PAUL

Paul Petrovich Romanov, September 20, 1754–March 12, 1801.

Emperor of Russia 1796–1801.

Paul was the son of Empress Catherine II (the Great). He was brought up by his father's aunt Empress Elizabeth who ruled from 1741 to 1761. From 1760 he was tutored by Nikita Ivanovich Panin. His father was officially Peter III but Catherine in her diary ascribes his paternity to her lover Sergei Saltykov. He succeeded to the throne on November 6, 1796, at the age of forty-two, from which he had been kept for thirty-four years by his mother.

After the overthrow of Peter III, he lived with his family in Gatchina Palace, given to him by his mother, where he had his own court and a small army. The violent events of his childhood and his estrangement from his mother made him irritable and suspicious of those around him. During that period his relations with Catherine had been strained. State affairs were never discussed with him. She even proposed nominating as her successor (Peter I's edict of 1722 decreed that tsars should designate their successors) his son Alexander, whom she separated from his father and had brought up under her own supervision.

Paul married twice, first Wilhelmina, princess of Hesse-Darmstadt (Natalya Alexeyevna), who died in childbirth three years later in 1776, leaving no issue. His second wife was Sophia Dorothea, princess of Württemberg, who took the name of Maria Feodorovna on admission to the Orthodox Church. They had five daughters and four sons, including Alexander and Nicholas, who became the next two tsars.

Paul conceived a bitter hatred of Catherine's policy, which, even in small details, he reversed immediately on his accession. One of

Paul I. Portrait by Stepan Schukin. The State Hermitage Museum, St Petersburg.

the major acts of his reign was the law of April 5, 1797, promulgated on the day of his coronation, establishing the succession to the throne on the basis of primogeniture, thus reversing Peter I's 1722 edict. This remained in force until 1917 and as a result dynastic upheavals were at an end, except for the crisis of December 1825.

Paul also revoked many of the privileges that Catherine had granted to the gentry. He issued a decree limiting the forced service landowners might exact from their serfs to three days a week, but it had little practical importance because it was impossible to enforce it. He continued, as Catherine had done, to give away to favorites large grants of crown land, with peasants, thus enlarging the area of serfdom. He imposed the sternest discipline in the army, modeled, as were the soldiers' uniforms, on the Prussian style. In order to combat the spread of revolutionary ideas, Paul recalled Russians from abroad and prohibited the import of foreign books.

None of his subjects, and least of all those in his immediate entourage, felt secure, and a plot to remove him was headed by Count Peter Alexeyevich Pahlen (1745–1826), military governor of St. Petersburg. Paul was strangled in his bedroom by a group of officers on the night of March 12, 1801. Russian historians allege that the plot was encouraged by the English minister in

One of the major acts of his reign was the law of April 5, 1797, promulgated on the day of his coronation, establishing the succession to the throne on the basis of primogeniture, thus reversing Peter I's 1722 edict.

Russia owing to English dissatisfaction with his foreign policy. Paul had thrown over his alliance with England, come to an understanding with Napoleon, changing from war with France to union with her, and dispatched a military force to conquer India. This was probably one of the main reasons for his murder. He was buried in the Cathedral of the St. Peter and St. Paul Fortress in St. Petersburg.

CHRONOLOGY

1754 Paul born (September 20).

1796 Accession to the throne (November 6).

All people detained by the Secret Chancellery freed and a general amnesty declared for all officials facing prosecution.

Article 15 of the Charter of 1785 is abolished. This exempts the nobility from corporal punishment.

1797 Coronation of Tsar Paul.

Law on succession to the throne according to genealogical seniority.

1801 Paul strangled (March 12).

BIBLIOGRAPHY

Almedingen, E. M. *So Dark a Stream: A Study of the Emperor Paul I of Russia 1754–1801.* 1959.

Ragsdale, H. *Tsar Paul and the Question of Madness.* 1988.

15
ALEXANDER I

Alexander Pavlovich Romanov, December 12, 1777–November 19, 1825.

Emperor of Russia 1801–1825.

Alexander was the son of Emperor Paul and Princess Sophia Dorothea of Württemberg (Empress Maria Feodorovna). In infancy he was removed from the care of his parents by his grandmother Catherine II (the Great), who had him educated under her own supervision and according to a set of instructions, based on eighteenth-century humanitarian philosophy, which she drew up herself. She appointed as her grandson's principal tutor Frédéric-César de La Harpe (ca. 1754–1838), a Swiss revolutionary and an ardent republican, and a follower of Jean Jacques Rousseau (1712–1778) the French political philosopher. La Harpe's teaching included a belief in the rule of law and a hatred of despotism. It is sometimes felt that his teaching had little in common with Russian reality, and that this is partly responsible for the contrast between the theory and practice of Alexander I's reign. In view of the strained relations between Paul and Catherine he could show affection for neither without risk of offending the other, so he became used to concealing his real feelings.

In view of the strained relations between Paul and Catherine he could show affection for neither without risk of offending the other, so he became used to concealing his real feelings.

Alexander knew of the plot that removed Emperor Paul and stipulated that his father's life should be spared. His earliest steps as emperor, together with the known liberalism of his views, inspired many Russians with hope for the future. No reform could take place

Alexander I.
Anonymous
artist. The State
Hermitage
Museum,
St Petersburg.

without a thorough study of his country's needs. He formed a small "unofficial private committee" of four young men, Nikolai Novosiltsev, Pavel Stroganov, Viktor Kochubey, and Adam Csartoryski, who shared his views. They discussed a whole range of political, economic, and social conditions in Russia. The principal practical result of the discussions was the creation of ministries instead of the colleges established by Peter the Great. He entrusted another adviser, Count Mikhail Mikhailovich Speransky (1772–1839), the minister of state and political reformer, with the task of planning a comprehensive reorganization of the government. Speransky's plan was one of the most remarkable documents of Russian political history, but, again, Alexander picked from it and carried out only one or two items; the intrigues of the opposition drove Speransky from office and nullified his work.

Much of Alexander's activities were concentrated on the struggle with France in the early part of his reign, culminating in his triumphant entry into Paris. Both Paul and Alexander vacillated in their approach to the struggle with France. In 1805 Alexander joined the Austrians and British in the Third Coalition against France. The Battle of Austerlitz on November 20, 1805, was an appalling defeat. A fourth coalition was established in 1806 consisting of Russia, Britain, Prussia, and Sweden. More troubles followed; Turkey closed the Dardanelles and the French won the Battle of Friedland on June 2, 1807. As a result, a meeting was held between Napoleon Bonaparte, Frederick Wilhelm III of Prussia, and Alexander where the Treaties of Tilsit were signed following the defeat of the Prussians at Jena and Auerstadt and the Russians at Friedland. Russia became an ally of France, and Prussia, its territory considerably reduced, was occupied by French troops. Both Russia and Prussia joined the Continental System of blockade against British trade. A further conference was held in March 1808 at Erfurt, which was meant to consolidate the Tilsit treaties. Relations between Russia and France began to cool because Russia was not enthusiastic about fighting a war against Austria. During 1811 Russo-French relations deteriorated further partly because Napoleon had seized the duchy of Oldenburg, the security of the duchy having been guaranteed in the Tilsit Treaties. Alexander protested but these protests were rejected. On June 12, 1812, the French Grand Army crossed the river Niemen and the invasion of Russia began.

The calendar of events was that by June 16 the French had reached Vilna and on July 16 Vitebsk was lost, followed by Smolensk on August 6. On August 8 Prince Mikhail Kutuzov replaced Prince Michael Barclay de Tolly who was accused of having opened the way for the enemy to move on Moscow. On August 26 the Russians were defeated at the Battle of Borodino. Kutuzov then reverted to de Tolly's tactics.

Napoleon's troops entered Moscow, which had been evacuated by Russian forces and by some of the city's population. Fire broke out destroying two-thirds of the city. The advent of winter caused Napoleon to begin his disastrous retreat. Of the 450,000 soldiers of the French army only 100,000 had reached Moscow and only 25,000 crossed the Niemen River in December; the rest being lost by battle, disease, starvation, and harsh weather. Kutuzov won a victory at Smolensk and harassed the Grand Army continuously on its homeward route. By December 1812 the entire remnant of the Grand Army had left Russian soil. Russian forces participated in the allied invasion of France in January and February 1814 and Paris surrendered on March 18. Allied forces entered the city with Alexander I at the head of the Russian troops.

By the end of the Napoleonic Wars, Russia had become the dominant military power in Europe. At the Congress of Vienna (1815), which took place following the downfall of Napoleon, Russia gained most of the Duchy of Warsaw, which became the constitutional Kingdom of Poland in union with Russia. Poland remained under Russian rule until 1918.

Varying in approach, the leading diplomats in Europe, Alexander I, Castlereagh, Metternich, and Talleyrand, saw the congress as the first act of a permanent system of diplomacy, a "Concert of Europe"; and Vienna was indeed the first of a series of congresses (Aix-la-Chapelle, Laibach, Troppau, and Verona) that met in an endeavor to resolve European problems in the decade following Napoleon's overthrow. Alexander had felt himself designated by Divine Providence to save Europe from the tyrant. The same spirit of religious mysticism inspired him with the idea of the Holy Alliance of monarchy, which he proposed as the basis of the reorganization of Europe.

After 1815 Alexander continued from time to time to profess himself still a liberal but for reform in Russia nothing else was done. Alexander's policy became more and more reactionary, to the disappointment of many of his subjects who had become acutely aware of the backwardness of Russia. Groups formed for discussion of political and social affairs eventually developed into secret societies with more or less radical programs of reform. These societies were small and Alexander took no measures to curtail their activities, believing that the organizers held the same views that he held in his youth and they should not be punished.

Alexander married Princess Louise of Baden (Empress Elizabeth Alexeyevna) and had two daughters, Maria (died 1799) and Elizabeth (died 1806). Thus, he left no direct heir and after his death was followed by his brother Nicholas. During his last years he had frequently expressed a desire to abdicate. As Alexander's body was not publicly displayed at his funeral, the story arose that he had not died in 1825 but had retired to Siberia and lived as a hermit or wandering holy man under the name of Kuzma.

CHRONOLOGY

1777	Alexander I born (December 12).
1801	Alexander I ascends throne (March 12).
1807	Treaty of Tilsit with Napoleon (June 25).
1812	French invade Russia and take Moscow (September 12).
1814	Paris taken and Alexander enters at the head of his troops (March 18–19).
1814–1815	Alexander I leads the Russian delegation at the Congress of Vienna.
1825	Death of Alexander I at Taganrog; buried in the Cathedral of the St. Peter and St. Paul Fortress in St. Petersburg.

BIBLIOGRAPHY

Almedingen, E. M. *The Emperor Alexander I.* 1964.

Gribble, F. *Emperor and Mystic: The Life of Alexander I of Russia.* 1931.

Palmer, A. *Alexander I: Tsar of War and Peace.* 1974.

16

NICHOLAS I

Nikolai Pavlovich Romanov, June 25, 1796–February 18, 1855.

Emperor of Russia 1825–1855.

Nicholas I was born at Gatchina near St. Petersburg, the third son of Emperor Paul. He was not considered likely to succeed to the throne and received education in military engineering. He held the post of inspector general of the army's engines and also became commander of the First Guards Division.

Alexander I died in Taganrog on November 19, 1825, and news reached St. Petersburg on November 27. Grand Duke Constantine was considered by most to be heir presumptive, but in 1822 he had sent Alexander a formal letter stating that he was unwilling to succeed to the throne. In 1823 Alexander signed a manifesto declaring Grand Duke Nicholas successor. However, Alexander decided to keep this information secret and Constantine continued to use the title Tsarevich.

The news of Alexander's death did not reach Constantine until December 7, 1825, when he immediately proclaimed Nicholas as tsar. The same news reached Nicholas on December 9 and he proclaimed Constantine as tsar. Constantine was Russian commander-in-chief of the Polish army at that time and refused to leave Warsaw. After an exchange of messages between Moscow and Warsaw, Nicholas claimed the throne for himself. *The Times* of London said, "The Empire is in the strange position of having two self denying Emperors and no active ruler." He ascended the throne on December 14, 1825, and was crowned in the Dormition Cathedral of the Moscow Kremlin on August 22, 1826. He married Frederica

Louisa Charlotta Wilhelmina (Alexandra Feodorovna) daughter of King Friedrich William III of Prussia and they had seven children.

On December 14, 1825, only hours after Nicholas I was declared emperor, troops occupied Senate Square in St. Petersburg and declared their allegiance to Constantine and demanded a constitution. The origins of the Decembrist insurrection arose from the many secret societies that had sprung up after the war with Napoleon Bonaparte of 1812–1815. All secret societies were banned in 1822.

Nicholas I.
Portrait by Horace
Vernet, 1830s. The
State Hermitage
Museum,
St Petersburg.

Leading societies included the following:

1816 Union of Salvation, St. Petersburg (renamed Union of Welfare, 1818)

    leading members: Prince Sergei Trubetskoy

                       Matvey and Sergei Muravyov-Apostol

                       Aleksandr and Mikhail Muravyov

                       Pavel Pestel

1817 Union of Public Good re-established as

1822 Northern Society (Society of the North)

    leading members: Nikita Muravyov

                       Prince Sergei Trubetskoy

                       Prince Yevgeny Obelensky

                       Nikolai Turgenev

                       Kondraty Ryleyev

1821 Southern Society

1823 Society of United Slavs founded by Pyotr Borisov

1825 Merged with the Southern Society

The Northern Society advocated a British-style constitutional monarchy, the abolition of serfdom, and equality before the law.

The Southern Society was republican and aimed at the abolition of the monarchy. It also aimed at devolution, giving areas such as the Ukraine far more power over their own affairs. It was also advocated that 50 percent of the land should be taken into state ownership and the balance be divided among the peasants. It wanted a federal union with Poland and their ideas and ideals were dominated by Panslavism.

There were several moves to bridge the gap between the ambitions of the two societies but this had not been achieved by the time of the death of Alexander I and the confusion concerning the succession.

The insurrection was on December 14, 1825 and it proved to be a fiasco. It was arranged for the day on which soldiers were to take the oath of loyalty to Nicholas I. It was hoped that the soldiers would refuse. In fact only 3,000 soldiers and sailors refused to take the oath. The rebellious regiments went to Senate Square but were without effective leadership and unprepared for action. The rebels found themselves surrounded and surrendered, but not before they killed Governor General Miloradovich; Pyotr Kakhovsky fired the shot.

The St. Petersburg insurrection was followed by the rebellion of the Chernigov regiment on December 29, 1825, which was put down at Kovalevka in the Ukraine on January 3, 1826.

About 579 individuals were investigated for being involved in the uprising; 79 percent were army personnel and 121 were brought to trial.

Five were hanged: Pestel, Sergei Muravyov-Apostol, Bestuzhev-Ryumin, Kakhovsky, and Ryleyev. Thirty-one went into penal servitude. The rest were deported. Many of the soldiers were forced to run the gauntlet, and the Chernigov regiment was sent to the war in Caucasia.

This was the first rebellion against the tsar in modern times and paved the way for future revolutionary movements.

Only when Alexander II came to the throne in 1855 were the surviving Decembrists released from imprisonment. Nicholas's first priority after his accession was to deal with the arrested Decembrists; he took an active part in the official investigation.

An extract from the report of the Supreme Criminal Court dated July 13, 1826, states:

> Your Imperial Majesty will graciously observe:
>
> That, of the 121 defendants sentenced by the Supreme Criminal Court, 5 persons designated outside the categories are condemned to death by quartering; 31 persons, in the first category, are condemned to death by beheading; 17 persons, in the second category, are sentenced to civil death, exiled for life at hard labor; 2 persons, in the third category, are exiled to hard labor for life; 38 persons, in the fourth, fifth, sixth, and seventh categories, are sentenced to hard labor for specified terms, and then to penal settlement; 15 persons, in the eighth category, upon divestment of their rank and nobility, are sentenced to penal settlement for life; 3 persons, in the ninth category, upon divestment of their rank and nobility, are sentenced to banishment to Siberia for life; 1 person, in the tenth category, upon divestment of his rank and nobility, is sentenced to service as a common soldier until he earns promotion; 8 persons, in the eleventh category, upon divestment of their rank, are sentenced to service as soldiers with the right to earn promotion.

The effect of the sentences on the public was heightened because capital punishment had not been used as a legal penalty in Russia for fifty years.

Nicholas next aimed to strengthen the security system. In 1826, six months after the Decembrist uprising, he formed the Third Section, a department of secret police. It was a secret police force responsible for political security and was the tsar's chief weapon against subversion; it symbolized his reign. Designed by Count Aleksandr Benckendorff, head of the department (1826–1844), its chief functions were surveillance, the gathering of information on undesirables such as political dissidents and foreigners, the running of state prisons, prosecution of forgers, banishment of political criminals, and censorship. The department had a vast network of spies and informers and the cooperation of the military corps of gendarmes, established in 1836.

The actual decree establishing the Third Section was published on July 3, 1826:

Deeming it necessary to establish a Third Section in my own chancery, to be headed by Adjutant General Benkendorf, I command that the Special Chancery of the Ministry of Internal Affairs be abolished.

The matters to occupy this Third Section of my own chancery shall be as follows:

1. All instructions and announcements of the higher police on all matters.
2. Intelligence concerning the number of various sections and schismatic [religious] groups existing within the state.
3. Information concerning the discovery of counterfeit bank notes, coins, stamps, documents, and so on, the investigation and further prosecution of which remains under the jurisdiction of the Ministries of Finance and Internal Affairs.
4. Detailed intelligence concerning all persons under police surveillance, as well as all orders bearing on this matter.
5. The exile and placement of suspicious and harmful persons.
6. Supervisory and economic management of all places of internment where state criminals are kept.
7. All edicts and instructions concerning foreigners residing in Russia, arriving within its borders, and leaving it.
8. Reports on all events, without exception.
9. Statistical information relevant to the police.

The department, although supposed to protect the proletariat and to root out corruption, became increasingly repressive, causing the arrest of many populists (*narodniki*) and other subversives. This led to the assassination of the then head of the Third Section, General N. V. Mezentsov, in 1878.

The failure of the department to achieve much, largely due to the proliferation of false reports brought in by informers, resulted in its closure in 1880 by General Mikhail Loris-Melikov. Its functions were transferred to the Ministry of the Interior.

That Nicholas was not in principle opposed to reform is shown by the fact that soon after his accession he appointed a committee to discuss the reorganization of the country. The committee sat for ten years without producing any plans that gained the tsar's approval. But, while not opposed to reform in principle, Nicholas from the outset made it clear that reform should come from above, on the initiative of authority, and not as the result of demands from below. Nicholas was cautious in his approach to the revolutions that had broken out in many European countries in 1848 but repression was increased. This included the establishment of the Corps of Gendarmes, increased censorship, and many repressive measures in the universities such as reduction of the number of students and removing constitutional law from the curriculum.

The outstanding achievement of Nicholas's reign was the publication in 1830 of the *Complete Collection of Laws of the Russian Empire,* which was a forty-five-volume compilation of Russian laws, the first issued since the Code of 1649. It was compiled by Count Mikhail Mikhailovich Speransky (1772–1839) who was a minister of state under Alexander I and who had taken a prominent part in the proceedings against the Decembrist conspiracy. He also provided for keeping the code up to date.

Industrialization accelerated by using protectionist policies, particularly in the textile industry.

Throughout his reign Nicholas played the role of the policeman of Europe, actively intervening in defense of the principle of absolutism wherever it was threatened. The outstanding example of such intervention occurred in 1849, when a Russian army quelled the revolt of Hungary against the emperor of Austria. Nicholas's antirevolutionary views, however, did not prevent him from interfering in one area to defend subjects who had revolted against legitimate authority. This was in the Balkans, where the Greeks had risen in rebellion against the Ottoman Empire.

On March 15, 1854, France and Britain declared war on Russia in what was to be called the Crimean War. Russia had invaded Ottoman territories because of a dispute over who should protect the Christian shrines in the Ottoman-controlled Holy Land. When the Ottomans disagreed with Russia, Russia marched in and Britain and France issued an ultimatum for the tsar to withdraw. Napoleon III of France was a willing ally as he needed some military glory to raise his popularity at home. Britain was not at all happy about Russia's invasion as a Russian occupation of Istanbul would have been a serious threat to vital communications with India.

Nicholas told his son, Alexander, just before he died: "I am handing the country to you in a poor state." Nicholas I died on February 18, 1855, before the Crimean War ended. He was buried in the Cathedral of the St. Peter and St. Paul Fortress in St. Petersburg.

CHRONOLOGY

1796	Nicholas I born (June 25).
1825	Accession to the throne (December 14).
	Decembrist insurrection (December 14).
1853–1856	Crimean War.
1855	Nicholas I died (February 18).

BIBLIOGRAPHY

Lincoln, W. B. *Nicholas I: Emperor and Autocrat of All the Russias.* 1978.

Presniakov, A. E. *Emperor Nicholas I of Russia: The Apogee of Autocracy, 1825–1855.* 1974.

Riasanovsky, N.V. *Nicholas I and Official Nationality in Russia, 1825–1855.* 1959.

17

ALEXANDER II

Alexander Nikolaievich Romanov, also called the Tsar–Liberator,
April 29, 1818–March 1, 1881.

Emperor of Russia 1855–1881.

Alexander II was the eldest son of Nicholas I. In 1841, he married Princess Maria of Hesse-Darmstadt (Maria Alexandrovna), by whom he had six sons and two daughters. On his wife's death in 1880 he married morganatically Princess Catherine (Katia) Mikhailovna Dolgorukaya, on whom he conferred the title of Princess Yurievsky. There were two sons and two daughters by this union.

Alexander ascended the throne on February 19, 1855, at a critical point in Russian history. Russia had been defeated in the Crimean War but the war was not yet officially over. In December, Austria threatened to join the war against Russia, which caused Alexander to discuss peace terms and these were laid down in the Treaty of Paris of March 1856. Russia was forced to cede Southern Bessarabia to Moldavia. She had to give up her Black Sea fleet and her claim to an exclusive protectorate over Christians living in the Turkish empire.

Alexander II saw the causes of defeat in the Crimean War and started to bring about great fundamental changes—greater than any since Peter I (the Great). In 1841 A. P. Zablotskiy-Desyatovskiy, a government official under Alexander II, produced a report on the condition of the serfs, mainly in central European

Better to begin to abolish serfdom from above than to wait until it begins to abolish itself from below.

Russia, which gave a horrifying account of the lives of peasant serfs and the callousness of the average landlord. Alexander chose first the peasant problem and in 1856 advocated the abolition of serfdom and appointed a Select Committee. Alexander stated, "Better to begin to abolish serf-

Alexander II. Anonymous artist. The State Hermitage Museum, St Petersburg.

dom from above than to wait until it begins to abolish itself from below."

The Edict of Emancipation of the serfs (March 3, 1861) liberated serfs, hitherto regarded as chattels of the landowner. Ten million male peasants and their families were given their personal freedom without payment. Although a landmark in the history of Russia—the serf could marry, take legal action, own property in his name, and engage in business or trade—he was in fact economically dependent on the landlord. The serf had to buy the land from his previous owner; the amount and type of land often depended on the individual landowner's whim. The land could be redeemed by thirty to forty days' labor annually, or by *obrok*, a 6 percent tax paid to the landowner. In many cases the serfs were worse off following the 1861 edict.

THE MANIFESTO OF HIS MAJESTY, THE EMPEROR:

By the grace of God, we, Alexander II, Emperor and Autocrat of all the Russias, King of Poland, Grand Duke of Finland, etc., to all our faithful subjects make known:

Called by Divine Providence and by the sacred right of inheritance to the throne of our ancestors, we took a vow in our innermost heart so to respond to the mission which is intrusted to us as to surround with our affection and our Imperial solicitude all our faithful subjects of every rank and of every condition from the warrior who nobly bears arms for the defense of the country to the humble artisan devoted to the works of industry . . . .

We thus came to the conviction that the work of a serious improvement of the condition of the peasants was a sacred inheritance, bequeathed to us by our ancestors—a mission which, in the course of events, Divine Providence called upon us to fulfil.

We have commenced this work by an expression of our Imperial confidence towards the nobility of Russia, which has given us so many proofs of its devotion to the Throne and of its constant readiness to make sacrifices for the welfare of the country . . . .

Having invoked Divine assistance, we have resolved to carry this work into execution.

In virtue of the new dispositions above mentioned, the peasants attached to the soil (*attachés à la glebe*) will be invested within a term fixed by law with all the rights of free cultivators.

The proprietors retaining their rights of property on all the land belonging to them, grant to the peasants for a fixed regulated rental the full enjoyment of their close (*enclos*); and, moreover, to assure their livelihood and to guarantee the fulfilment of their obligations towards the Government, the quantity of arable land is fixed by the said dispositions as well as other rural appurtenances (*ougodie*).

But, in the enjoyment of these territorial allotments, the peasants are obliged, in return, to acquit the rentals fixed by the same dispositions to the profit of the proprietors. In this state, which must be a transitory one, the peasants shall be designated as "temporarily bound" (*temporairement obligés*).

At the same time they are granted the right of purchasing their close (*enclos*) and, with the consent of the proprietors, they may acquire in full property the arable lands and other appurtenances which are allotted to them as a permanent holding (*jouissance*). By the acquisition in full property of the quantity of land fixed the peasants are free from their obligations towards the proprietors of land thus purchased, and they enter definitively into the condition of free peasants—landholders (*paysans libres—propriétaires*).

By a special disposition concerning the domestics (*gens de la domesticité—dvorovye*) a transitory state is fixed for them adapted to their occupations and the exigencies of their position. On the expiration of a term of two years, dating from the day of the promulgation of these dispositions, they shall receive their full enfranchisement and some temporary immunities . . . .

We also count upon the generous devotion of our faithful nobility, and we are happy to testify to that body the gratitude it has deserved from us, as well as from the country, for the disinterested support it has given to the accomplishment of our designs. Russia will not forget that the nobility, acting solely upon its respect for the dignity of man and its love for its neighbor, has spontaneously renounced rights given to it by serfdom actually abolished, and laid the foundation of a new future, which is thrown open to the peasants . . .

And now, pious and faithful people, make upon the forehead the sacred sign of the cross and join thy prayers to ours to call down the blessings of the Most High upon the first free labors, the sure pledge of thy personal wellbeing and of the public prosperity.

Given at St. Petersburg, the 19th day of February [March 3] of the Year of Grace 1861, and the seventh of our reign.

ALEXANDER

Prince Peter Kropotkin (1842–1921) was a student in the Corps of Pages in 1861 when a statute abolishing serfdom was enacted. This extract from his *Memoirs of a Revolutionist* (1899) recalls the reaction to emancipation in St. Petersburg and on a family estate at Nikolskoye, Kaluga:

On 21 February 1861 we went on parade; and when all the military performances were over, Alexander II, remaining on horseback, loudly called out, "The officers to me!" They gathered round him, and he began, in a loud voice, a speech about the great event of the day.

"The officers . . . the representatives of the nobility in the army"—these scraps of sentences reached our ears—"an end has been put to centuries of injustice . . . I expect sacrifices from the nobility . . . the loyal nobility will gather round the throne" . . . and so on. Enthusiastic hurrahs resounded amongst the officers as he ended.

We ran rather than marched back on our way to the corps—hurrying to be in time for the Italian opera, of which the last performance in the season was to be given that afternoon; some manifestation was sure to take place then. Our military attire was flung off with great haste, and several of us dashed, lightfooted, to the sixth-story gallery. The house was crowded.

During the first entr'acte the smoking-room of the opera filled with excited young men, who all talked to one another, whether acquainted or not. We planned at once to return to the hall, and to sing, with the whole public in a mass choir, the hymn "God Save the Tsar."

However, sounds of music reached our ears, and we all hurried back to the hall. The band of the opera was already playing the hymn, which was drowned immediately in enthusiastic hurrahs coming from all parts of the hall. I saw Bavéri stopped, but the hurrahs continued. I saw the stick wave again in the air; I saw the fiddle-bows moving, and musicians blowing the brass instruments, but again the sound of voices overwhelmed the band. Bavéri began conducting the hymn once more, and it was only by the end of that third repetition that isolated sounds of the brass instruments pierced through the clamor of human voices.

The same enthusiasm was in the streets. Crowds of peasants and educated men stood in front of the palace, shouting hurrahs, and the tsar could not appear without being followed by demonstrative crowds running after his carriage. Herzen was right when, two years later, as Alexander was drowning the Polish insurrection in blood, and "Muravioff the Hanger" was strangling it on the scaffold, he wrote, "Alexander Nikolaevich, why did you not die on that day? Your name would have been transmitted in history as that of a hero."

Where were the uprisings which had been predicted by the champions of slavery? Conditions more indefinite than those which had been created by the Polozhenie (the emancipation law) could not have been invented. If anything could have provoked revolts, it was precisely the perplexing vagueness of the conditions created by the new law. And yet, except in two places where there were insurrections, and a very few other spots where small disturbances entirely due to misunderstandings and immediately appeased took place, Russia remained quiet,—more quiet than ever. With their usual good sense, the peasants had understood that serfdom was done away with, that "freedom had come," and they accepted the conditions imposed upon them, although these conditions were very heavy.

I was in Nikolskoye in August 1861, and again in the summer of 1862, and I was struck with the quiet, intelligent way in which the peasants had accepted the new conditions. They knew perfectly well how difficult it would be to pay the redemption tax for the land, which was in reality an indemnity to the nobles in lieu of the obligations of serfdom. But they so much valued the abolition of their personal enslavement that they accepted the ruinous charges—not without murmuring, but as a hard necessity—the moment that personal freedom was obtained . . . .

When I saw our Nikolskoye peasants, fifteen months after the liberation, I could not but admire them. Their inborn good nature and softness remained with them, but all traces of servility had disappeared. They talked to their masters as equals talk to equals, as if they never had stood in different relations. Besides, such men came out from among them as could make a stand for their rights.

Emancipation of the serfs left a gap in rural life that was partly filled by the establishment in 1864 of district and provincial councils (*zemstvos*) elected by all classes of the population. In 1870 municipal government was reformed.

There were legal reforms of 1864, which brought in legislation that separated the judiciary from the executive government and reformed court procedures. Formerly a branch of general administration, with all cases relying on secrecy and written evidence, the judiciary acquired independent judges and public hearings in court, with cases debated by lawyers. Procedure was simplified by introducing two ways of conducting a case, the general and the abbreviated procedure. Minor cases came before justices of the peace; serious criminal cases were tried by jury. The system did not apply to military courts. The central government attempted to sidestep the new legislation (when dealing with suspected revolutionary activity) by reserving certain categories of offense for special courts-martial. The reform is considered the most important and most successful of the Great Reforms of the 1860s.

Education saw changes. The universities regained their autonomy. In secondary education "modern" schools were introduced. More attention was paid to the education of girls. Primary education was left to the care of the local councils.

The Crimean War showed up also the weaknesses of Russia's military system. The most important reform in this sphere was the introduction in 1874 of conscription for the whole male population irrespective of status. Military justice was reformed and measures were taken to raise the educational standards of both officers and men.

A great influence on Russian affairs was Aleksandr Ivanovich Herzen (1812–1870), a radical journalist and political thinker and probably the greatest European publicist of his day. He disliked the social order of Russia and as a result of his association with a radical discussion group he was exiled (1834–1842). His father, who died in 1846, left him a fortune, and Herzen left Russia the following year, never to return. He was much influenced by the revolutions of 1848, and lived mainly in London, where he set up the Free Russian Press and published *The Bell* (*Kolokol*), the first Russian émigré journal, which had considerable influence inside Russia.

Under Alexander, Russia concentrated on strengthening its borders. In 1867 Alaska and the Aleutian Islands were sold to the United States. Alexander's greatest foreign policy achievement was the successful war of 1877–1878 against the Ottoman Empire, resulting in the liberation of Bulgaria and annulment of the conditions of the Treaty of Paris of 1856, imposed after Russia's defeat in the Crimean War.

There were attempts on the life of Alexander in 1866 and twice in 1879, and again in 1880, but on March 1, 1881, in St. Petersburg, Alexander was mortally wounded by a bomb thrown by a student, a member of the revolutionary organization *Narodnaya Volya* (The National Will). This revolutionary organization came into being in 1879. It concentrated on the killing of high government officials. Later, led by Ulyanov, Lenin's older brother, the St. Petersburg group attempted the assassination of Alexander III.

The Cathedral of the Resurrection was erected (1883–1907) on the site of the murder of Alexander II. He was buried in the Cathedral of the St. Peter and St. Paul Fortress in St. Petersburg.

CHRONOLOGY

1818 Alexander II born (April 29).

1856 Treaty of Paris ends Crimean War.

1861 Emancipation of serfs.
Army ceases to be used as punishment for criminals.

1870 Lenin born in Simbirsk (April 22).

1879 Attempts on life of Alexander II.

1880 Unsuccessful attempt on life of Alexander II.

1881 Alexander II assassinated in St. Petersburg by the National Freedom group, on the day he agrees to discuss political change.

BIBLIOGRAPHY

Almedingen, E. M. *The Emperor Alexander II.* 1962.
Graham, S. *A Life of Alexander II, Tsar of Russia.* 1935.
Mosse, W. E. *Alexander II and the Modernization of Russia.* 1958.

18

ALEXANDER III

Alexander Alexandrovich Romanov, February 26, 1845—October 20, 1894.

Emperor of Russia 1881—1894.

Alexander III was the second son of Alexander II. On the death of his elder brother Nicholas in 1865 he became heir to the throne and succeeded to it on the assassination of his father March 1, 1881. He was crowned in the Dormition Cathedral of the Moscow Kremlin on May 15, 1883. Alexander III married Princess Dagmar of Denmark (Maria Fyodorovna), who was formerly betrothed to Nicholas, and had four sons and two daughters. His eldest son became Nicholas II. Fearing for his life Alexander III refused to live in the Winter Palace and resided in Gatchina. This palace was designed by Emperor Paul and was in fact a fortress, surrounded by watchtowers and ditches. Alexander quickly had his father's assassins arrested and tried. They were publicly hanged. Earlier Leo Tolstoy wrote to Alexander pleading for the lives to be spared, but the letter was not passed on.

Soon after his accession on April 29, 1881, an Imperial Manifesto confirmed the emperor's determination to maintain the autocracy. It was drafted by Konstantin Petrovich Pobedonostsev (1827—1907). Alexander III depended heavily on his advice, together with that of Count Dmitry Tolstoy (1823—1889). Pobedonostsev was tutor to both Alexander III and Nicholas II and was reactionary. He was responsible for the illiberal schemes in Alexander III's reign, fighting against a constitution, freedom of the press, and trial by jury. Tolstoy was a lesser but important influence and was *Oberprokuror* of the Holy Synod in 1864 and became a reactionary minister of education in 1866. He felt that more concentration on classical languages would distract students from the issues of the day. In 1882 he was appointed interior minister.

Alexander III was more in sympathy with the views held by Nicholas I than with his father Alexander II, who he felt had weakened the monarchy. He canceled the idea of the so-called constitution his father had proposed to promulgate, and he issued a manifesto asserting his "faith in the principle of autocracy," which he felt himself called to "reinforce and protect from any infringement." He had a stubborn nature and this caused him to persist obstinately with any policy on which he had set his mind.

Alexander III. Portrait of Crown Prince Alexander Alexandrovich, by Vasily Pavlovich Hudoyarov, late 1870s to early 1880s. The State Hermitage Museum, St Petersburg.

His actions resulted in undoing much of what his father had achieved.

Alexander III's aim was to achieve a political ideal of a nation containing one nationality, one language, and one religion. He wished to curb the reforms brought about by his father, Alexander II, and in August 1881 issued the Temporary Regulations of 1881. These and other measures included:

The power of officials to (i) search, (ii) exile, (iii) try by courts-martial anyone considered to be a threat to the state;

The post of land captain (*zemsky nachalnik*) was introduced so that peasants were under more restrictions (1889). The land captain acted as justice of the peace;

The State Gentry Bank was established (1885);

Town government (1892) and the *zemstvo* system (1890) were reorganized and the electorate decreased, thus restricting the peasant vote. The electorate of St. Petersburg decreased from 21,000 to 8,000 and Moscow from 20,000 to 7,000;

The University Statute of 1884 brought higher education back under the complete control of the state;

Higher education for women abolished;

Russification of minorities such as Poles, Georgians, Armenians, and Finns;

Restrictions of Jews—from 1881 pogroms occur and increased official anti-Semitism;

Pressure brought on all those not of the Orthodox faith;

Press regulation made it impossible for radical journals to be published.

The reign coincided with an industrial revolution in Russia, and under a succession of enlightened finance ministers steps were taken to help the peasants. These included reducing the soul tax, which was finally abolished in 1887, and the establishment of a Peasant Land Bank in 1882.

Industry and trade were aided by the further extension of the railway system and by currency reforms. The protectionist economic policy helped the rapid industrial development of the country that resulted in great increase of the number of industrial workers and the spread of Marxist and social democratic ideas. In 1882 the employment of children below twelve years was banned and the working hours of those under fifteen years were limited. Factory inspectors were introduced and strikes were made illegal.

Alexander was fortunate in his finance ministers, who stabilized the whole financial system and built up Russia's gold reserves and achieved a surplus on the trade account, largely due to the export of grain. In 1891–1892 there was a great famine. The government ordered that the word famine should not be used in the press. Because there were delays in banning grain exports, opposition to the government began to grow.

Alexander was anti-German, unusual in a tsar who had German blood (his greatuncle was Wilhelm I of Germany). Initially, however, he believed that good relations with Germany were vital to Russia's interests. He was also anti-Semitic and believed that the attempt on his life was inspired by Jews. He was, however, unique as a tsar in that there was peace throughout his reign.

Alexander III died on October 20, 1894, in Livadia, in the Crimea, and was buried in the Cathedral of the St. Peter and St. Paul Fortress in St. Petersburg.

CHRONOLOGY

1845   Alexander III born (February 26).

1881   Accession to the throne (March 1).

Establishment of the *Okhrana*, Department for Safeguarding Public Security and Public Order.

1886   Abolition of soul tax (except in Siberia).

1887   Attempt on the life of Alexander III (March 1).

1894   Death of Alexander III at Livadia in the Crimea (October 20).

BIBLIOGRAPHY

Whelan, H. W. *Alexander III and the State Council.* 1982.
Zaionchkovskii, P. A. *The Russian Autocracy under Alexander III.* 1976.

19

NICHOLAS II

Nicholas Alexandrovich Romanov, May 6, 1868–July 17, 1918.

Emperor of Russia 1894–1917.

Nicholas II, the last Russian emperor, was the eldest son of Alexander III and ascended the throne on October 20, 1894. Less than a month after his accession Nicholas married Princess Alix of Hesse-Darmstadt (Alexandra Fyodorovna). They had four daughters (Olga, Tatiana, Maria, Anastasia) and a son, Alexis, who suffered from hemophilia. Nicholas's coronation on May 14, 1896, was followed four days later by a disaster. Owing to official mismanagement, panic broke out among a vast crowd (numbering about 500,000) assembled as part of the coronation festivities on a military training field at Khodynka, outside Moscow. A large number (estimated at 2,000 to 3,000) lost their lives, while many more were seriously injured.

Nicholas II was happy in his family life but was very different from his father. He was weak-willed and easily swayed. He shared Alexander III's belief in the infallibility of the principle of autocracy, though by his own lack of political insight he was to be the first and last Russian monarch to allow serious inroads to be made into his absolute power, and ultimately was largely responsible for the overthrow of his dynasty and of the monarchy as an institution in Russia. He struggled desperately to hold on to power during both the 1905 and the 1917 revolutions. In 1895, in a speech, Nicholas II stated:

> I know that recently, in *zemstvo* assemblies, there have been heard voices carried away by senseless dreams about the participation of *zemstvo* representatives in governmental affairs. Let everyone know that, devoting all my strength to the good of my people, I will preserve the principles of autocracy as firmly and

Nicholas II. Portrait of Emperor Nicholas II with Remarque-Portrait of Tsarevich Alexei Nikolayevich, by Mikhail Victorovich Rundaltsov, 1913. The State Hermitage Museum, St Petersburg.

undeviatingly as did my unforgettable late father.

Throughout history the Romanovs tended to show a reaction against their predecessors; Catherine II (the Great) and Paul, and Alexander II and Alexander III are examples. Nicholas's affirming his unswerving belief in the principle of autocracy, as did his father, Alexander III, led to the inevitability of the Revolutions of 1917.

During his reign Russia was involved in two wars. The first was the Russo-Japanese war of 1904–1905 in which over 400,000 Russians were killed, wounded, or captured; Japan lost 170,000 personnel. Russia, in order to become a great Pacific naval power, needed an ice-free port in the Far East. In 1896 it obtained a lease for Port Arthur from China and connected this port with St. Petersburg by means of the Trans-Siberian Railway. In 1900 Russia assumed power over the Chinese province of Amur, but this was opposed by Japan and Britain. Russia eventually agreed to evacuate the area it had occupied but, in fact, failed to keep the agreement.

In 1903 suggestions were made to clarify the integrity of China, Manchuria, and Korea. Russia failed to respond to these overtures and Japan withdrew its minister from St. Petersburg. Two days later Japan landed troops at Chemulpo and on February 8, 1904, there was a surprise attack on the Russian Far Eastern fleet in the harbor of Port Arthur. The Japanese did not declare war until six days later and subsequently they besieged the city, finally taking it on December 19, 1904. The Japanese army captured Korea and much of Manchuria and decisively defeated the Russian army at Mukden in March 1905.

In October 1904 the Russian Baltic fleet sailed to the Far East under Admiral Zinovi Rozhestvenskii and created an international incident (known as the Dogger Bank Incident) when the Russian vessels fired on some English fishing trawlers on the Dogger Bank, an extensive sandbank in the North Sea, and inflicted casualties. Russia claimed by way of excuse that there were Japanese torpedo boats with the fishing boats. Poorly maintained and obsolete, the Russian fleet was destroyed by the Japanese on May 27, 1905, at the Battle of Tsushima. Russia lost eight battleships, several cruisers, and five destroyers; five ships were captured and only three returned to Vladivostok. Japan lost three torpedo boats. The war ended with the Treaty of Portsmouth (New Hampshire) and was mediated by U.S. President Theodore Roosevelt. Japan gained Port Arthur, half of Sakhalin Island, and an important role in Korea. Both Russia and Japan left Manchuria, and Chinese exclusive administration was resumed.

By the end of the Russo-Japanese war a revolutionary crisis was looming. The refusal to allow the *zemstvo* movement a national assembly had outraged many liberals. On January 9, 1905, many innocent, peaceful demonstrators were fired upon by troops in St. Petersburg; it marked the beginning of the 1905 Revolution. The employees of the Putilov factory who were members of Father Georgii Gapon's organization of workers felt that some of their members had been victimized and had gone on strike. The employers decided upon a lockout, whereupon the workers decided to present their grievances to the tsar in the form of a petition; a certain number of political demands were also included by intellectuals. Having told the authorities of this planned march the demonstrators were fired on by troops; as a result 96 people were killed and 339 wounded.

The petition read:

> We working men of St. Petersburg, our wives and children, and our parents, helpless and aged men and women, have come to you, our ruler, in quest of justice and protection . . . . We have no strength at all, O Sovereign. Our patience is at an end. We are approaching that terrible moment when death is better than the continuance of intolerable sufferings . . . .

Our first wish was to discuss our needs with our employers, but this was refused to us; we were told that we have no legal right to discuss our conditions . . . .

Every worker and peasant is at the mercy of our officials, who accept bribes, rob the Treasury and do not care at all for the people's interests. The bureaucracy of the government has ruined the country, involved it in a shameful war and is leading Russia nearer and nearer to utter ruin. We, the Russian workers and people, have no voice at all in the expenditure of the huge sums collected in taxes from the impoverished population. We do not even know how our money is spent. The people are deprived of any right to discuss taxes and their expenditure. The workers have no right to organize their own labor unions for the defense of their own interests.

Is this, O Sovereign, in accordance with the laws of God, by whose grace you reign? And how can we live under such laws? Break down the wall between yourself and your people . . . . The people must be represented in the control of their country's affairs. Only the people themselves know their own needs. So do not reject their help, accept it, command forthwith that representatives of all classes, groups, professions, and trades shall come together. Let capitalists and workers, bureaucrats and priests, doctors and teachers meet together and choose their representatives. Let all be equal and free. And to this end let the election of members to the Constitutional Assembly take place in conditions of universal, secret and equal suffrage.

This is our chief request; upon it all else depends; this is the only balm for our sore wounds; without it our wounds will never heal, and we shall be borne swiftly to our death.

The Bloody Sunday massacre precipitated nationwide strikes, uprisings, and mutinies (most notably the mutiny on the battleship *Potemkin*). The situation created a serious threat to the régime. By October, Russia was gripped by a general strike. The St. Petersburg

Soviet (workers' council), dominated by the Mensheviks, was established. In August the tsar promised to create an elected national institution, the Duma. The insurrection continued until October. Nicholas II issued his October manifesto promising a constitutional monarchy. The revolution was substantially crushed by the end of December.

The main clauses of the October manifesto were:

We impose upon the government the duty to execute Our inflexible will:

To grant the population the inviolable foundations of civic freedom based on the principles of genuine personal inviolability, freedom of conscience, speech, assemblies, and associations.

Without postponing the scheduled elections to the State Duma, to admit in the participation of the Duma insofar as possible in the short time that remains before its scheduled meeting all those classes of the population which presently are completely deprived of voting rights, and to leave further development of general elective law to the future legislative order;

To establish as an unbreakable rule that no law shall become effective without the confirmation by the State Duma, and that the elected representatives of the people shall be guaranteed an opportunity of real participation in the supervision of the legality of the acts by authorities whom We shall appoint.

The Duma was established in response to the 1905 revolution and the consequences of Bloody Sunday. Freedoms granted in the manifesto were soon annulled. The tsar could rule absolutely when the Duma was not in session and he could dissolve it at will.

The Union of October 17, known as Octobrists, was a political party founded in November 1905 with the aim of ensuring the implementation of the promises made in Nicholas II's manifesto of 1905, which granted a constitution. The party was led by Aleksandr Ivanovich Guchkov (1862–1936), and the party won twelve seats in the first Duma, thirty-two in the second, 150 in the third, and ninety-seven in the fourth. In the third and fourth Dumas, the Octobrists had an overall majority. They joined the progressive bloc in 1915 and took part in the provisional government of 1917.

Petr Arkadevich Stolypin (1862–1911) was premier from 1906 to 1911 and his policy was, on the one hand, firm suppression of the revolution and, on the other, reforms designed to remove the causes of discontent. He was not afraid of using unpopular measures—he dissolved two Dumas—or even unconstitutional ones, such as the reform of electoral law in 1907 by imperial decree.

During Stolypin's premiership reactionary populist groups known as the Black Hundreds were particularly active. While endorsing national representation and the need to improve the life of peasants and workers, they also supported absolutism and anti-Semitism. The least harmful activity was the staging of popular demonstrations at which the crowds would carry icons and portraits of the royal family, accompanied by patriotic and religious songs. More sinister was the hatred of the Jews, which was encouraged. They organized pogroms directed against Jews and general terror against university students and members of free professions; "Beat the Yids and the Intelligents; Save Russia" became their slogan. The authorities tended to ignore the pogroms, and Nicholas II thanked the Black Hundreds for their support.

Stolypin's agrarian reforms (1906–1911) enabled the peasants to leave the village communities and set up separate farms. Stolypin also facilitated purchase of land by the peasants through the Peasant Bank and colonization of Siberia and Russian Central Asia by peasants from overpopulated provinces of European Russia. A liberal conservative, Stolypin was opposed both by the radicals and the extreme right. He was assassinated in 1911 by a Socialist Revolutionary terrorist who was also a police agent.

Stolypin's predecessor was Count Sergei Yulievich Witte (1849–1915), who was prime minister from 1903 to 1906. He negotiated the Treaty of Portsmouth, which ended the Russo-Japanese War, and suggested to Nicholas II the granting of a constitution providing for a legislative duma. A moderate conservative, Witte incurred the suspicion of both the liberals and the extreme right, including the emperor, who suddenly dismissed him in 1906.

Another important figure in this period was Vyacheslav Konstantinovich Plehve (1846–1904), a staunch supporter of the autocracy, who was the minister of the interior from 1902 until he was assassinated in 1904.

In April 1912 workers in the Lena goldfield went on strike in order to obtain better living and working conditions and higher wages. About 5,000 protesters were brutally repressed by troops, who fired on them, killing approximately 200 and wounding many others. As a result, the Russian workforce became incensed, and during that year some 725,000 workers went on strike. The Duma, also angered, called for an investigation of the massacre, which resulted in heavy criticism of the way in which the goldfield was managed.

Duma had been the name of a Kievan political institution consisting of a council of boyars, but is better known as the elected legislative assemblies, which, with the Council of the Empire, comprised the Russian legislature from 1906 to 1917, and which were established in response to the 1905 Revolution. The First State 442-member Duma, elected by universal male suffrage, met for 73 days in 1906, and the second met in 1907 for 102 days. The first and second Dumas were unsuccessful in that, although it was expected that the representatives would be conservative, they were mainly liberal and socialist, and their demands for reform were totally unacceptable to the government.

About 180 deputies met in Vyborg to protest against the dissolution of the first Duma by Nicholas II in July 1906. The largest majority were Kadets (Constitutional Democratic Party), and the manifesto urged the people not to pay taxes or undertake military service when conscripted. The plan failed and the deputies were arrested, given three months' imprisonment, and, probably more important for Russia, deprived of their right to stand for election to the second Duma.

In 1906 the Council of the Empire was attached to the Duma as an upper house with 196 members, 98 of them nominated by the tsar and 98 elected by the clergy, the corporations of nobles, and other academic, civic, and commercial bodies. Both houses had the same powers. The Duma had limited competence and could not consider the army or navy; all laws had to be proposed to a minister who would consider them and prepare his own draft; and ministers were responsible to the tsar. A preliminary report of all measures had to be submitted to the Council of the Empire and the tsar for approval. A majority vote of the Duma was submitted to the upper house, and in case of disagreement the tsar could intervene.

The third Duma ran its full five-year term (1907–1912) and gave support to the government's agrarian reforms and military reorganization. The fourth Duma sat from 1912 to 1917, but it gradually became opposed to the government's war policy and increasingly critical of the imperial régime. On the abdication of Nicholas II the provisional committee established by the Duma asked Prince Lvov to form a provisional government.

International conferences known as the Hague Conventions were convened by Nicholas II and met May 18 to July 19, 1899 and June 15 to October 18, 1907 in the Netherlands with the aim of "a possible reduction to the excessive armaments which weigh upon all nations" by "putting a limit on the progressive development of the present armaments." Twenty-six countries were represented. The first convention's achievements were limited but did include agreement on the use of gas, expanding bullets, and banning of explosives launched from balloons, and the creation of a court of arbitration (the International Court of Justice). The second convention reached agreement on a number of naval matters and on the employment of force to recover debts but failed to reach any consensus on major issues. A further convention was planned for 1915 but because of World War I did not meet. The two conventions did influence the planning for the League of Nations.

A great influence on the royal family was a Siberian peasant who exerted a pernicious influence at court and on political affairs. He was Grigory Yefimovich Rasputin (1872–1916). Although without education, he allegedly possessed hypnotic powers, and he claimed to be able to work miracles, preaching that physical contact with himself had a healing effect. As a youth Rasputin had been influenced by the *Khlysty* (flagellants) sect. In 1903 Rasputin arrived in St. Petersburg as a *starets* (holy man) and as such gained access to the highest circles of society. He exercised virtually unlimited influence on Tsarina

Rasputin arrived in St. Petersburg as a starets (holy man) and as such gained access to the highest circles of society.

Alexandra by using hypnotism to stop the hemophiliac tsarevich's bleeding. She viewed him as a divine missionary sent to save the dynasty. The church denounced him as an imposter, and in 1912 he was sent back to Siberia. In 1914 he returned, and in 1915, when the tsarina was left in charge of domestic affairs following Nicholas's decision to assume full command of the army forces, Rasputin's influence was considerable, and many of the more capable ministers were dismissed. He was assassinated in 1916.

Boris Vladimirovich Stürmer (1848–1917) was appointed prime minister in 1916 and was also in charge of the ministry of foreign affairs. A puppet of Rasputin, he was not liked and was dismissed from the Duma on November 23, 1916.

On July 19, 1914, Russia and Germany declared war against each other; Austria joined Germany on July 25. France and Britain who were bound by treaties declared war against Germany and Austria on August 4. The Russian army had a war strength of 5,500,000 by August 1914, having recovered from the Russo-Japanese war. It was, however, much inferior to the German army in artillery, machine guns, planes, and communications, although stronger than the Austrians. To relieve the French, the army invaded East Prussia, suffering defeats at Tannenberg and the Masurian Lakes. It also overran Galicia, although by early 1915 its ammunition was spent. In May the Germans attacked with overwhelming artillery and drove the Russians back with frightful losses to a line from Riga to Galicia. In September, Nicholas assumed supreme command of the armed forces. When the offensive halted in October, the Russians rebuilt the army, which had lost 3,400,000 men since August 1914, and by June 1916 it was stronger than ever.

Under General Aleksei Alekseyevich Brusilov, the Russians overran the Austrians and by September had taken 400,000 prisoners. But the

Russian losses of almost 2,500,000 men during 1916 demoralized the soldiers, who were already deserting in large numbers. On the Turkish front the Russians also achieved considerable but indecisive successes. By early 1917 the Russian army was close to collapse and in March Nicholas left Petrograd (the new name for St. Petersburg) for army general headquarters. On March 2, 1917, Nicholas II abdicated in favor of his brother Grand Duke Michael Alexandrovich (1878–1918).

Nicholas II sent this message to his people:

In the days of great struggle with an external foe, who has been striving for almost three years to enslave our native land, it has been God's will to visit upon Russia a new grievous trial. The internal disturbances which have begun among the people threaten to have a calamitous effect on the future conduct of a hard-fought war. The destiny of Russia, the honor of our heroic army, the welfare of the people, the whole future of our beloved fatherland demand that the war be carried to a victorious conclusion no matter what the cost. The cruel foe is straining his last resources and the time is already close at hand when our valiant army, together with our glorious allies, will be able to crush the foe completely. In these decisive days in the life of Russia, We have deemed it Our duty in conscience to help Our people to draw closer together and to unite all the forces of the nation for a speedier attainment of victory, and, in agreement with the State Duma, We have judged it right to abdicate the Throne of the Russian State and to lay down the Supreme Power. Not wishing to be parted from Our beloved Son, We hand over Our succession to Our Brother, the Grand Duke Mikhail Alexandrovich, and bless Him on his accession to the Throne of the Russian State. We enjoin Our Brother to conduct the affairs of the state in complete and inviolable union with the representatives of the people in the legislative bodies on the principles to be established by them, and to take an inviolable oath to this effect. In the name of the dearly beloved native land, We call upon all true sons of the Fatherland to fulfil their sacred duty to it by their obedience to the Tsar at this time of national trial and to help Him, together with the people's representatives, to lead the Russian State onto the path of victory, prosperity, and glory. May the Lord God help Russia!

NICHOLAS

Pskov, March 2, 1917. 3:00 p.m.

On March 3 the Grand Duke refused the throne, consenting to accept it only if he were offered it by a democratically elected constituent assembly. Although Pavel Nikolaevich Milyukov (1859–1943), the leading liberal in Russia from 1905 to 1917, and Aleksandr Ivanovich Guchkov (1862–1936), head of the Octobrist party, both members of the provisional government, implored Michael to accept the throne, he declined, thus bringing to an end the Romanov dynasty.

Prince Georgy Yevgonevich Lvov (1861–1925) formed a provisional government at the request of the provisional committee of the Duma following the abdication of Nicholas II and was prime minister until Aleksandr Kerensky replaced him in July 1917.

Nicholas and his family lived quietly, under arrest, in their palace at Tsarskoye Selo from March to August 1917. In August they were sent to Tobolsk in Siberia. After the Bolsheviks seized power in November 1917, they were transferred to Ekaterinberg, where on July 17, 1918, the entire family was shot by order of the local soviet. On August 14, 2000, at a meeting in Moscow, the Jubilee Bishops' Council of the Russian Orthodox Church voted for the canonization of Nicholas II.

CHRONOLOGY

1868	Nicholas II born (May 6).
1894	Accession to throne (October 20).
1904–1905	Russo-Japanese war.
1904	Tsarevich Alexis is born (August).

1905	Surrender at Port Arthur (January).
	Bloody Sunday (January).
	Destruction of Russian fleet at Tsushima by Japanese (May).
	Mutiny on the battleship *Potemkin* (June).
	Tsar issues manifesto promising a constitution and an elected parliament with genuine legislative power. The tsar also grants freedom of the press, free speech and religious toleration (October).
1906	First Duma assembles; votes no confidence in the government (May).
	Deadlock over the constitutional issue leads to the dissolution of the Duma (July).
1912	Term of third Duma ends (June).
	Elections to the fourth Duma (November).
1914	Germany declares war on Russia (August).
1915	Austro-German offensive in Galicia defeats Russians (May).
	Duma meets to consider the way the war is being conducted (August).
	Tsar assumes supreme command of the armed forces (September).
1917	Duma meets (February).
	Tsar leaves Petrograd for army general headquarters (March).
	Tsar Nicholas II, in Pskov, abdicates for himself and for his son, in favor of his brother, Grand Duke Michael, at the same time confirming the new ministry and asking the country to support it.
	Grand Duke Michael chooses not to accept the throne unless he is asked by a constituent assembly (March 2).
	Imperial family arrested (March).
	A Bolshevik government is formed (November).

1918	Russians sign Treaty of Brest-Litovsk, giving up large areas of pre-Revolutionary Russia (March).
	Execution of imperial family at Ekaterinburg (July 17).
1991	Bones of Nicholas II and family exhumed.
1998	Remains interred in the St. Catherine's Chapel of the St. Peter and St. Paul Cathedral, St. Petersburg.

BIBLIOGRAPHY

Lieven, D. C. B. *Nicholas II: Emperor of All the Russias.* 1993.

Nicholas II. Letters of the Tsar to the Tsaritsa, 1914–1917. 1929.

Radzinsky, E. *The Last Tsar: The Life and Death of Nicholas II.* 1992.

20

KERENSKY

Aleksandr Fedorovich Kerensky, April 22, 1881–June 11, 1970.

Prime Minister July 15, 1917–October 25, 1917.

Kerensky was born in Simbirsk (Ulyanovsk) and graduated in history and law at St. Petersburg University and was noted for his role as defending counsel in political trials. In 1912 he traveled to Siberia to investigate the Lena Goldfield Massacre.

He joined the Socialist Revolutionary party in 1905, was arrested, and exiled but returned in 1906. He was elected in 1912 to the fourth Duma as a *Trudovik* (Labor) delegate. His eloquence and fearless directness made him a popular opposition leader. He was considered an outstanding non-Bolshevik politician, and in March 1917 he became vice-president of the Petrograd soviet and minister of justice in the first provisional government.

The provisional government had been formed by the Duma in February 1917 in Petrograd upon the collapse of the autocracy. It promised to form a constitutional assembly and to hold free elections. It abolished the secret police and granted religious freedom. Many of its leaders were of a conservative outlook, although Kerensky was a moderate socialist. Because of the war effort, grave problems, such as redistribution of land and the rights of non-Russian people to self-government, could not be resolved. As a result, discontent continued to grow.

Taking over the war ministry in May 1917, Kerensky attempted to reorganize the army and in July under Allied pressure launched a short-lived offensive. Lack of clarity in his dealings with General Lavr Georgevich Kornilov (1870–1918) led to Kerensky's downfall. Kornilov was the Petrograd military commander in 1917 and was responsible for the arrest of Nicholas II and his family. As commander in chief of all Russian forces in August 1917, he believed that the provisional government was incapable of dealing with any threat from the Bolsheviks. Mistakenly believing that Kerensky was in agreement, he organized his troops to march on Petrograd but was arrested on Kerensky's orders. This action strengthened the Bolsheviks, and, after the fall of Kerensky, Kornilov escaped to join the anti-Bolshevik forces of Anton Denikin on the Don, where he was killed in action.

On July 15, 1917, Kerensky became head of a reconstructed government but the task of rallying the workers and a distracted country of weakened by war proved beyond his powers. Critics blamed him for the seizure power by the Bolsheviks. The Petrograd Soviet of Workers' Deputies was established at the same time as the provisional government and this had the support of industrial workers and socialists, and in October 1917 the Soviet overthrew the provisional government. After trying various expedients to establish a unified authority he was driven out of power. Settling in Paris, he became leader of the émigré Social Revolutionaries and edited their paper, *Dni*. In 1940 he went to Australia and in 1946 settled in the United States.

Sir George Buchanan, who was British ambassador in Petrograd 1910–1918, recorded in his memoirs:

> Kerensky's Government had fallen, as the Empire had fallen, without a struggle. Both the Emperor and he had been wilfully blind to the dangers which threatened them, and both had allowed the situation to get beyond their control before taking any measures for their own protection. It was only when his hour had already struck and when, as Rodzianko telegraphed, it was too late that the Emperor consented to grant a constitution. It was the same with Kerensky. He waited and procrastinated. When at last he made up his mind to act, he found that the Bolsheviks had secured the support of the garrison and that it was he, and not they, who was to be suppressed. If I had to write the epitaphs of the Empire and the Provisional Government, I would do so in two words—lost opportunities.

R. H. Bruce Lockhart in his *Memoirs of a British Agent* (1932) wrote:

Kerensky was the victim of the bourgeois hopes which his short-lived success aroused. He was an honest, if not a great, man—sincere in spite of his oratorical talents, and, for a man who for four months was worshipped as a god; comparatively modest. From the start he was fighting a hopeless battle, trying to drive back into the trenches a nation which had already finished with the war. Caught between the cross-fires of the Bolshevik Left, which was screaming peace at every street-corner and in every trench, and of the Right and of the Allies, who were demanding the restoration of discipline by Tsarist methods, he had no chance. And he fell, because whoever had tried to do what he did was bound to fall.

From the start he was fighting a hopeless battle, trying to drive back into the trenches a nation which had already finished with the war.

CHRONOLOGY

1881	Kerensky born in Simbirsk (Ulyanovsk) (April 22).
ca. 1905	Joined the Socialist Revolutionary party.
1912	Elected to the fourth Duma.
1917	Minister of justice (March).
	Minister of war and of the navy (May).
	Prime minister (July).
	Supreme commander-in-chief (September).
	Escaped to the front following the October Revolution (October 25).
1970	Died in New York City (June 11).

BIBLIOGRAPHY

Abraham, R. *Alexander Kerensky, the First Love of the Revolution.* 1987.

Kerensky, A. F. *The Kerensky Memoirs: Russia and History's Turning Point.* 1987.

Kerensky, A. F. *The Road to Tragedy.* 1935.

Kerensky, A. F. and R. P. Browder. *Documents.* 1961.

21

LENIN

Vladimir Ilyich Lenin (Ulyanov), April 22, 1870–January 21, 1924.

President of the Council of People's Commissars, 1917–1922.

Lenin was born at Simbirsk (later renamed Ulyanovsk) on the middle Volga. His elder brother, Alexandr Ilyich Ulyanov, was a member of the People's Will and the manufacturer of the bombs intended for the assassination of Alexander III. Ulyanov was hanged in the Schlüsselburg prison in St. Petersburg on May 8, 1887. His involvement in the revolutionary movement and his execution made a great impact on Lenin's subsequent development. At Simbirsk grammar school he was awarded a gold medal. The headmaster, Fyodor Kerensky, father of a later prime minister, Alexandr Kerensky, said of him, "He is quite talented, invariably diligent, prompt and reliable."

He was expelled from Kazan University in 1887, having taken part in a student demonstration. Lenin read widely including the works of Marx and of other Russian revolutionary writers and took his law examinations externally. In his early twenties, Lenin founded the St. Petersburg League of Struggle for the Emancipation of the Working Class, prototype of the Bolshevik party, and stated that the workers would with the aid of the peasantry overthrow first the monarchy and then capitalism in Russia.

Early in 1897, the government exiled Lenin to eastern Siberia where in the following year he married Nadezhda Konstantinovna Krupskaya, a St. Petersburg revolutionary colleague. In Siberia, Lenin and his wife jointly translated the Webbs' *History of Trade Unionism*, and Lenin completed his *Development of Capitalism in Russia*. Before leaving Russia in 1900 after his release, he organized correspondents, publication and distribution for *Iskra* (The Spark), an illegal Marxist paper, which he thereafter edited in Munich and London. This journal

Vladimir Lenin poses in his study at the Kremlin in October 1918.

with his book *What Is to Be Done?* helped to provide an ideology and create an organization for a Russian Marxist party. The Russian Social-Democratic Labor party was formally established at a London congress in 1903. Lenin insisted that members must be active in the party and disciplined, but disagreement over a number of issues led to the emergence of two main groups, the Bolsheviks who were of the radical faction, and the Mensheviks. The Bolsheviks, meaning the majority, were headed by Lenin. Many of the Mensheviks were the followers of Pavel Borisovich Axelrod (1850–1928) and Leo Trotsky (Lev Davidovich Bronstein) (1879–1940). In 1922 the Mensheviks were suppressed and in 1931 a show trial took place in Moscow.

After the 1903 congress Lenin lost control of *Iskra* but continued to influence the movement in Russia through other newspapers, personal contacts, polemical books, and correspondence amounting to 300 political letters a month. During the revolutionary uprisings of 1905, he returned in disguise to Russia, working there illegally until the end of 1907 when he escaped to Geneva. In the period of intensified reaction after 1907 many intellectuals left the Bolsheviks.

Lenin's main work of organization in these years was to keep the Bolsheviks together, using all opportunities for open activity while strengthening their underground organization so as to be able to guide the next wave of popular opposition to the tsarist government. This began with the Lena goldfields strike and massacre of 1912; that same year at the Prague conference the Bolshevik party was formed by expelling Mensheviks from the Social Democratic Labor party.

The March Revolution of 1917 made it possible for Lenin and his fellow émigrés to return to Russia. The "Sealed Train" took Lenin—and thirty of his comrades—from Zurich, Switzerland, to the Finland Station in Petrograd in April 1917. The journey through Germany, Sweden, and Finland was arranged by the German government with the aim of helping to bring to an end the fighting on the Eastern Front and so free a million troops to reinforce its armies in France.

Leon Trotsky sings and addresses a huge assemblage during the session of the Third International in Moscow, December 1921.

Lenin's *April Theses*, produced on reaching Petrograd, outlined the Bolsheviks' path to power. While in hiding to escape arrest after street clashes that took place in July, he wrote the famous unfinished work *State and Revolution* and directed the political preparation for the seizure of power by the soviets, the local ad hoc "parliaments," in the largest of which the Bolsheviks now had a majority.

As head of the government formed after the Bolshevik revolution, Lenin played as dominant a part in building up, guiding, and consolidating the new state as he had done in creating the Bolshevik party. His insistence on immediate peace with Germany overcame the opposition within the party and led to the treaty of Brest-Litovsk. An armistice was concluded with Germany early in December, and peace negotiations were begun at the headquarters of Prince Leopold of Bavaria at Brest-Litovsk. The treaty was signed on March 3, 1918.

The chief terms of this treaty were: (1) All mutual agitation and propaganda to cease; (2) Soviet Russia agreed to renounce control of certain territories that formerly belonged to Tsarist Russia; (3) Germany to evacuate certain parts of Russia then occupied; (4) Russia to evacuate the east Anatolian provinces of Turkey, as well as the districts of Kars, Ardahan, and Batumi, and Estonia, Livonia, Finland, and the Aaland Islands; (5) Russia to demobilize its army completely and keep all warships within its harbors; (6) Russia to recognize the treaty of peace concluded by the Central Powers and the Ukrainian People's Republic; (7) Iran and Afghanistan to be respected as free and independent states; (8) mutual renunciation of payment of war costs.

Seriously wounded in an attempted assassination (August 1918), Lenin recovered to see Russia through the civil war and the subsequent beginnings of economic rehabilitation, the outstanding fruits of his intense activity being the establishment of the Communist International in 1919, early plans for the Soviet Union's social and industrial development, and the realistic New Economic Policy (NEP) of 1921, which was introduced as a compromise after war communism had failed. War communism was the name given to the Bolshevik government's social and economic policies of 1918–1921. In order to support the Bolsheviks in the civil war fully and to build communism in general, war communism was characterized by the nationalization of industry and trade, wages in kind for workers, and enforced labor service. These measures were unpopular, and in 1921 there occurred several uprisings.

NEP was not well received by communists; for some it was considered a defeat and a retreat from socialism. Under NEP energy, communications, heavy industry, and so on, stayed in state hands, while light industry and agriculture reverted to private ownership. Trade was again legal and Soviet Russia recovered. For the peasant it was the golden era of Soviet rule. NEP was brought to an end when Stalin launched the first Five-Year Plan (October 1928–1932). During NEP there was a developed system of producers' and consumers' cooperatives, and many cottage industries, but all this was destroyed by Stalin who forced peasants to join collectives (*kolkhoz*) and state (*sovkhoz*) farms.

Work became increasingly difficult for Lenin from the beginning of 1922 when his injury and the intensity and hardness of his life began to tell. Working to the end even during attacks of paralysis, he died on January 21, 1924. Succession to the leadership had exercised his mind during his last years. He had fears about the two main contenders, Trotsky and Stalin.

Leo Trotsky (Lev Davidovich Bronstein) was a theorist and revolutionary born at Yanova in Ukraine, and in 1897 he became a leader of the south Russian labor union in Odessa, being arrested in 1898. Exiled to Siberia in 1900, he escaped abroad. In 1905 he returned to Russia and became president of the St. Petersburg soviet but was again arrested. After a second escape from Siberia in 1907, he lived until 1914 in Austria. That year Trotsky went to France and from there he went to Spain, where he was imprisoned, and on to the United States. In 1917 he returned to Russia, but was imprisoned by the provisional government. He joined the Bolsheviks and he took a prominent part in seizing power on behalf of the Petrograd soviet of which he was again president, and was Lenin's chief partner in the October Revolution.

As commissar for foreign affairs, Trotsky led the Russian delegation at Brest-Litovsk but was opposed to the conclusion of the treaty and resigned. As commissar for war (1918–1925), he conducted operations on many fronts during the civil war. In the years 1920 to 1926 he elaborated his theory, formed in 1905, of "permanent revolution," according to which socialism could not be built in Russia without revolutions in the West, and led various opposition factions inside the Bolshevik party. In 1927 he was expelled from the party. Exiled to Alma Ata, he continued to conduct political activities by correspondence with his followers and was deported to Turkey in 1929. Trotsky subsequently lived in France, Norway, and Mexico. At the Moscow trials (1936–1938), he was depicted as a traitor to Russia and to socialism. He was assassinated in Mexico in 1940, probably by a Soviet agent.

Lenin wrote, "Comrade Trotsky . . . is personally perhaps the most capable man in the present Central Committee but he has displayed excessive self-assurance." "Comrade Stalin having become General Secretary has unlimited authority and I am not sure that he will always be capable of using that authority with sufficient caution . . . ." "These two qualities of the two outstanding leaders of the present can inadvertently lead to a split."

> *Comrade Trotsky . . . is personally perhaps the most capable man in the present Central Committee but he has displayed excessive self-assurance.*

In January 1923, Lenin wrote, "Stalin is too rude . . . which becomes intolerable in a General Secretary. That is why I suggest that the comrades think about a way of removing Stalin from that post."

CHRONOLOGY

1870 Vladimir Ilyich Ulyanov, who later adopted the pseudonym Lenin, is born in Streletskaya Ulitsa (now Ulyanovsk), Simbirsk (April 22).

1887 Lenin takes part in student demonstrations, he is arrested and expelled from the University of Kazan.

1895 Lenin founds the Union of Struggle for the Liberation of the Working Class in St. Petersburg (November).

The majority of members of the union are arrested and Lenin's sentence is fifteen months in prison and exile to Siberia for three years (December).

1900 Lenin leaves Russia to live abroad.

1902 Lenin's *What Is to Be Done?* is published.

1907 Lenin emigrates and will not return to Russia for ten years.

1917 Lenin arrives back in Petrograd and gives the address known as "The April Theses."

Fearing arrest, Lenin flees to Finland (July).

Lenin secretly returns to Petrograd from Finland (October).

The Winter Palace cut off and ministers of provisional government arrested. Kerensky flees. Lenin announces the transfer of power to the Military Revolutionary Committee and the victory of the socialist revolution (November).

1921 New Economic Policy (NEP) introduced.

1923 Lenin suffers a further stroke and this ends his participation in political affairs.

1924 Lenin dies (January 21).

Lenin is placed in the mausoleum in Red Square, Moscow (January 27).

BIBLIOGRAPHY

Service, R. *Lenin: A Political Life*. 3 vols, 1985–1995.
Volkogonov, D. *Lenin: Life and Legacy*. 1984.
Weber, G., and H. Weber. *Lenin: Life and Works*. 1980.

22

STALIN

Josif Vissarionovich Stalin (Djugashvili), December 6, 1878–March 5, 1953.

Secretary General of the Central Committee of the Communist Party from 1922 and Premier from 1941–1953. Leader of the World Communist Movement.

Stalin was born in Gori, Georgia, and was the son of a Georgian shoemaker. He was expelled from the Tbilisi Theological Seminary in 1899 as a result of his interest in the revolutionary movement. He then joined the Social Democratic Labor party; in 1903 when the party split, he joined the Bolsheviks under Lenin. Having worked in the underground movement in Transcaucasia, he was made part of the Bolshevik Central Committee by Lenin and Zinoviev. By this time he had adopted the name Stalin from the Russian *stal* (steel). He also briefly edited the Bolshevik newspaper *Pravda* before he was exiled to Siberia from July 1913 to March 1917. With the abdication of the tsar, Stalin was in charge of the party's affairs for three weeks until the arrival of Lenin in the "Sealed Train" from Switzerland, who proposed outright opposition to the war with Germany and overthrow of the provisional government.

In 1904, Stalin married Katherine Svanidze, by whom he had a son (later, during World War II, he was reported captured and killed by the Germans in 1944). Katherine died about 1907. In 1918 he married Nadezhda Allilueva, who is reported to have committed suicide; there was a daughter by this marriage.

After the February Revolution of 1917, Stalin served as a commissar for nationalities, in which post he organized the new structure of race relations and inaugurated the Union of Soviet Socialist Republics (USSR) in December 1922; he also served as commissar for worker-peasant inspection (1919–1923). His office was intended

Josef Stalin at the Kremlin, in an election photo issued in February 1950.

to bring democratic pressure on the bureaucratic administration; at this time he became a very close collaborator of Lenin. During the civil war he again served as a commissar for nationalities. In 1922 he was appointed Secretary General of the Central Committee, although Lenin, nurturing misgivings about Stalin's suitability for this position, was planning to remove him from it. Lenin's death, however, prevented this.

Together with Zinoviev and Kamenev, Stalin defeated Trotsky, and then with Bukharin and Rykov's help, he defeated Zinoviev and Kamenev in the struggle for power. Molotov, Voroshilov, Kaganovich, Ordzhonikidze, and Kirov then helped him defeat Bukharin's and Rykov's Right Opposition. From 1929 to 1934, he ruled with them, assuming the position of leader until they opposed him. This provided the catalyst for abandoning collective leadership and for instigating the Great Purge. Purges were campaigns by which the government wished to eliminate "socially alien" elements in trade unions, the party, and the bureaucracy. The old intelligentsia were purged in 1928–1931. The still more sinister Great Purge organized by Nikolai Yezhov occurred in 1936–1938. It is thought that between eight and ten million died in this purge. In 1939–1941 there were purges in the Baltic states, Bessarabia, part of Bukovina, and eastern Poland. There was also a wave of purges in 1944–1946 in territory that had been occupied by the enemy.

With Stalin as official head of government and chairman of the State Defense Committee, the reign of terror followed. The assassination in December 1934 of Sergei Mironovich Kirov (1886–1934) began the witchhunt that developed into the Great Purge, which resulted in the judicial execution of over one hundred suspected opponents of Stalin's régime. Kirov became a Bolshevik in 1904. His first task after the revolution was to establish Soviet power in the Caucasus. From 1926 he was party secretary in the Leningrad area and became a Politburo member in 1930. Kirov gave support to Stalin but opposed Stalin's personal rule after the seventeenth party congress in 1934.

The assassination in December 1934 of Sergei Mironovich Kirov (1886–1934) began the witchhunt that developed into the Great Purge, which resulted in the judicial execution of over one hundred suspected opponents of Stalin's régime.

Lavrenty Pavlovich Beria (1899–1953) served Stalin with admiration and was responsible for the deportation of thousands from eastern Poland and the Baltic states and was also in charge of the security police in the satellite states.

Stalinist Russia emerged in the mid-1930s with the essentials of modern industry, a controlled and heavily exploited peasantry, a monolithic ruling party working through a police state, a single focus of supreme authority in the person of Stalin, and a return to the traditions of patriotism and family stability. The first Five-Year Plan was launched in October 1928. It gave high priority to industrialization and in 1933 it was announced that the Five-Year Plan had been achieved nine months ahead of the scheduled date. In agriculture a shift to collectivization was undertaken, which was accelerated in 1929 when "the liquidation of the Kulaks as a class" was the order of the day. During 1936 to 1938 there was a period of staged trials and arrests designed to eliminate the revolutionary spirit still strong in the party. Between 1923 and the death of Stalin in 1953, a total of 3,600,000 citizens were "illegally punished" and 800,000 shot. A reversal of Stalinism later took place in 1987 with the vindication of the leadership killed in the purges of the 1930s. A rehabilitation law in 1991 ensured that all those illegally condemned between 1920 and 1988 could receive some compensation. The Stalin constitution adopted in December 1936, although an implicit promise of elementary democratic rights, contrasted grimly with the waves of arrests.

Stalin's foreign policy aimed to postpone war by collective security, and then to keep Russia out of it as long as possible by accommodation with either side. In August 1939, a Russo-German pact was signed. Stalin believed that Germany could not fight on two fronts and the pact also bought time.

Stalin formally assumed responsibility as premier in May 1941, an office he retained until his death. Germany invaded Russia on June 22, 1941; the operation was code-named "Barbarossa." The war caused great destruction and loss of life particularly in two great sieges. On June 22, 1941, the Germans had 500,000 troops over the Russian frontier, and by November 1941 the army was outside Leningrad (previously Petrograd). The Soviet forces, weakened by the Great Purge, were unprepared. Many officers had been promoted beyond their ability because of the purges. Leningrad was besieged and 750,000 people perished. Deaths during the siege of Leningrad alone were greater than all the civilian and military deaths of the Allies. On January 15, 1944, the Russians began to break out of the city, and on January 20 they succeeded in cutting the German corridor to the Gulf of Finland. On January 27 the two-and-a-half year siege ended.

In May and June 1942, German tanks, dive-bombers, and other forces were approaching the lower Volga River and the Caucasus. Having crossed the Don River, they reached the outskirts of Stalingrad and besieged the city. By mid-November 1942, the British victory at El Alamein in North Africa and the pursuit of the defeated Germans resulted in no more reinforcements for the German army near Stalingrad. Fresh Russian reinforcements were brought in, and on November 20, Yeremenko broke the enemy line. The Russians launched a great thrust from the north and Field Marshal Eric von Manstein was forced to retreat. The Germans under Field Marshal von Paulus (1890–1957) surrendered on February 2, 1943, having sustained a loss of 200,000 men.

A conference between President Franklin D. Roosevelt, Prime Minister Winston Churchill, and Premier Stalin was held at Yalta on February 4–11, 1945, to plan the final defeat and subsequent occupation of Nazi Germany. The Allied agreement that only unconditional surrender was acceptable was reaffirmed, and a four-power occupation of Germany was planned. A promise that the USSR would declare war against Japan was obtained. The USSR also agreed to join in the establishment of the United Nations.

After victory Stalin gradually withdrew from direct control of affairs but without abandoning the unprecedented power he had acquired. There was an alleged plot by some Moscow doctors to kill well-known government officials. The conspiracy was fully reported in the press in January 1953. The doctors, many of whom were Jewish, were said to have murdered Andrei Zhdanov (1896–1948), head of the Leningrad party organization. This was probably the pretext for starting another purge and was part of Stalin's anti-Semitic policy, but the death of Stalin in March 1953 saved the country from this. All but two of the doctors survived their ordeals and were released, and later Khrushchev stated that there had been no plot whatsoever and that it all had been engineered by Stalin. His death in 1953 was preceded by very cautious moves toward reform together with preparations for a new purge and official encouragement of anti-Semitism.

For details of the reversal of Stalinist policies and Khrushchev's "secret speech" at the XXth Party Congress, see page 119.

CHRONOLOGY

1878	Stalin born in Gori, Georgia (December 6).
	Stalin's "official" (incorrect) birthday (December 9).
1894	Admitted to Tiflis Theological Seminary.
1899	Expelled from seminary.
1912	Elected in absentia to Bolshevik Central Committee (January).
1913	Changes his name to Stalin (January).
	Returns to St. Petersburg as an editor of *Pravda* (February).
1917	Bolshevik coup in Petrograd (October 25).
1922	Stalin becomes secretary general of the Central Committee (April).
1936	Zinoviev and Kamenev tried and shot (August).
1937	Tukhachevsky and seven other marshals shot (May).

1939	Nazi-Soviet Nonaggression Pact signed in Moscow (August).
1940	Trotsky murdered in Mexico on Stalin's orders (August).
1941	Assumes responsibility as Premier (May).
	Germany invades USSR (June 22).
1945	Stalin hosts Allied talks in Yalta (February).
1953	Stalin dies (March 5).

BIBLIOGRAPHY

Applebaum, A. *Gulag: A History.* 2002.

Boobbyer, P. *The Stalin Era.* 2000.

Bullock, A. *Hitler and Stalin: Parallel Lives.* 1991.

Radzinsky, E. *Stalin.* 1996.

Sebag Montefiore, S. *Stalin: The Court of the Red Tsar.* 2002.

Shukman, H. *Stalin.* 1999.

Volkogonov, D. *Stalin.* 1994.

23

MALENKOV

Georgy Maksimilianovich Malenkov, January 8, 1902–January 13 (?), 1988.

Head of the Collective Leadership 1953 and Prime Minister 1953–1955.

Malenkov was born at Orenburg, Russia, and succeeded Stalin as head of the Communist party in 1953. He was succeeded by Nikita Khrushchev within two weeks but remained as prime minister until 1955.

Having joined the Red Army (1919) during the civil war that followed the October Revolution (1917), Malenkov joined the Communist party in 1920 and served as a political commissar for the Bolsheviks in Turkistan. Back in Moscow after the war, he studied engineering at the Higher Technical School (1922–1925). After graduation, he became a party official in the offices of the Central Committee. He then became closely associated with Stalin and in 1934 was placed in charge of the distribution of party personnel and the direction of local party organizations, which deeply involved him in the great party purge of the late 1930s.

In 1939 Malenkov was made head of the party's Cadres Directorate, which gave him authority over all personnel matters within the party bureaucracy; he also was elected a member and a secretary of the party's Central Committee and a member of its *Orgburo*, which was an agency established in 1919 to direct all Communist party organization. The Orgburo was abolished in 1952. In February 1941 he became a candidate member of the Politburo.

When Germany invaded the Soviet Union (June 1941), Malenkov was appointed to the State Defense Committee, the small group that directed the country during the war, and bore primary responsibility for the production of aircraft. He also became chairman of a committee that supervised the economic rehabilitation of areas liberated from German occupation (1943). After the war he was made a full member of the Politburo (March 1946), second secretary of the Central Committee, and deputy prime minister; he was generally regarded as one of Stalin's closest collaborators. During the immediate postwar period, he also became engaged in a bitter rivalry with Andrei Aleksandrovich Zhdanov (1896–1948), who, by instigating an attack on Malenkov's management of the dismantling and transport of German industrial equipment to the Soviet Union, caused his prestige and power to wane and contributed to the loss of his post in the party Secretariat by the end of 1946.

Within two years Malenkov had regained his position as one of Stalin's chief lieutenants, and, when Stalin died (March 1953), he assumed the post of senior party secretary as well as chairman of the Council of Ministers (i.e., prime minister). Malenkov ushered in a period of détente at home and abroad, promoting a more consumerist approach to economic growth. Although a few weeks later he was compelled to yield his top party post to Nikita Khrushchev, he worked for the next two years to reduce appropriations for arms production, increase the production of consumer goods at the immediate expense of heavy industry, and provide greater incentive for collective farm workers to increase agricultural production. His programs were opposed by other party leaders and in February 1955 he was also forced to resign as prime minister.

Subsequently, Malenkov's only government post was directing the ministry in charge of power stations. He retained his influential position on the party Presidium (formerly the Politburo) until 1957 when, after participating in the "anti-party group's" unsuccessful effort to depose Khrushchev, he was expelled from both the Presidium and the Central Committee and removed from his ministerial position. It was reported later that Malenkov had been placed in charge of a power station at Ust-Kamenogorsk in the Kazakh Soviet Socialist Republic. On retirement he moved to Moscow. His name disappeared from major Soviet reference books.

He died in 1988 but news of his death was delayed as relatives asked for the information to be withheld.

CHRONOLOGY

1902 Malenkov born (January 8).

1919 Joins Red Army.

1941 Candidate member of the Politburo.

1953 Becomes prime minister and party leader, but yields the leadership to Khrushchev within two weeks.

1955 Resigns as prime minister.

1957 Expelled from the Politburo, the Central Committee, and the Communist party.

1988 Malenkov dies (January 13 [?]).

BIBLIOGRAPHY

Ebon, M. *Malenkov, Stalin's Successor*. 1953.

24

KHRUSHCHEV

Nikita Sergeyevich Khrushchev, April 17, 1894–September 11, 1971.

Chairman of the Council of Ministers of the USSR 1953–1964.

The grandson of a former serf, and the son of peasants, Khrushchev was born at Kalinovka near the Ukrainian border, later moving with his family to Donetsk in the Ukraine and becoming an apprentice fitter. After a modest education and work in various Ukrainian industrial centers, he joined the Bolshevik party in 1918 and joined the Red Army as a political commissar in 1919, and in 1925 he began his full-time party work. He became a student of the industrial academy at Moscow in 1929 where Stalin's wife Nadezhda Allilueva befriended him. He entered the Moscow political world as party secretary of the academy and rose to party leadership of the capital by 1935.

From January 1938, following the elimination of the Ukrainian party leaders in the purge, to December 1949 Khrushchev was political head of the Ukraine, acting as political adviser on various fronts during the war. He was again in charge of Moscow and a secretary of the Central Committee when political power had to be allocated on Stalin's death in 1953. Khrushchev emerged victorious from a power struggle with Georgy Malenkov (1902–1988), becoming first secretary of the party in 1953 and forcing Malenkov out of his position as premier in 1955. By 1957 he had outwitted Malenkov, Beria, and Molotov and became the dominant national leader.

Lavrenty Pavlovich Beria (1899–1953) was born near Sukhumi, Georgia. He joined the Bolshevik party in 1917 and worked in the Cheka and the GPU (Gosudarstvennoye Politichskoe Upravleniye–State political administration) in Transcaucasia. From 1932 to 1938 he was virtual dictator of Transcaucasia. He was commissar for internal affairs from 1938 to 1945 and deputy prime minister for security from 1941 to 1953.

Nikita Khrushchev addresses the United Nations General Assembly in New York, October 3, 1960.

Beria played an important part in the development of forced labor camps (*gulags*). He was also responsible for the deportation of thousands of people from eastern Poland and the Baltic states and was in charge of the security police in the satellite states. In 1953 he was tried and shot. Among other charges he was accused of being an imperialist agent.

Vyacheslav Mikhailovich Molotov (1890–1986) was a party and government official whose real name was Skryabin. After joining the Bolsheviks in 1906, from 1909 to 1911 Molotov was banished for revolutionary activities to Vologda Guberniya. A contributor to the illegal paper *Zvezda*, he became the editorial secretary of *Pravda*. A member of the Russian bureau of the party's Central Committee, after the Bolshevik seizure of power he held a number of important positions, including head of the party organization in Ukraine (1920–1925); second secretary (after Stalin) of the Central Committee (1921–1930); member of the Politburo and the Presidium of the Executive Council; chairman of the Council of People's Commissars (1930–1940); deputy chairman of the State Defense Committee (1939–1949 and 1953–1956); and commissar for foreign affairs. He negotiated the Austrian State Treaty of 1955. Second only to Stalin, Molotov's influence waned after Stalin's death, but he was used by Khrushchev to outmaneuver Beria. In 1957, owing to his membership in the antiparty group, he was expelled from the Central Committee and its Presidium and relegated to the position of ambassador to the Mongolian People's Republic (1957–1960). In 1960 he served as the USSR's delegate to the International Atomic Energy Agency. In 1964 it was announced that he had been expelled from the Communist party.

In 1958 Khrushchev took over the post of prime minister from Marshal Nikolai Aleksandrovich Bulganin (1895–1975), who had joined the ill-fated antiparty group against Khrushchev. Bulganin was expelled from the Presidium and retired.

Khrushchev continued Stalin's emphasis on investment while taking emergency measures to improve consumption in the expanding economy and decentralizing the administration. At the XXth Party Congress convened in February 1956, Khrushchev laid bare Stalin's crimes since 1934 in his famous "secret speech." Although "secret," it was published by the United States government on June 4. He did not use the expression Stalinism to describe what he was analyzing but referred to it as the cult of the personality; on June 30 the Central Committee passed a resolution to eliminate the cult of personality and its consequences. This speech ended the claims to infallibility of the Communist party but provoked opposition from the conservative wing of the party. The concept of "peaceful coexistence" with the capitalist world was unveiled at the XXth Party Congress.

At the XXth Party Congress convened in February 1956, Khrushchev laid bare Stalin's crimes since 1934 in his famous "secret speech." Although "secret," it was published by the United States government on June 4.

One of Khrushchev's plans was the Council of the National Economy (*sovnarkhoze*). It was adopted in 1957 and initially there were 105 councils that covered the whole country and were responsible for all economic activity on their territory (except military, security, and other vital tasks that remained centralized). Khrushchev thought that by devolving decision making to the local level, economic efficiency would result. In fact the sovnarkhozes attempted to become ministates in their own right. By 1960 only 47 existed and they were abolished in 1965.

Khrushchev's policies brought about many changes in the Communist world and brought about some liberalization inside the USSR. Early in 1957 certain nationalities that were deported by Stalin to other regions of the USSR were rehabilitated and allowed to return to their regions of origin; these included Chechens, the Ingush, the Balkars, the Karachai, and the Kalmyks. Other changes included the removal of Stalin's body from the mausoleum in Red Square in Moscow and the renaming of the city of Stalingrad to Volgograd.

In 1954 the USSR recognized the sovereignty of East Germany and later in that year signed a treaty of friendship. Later in 1958 Khrushchev gave an ultimatum to the United States, France, and Great Britain on the status of Berlin. He aimed at a free, demilitarized city. Failing a resolution of the problem he threatened unilateral action. In August 1961 the construction of the Berlin Wall began.

An insurrection in Budapest, Hungary, caused Soviet troops to intervene in October 1956 and they completely crushed the uprising in November.

In his foreign policy Khrushchev alienated China: Mao Zedong felt that he should have been consulted before the anti-Stalin speech at the XXth Party Congress, and Khrushchev ended nuclear cooperation with China.

The USSR expressed its support for Cuba in the spring of 1962. In October that year the United States discovered Soviet nuclear missile installations in Cuba. President John F. Kennedy announced a naval blockade of the island and demanded that the missiles be removed immediately under threat of armed conflict. Later that month Khrushchev promised to remove the missiles in exchange for a promise that the United States would not invade Cuba.

The Cuban missile crisis, which could have caused a nuclear war by the super powers, the XXth Party Congress and the demolition of

Stalin, which infuriated Mao Zedong of China, together with Soviet action in the Hungarian Revolution of 1956 all led to reaction against Khrushchev. It was perhaps his failed agricultural policy that raised most criticism because he emphasized consumer production instead of heavy industry. His economic failure forced him out of office in 1964. Harold Macmillan, who was British prime minister, felt that Khrushchev was a sort of mixture between Peter the Great and Lord Beaverbrook— ruthless but sentimental. Khrushchev said of himself, "After I die they will place my actions on a scale—on one side evil; on the other good. I hope that the good will outweigh the bad."

CHRONOLOGY

1894   Khrushchev born at Kalinovka in Kursh Province, near the Ukrainian border (April 17).

1918   Khrushchev becomes a Bolshevik and joins the Red Army.

1939   Full member of the All-Union Politburo (March).

1953   Chairman of the Council of Ministers of the USSR.

1957   Khrushchev takes over Premiership from Bulganin (March).

1962   Cuban missile crisis (October).

1963   Nuclear Test-Ban Treaty.

1964   Resigns all offices (October 14).

1971   Khrushchev dies (September 11).

BIBLIOGRAPHY

Beschloss, M. *The Crisis Years: Kennedy and Khrushchev*. 1991.
Crankshaw, E. *Khrushchev*. 1966.
Frankland, M. *Khrushchev*. 1966.
Khrushchev, S. N. *Khrushchev on Khrushchev*. 1990.
McCauley, M. *Khrushchev and Khrushchevism*. 1987.
Taubman, W. *Khrushchev: The Man and his Era*. 2003.

25

BREZHNEV

Leonid Ilyich Brezhnev, December 19, 1906–November 10, 1982.

First Secretary (renamed General-Secretary in 1966) of the Communist Party 1964–1982, and Chairman of the Presidium of the Supreme Soviet of the USSR 1977–1982.

Brezhnev joined the Communist party in 1931. He had trained as a metallurgist, worked as an engineer, then took on full-time party work, becoming a regional first secretary in 1939. He was a political commissar during World War II and participated in the sovietization of western Ukraine, which was formerly Polish territory. In 1950 he became first secretary of the Communist party of Moldavia (now Moldova). Later in 1952 he was briefly a candidate member of the Presidium and a secretary of the Central Committee. After Stalin's death in 1953, Brezhnev was demoted, but Khrushchev, who had gained full power in Moscow, sent Brezhnev to Kazakhstan to supervise the "Virgin Lands" scheme; its success brought Brezhnev reelection to his posts in the party and he became a full Politburo member in 1957. From May 1960 to July 1964 he was chairman of the Presidium of the Supreme Soviet (titular chief of state).

He planned the fall of Khrushchev in 1964 with the help of Mikhail Andreyevich Suslov (1902–1982) who was one of the most powerful influences within the Communist party of the Soviet Union. Brezhnev became first secretary of the Communist Party Central Committee, with a title change to general secretary in 1966. At this point Aleksei Nikolaevich Kosygin (1904–1980) became prime minister and Nikolai Viktorovich Podgorny (1903–1983) became Soviet president.

President Nixon and Soviet Leader Leonid Brezhnev look over each other's signatures after they signed the compact pledging their countries to reach agreement in 1974 to permanently limit their offensive nuclear arsenals. June 21, 1973.

Brezhnev identified himself as a relatively successful reformer of agriculture, and in foreign affairs as one who did not tolerate backsliding in the Council for Mutual Economic Assistance (Comecon) group of countries. On September 28, 1968, *Pravda* published an article outlining how the USSR considered the sovereignty of the satellite states to be limited, and the USSR reserved the right to intervene in any Communist state where the régime was endangered by counterrevolution or by bourgeois nationalism. It became known as the Brezhnev Doctrine and was used to justify the invasion of Czechoslovakia in 1968 when the "Prague Spring" was gathering momentum and the Communist party of Czechoslovakia could have lost power. Brezhnev argued that Czechoslovakia was a socialist country and therefore was under the control of the Soviet Communist party. He derived some further influence from the meeting of Communist parties (except that of the Chinese People's Republic) in Moscow in 1969.

In June 1977 Brezhnev replaced Podgorny as president of the Presidium of the Supreme Soviet; the first person in Soviet history to hold the posts of party leader and chief of state simultaneously.

Brezhnev argued that Czechoslovakia was a socialist country and therefore was under the control of the Soviet Communist party.

He sought to normalize relations between West Germany and the Warsaw Pact countries and pushed for détente. Soviet-United States relations improved after President Richard M. Nixon visited Moscow in 1972, and Brezhnev returned the visit the following year. In 1975 he signed the Helsinki Final Act, which ruled that the post-1945 frontiers of countries could only be altered after negotiations. Though Brezhnev met President Jimmy Carter in Vienna in 1979 to sign a new bilateral strategic arms limitation treaty (SALT II), the U.S. Senate refused to ratify the treaty, and it was considered the end of détente. The rift came about due to the Soviet army's intervention in Afghanistan in December 1979.

Premier Kosygin launched what became known as the Kosygin Reforms, which aimed to give enterprise more control over what they produced and marketed. One of his problems was what to do with surplus labor in an enterprise as the law did not allow for their dismissal. The reforms promised much for Russia and the improving of the national economy, but were interrupted by the invasion of Czechoslovakia in August 1968. Afterward centralization was reimposed. Kosygin lacked the will to fight for power and was gradually pushed aside by Brezhnev. It has been said that abandoning the Kosygin Reforms was one of the reasons for the decline of the Soviet economy.

Brezhnev remained as head of the Communist Party of the Soviet Union (CPSU) for eighteen years, longer than any Soviet leader other than Stalin.

CHRONOLOGY

1906 Brezhnev born in Kamenskoye (now Dneprodzerzhinsk), Ukraine (December 19).

1931	Joins the Communist party.
1950	Becomes first secretary of the Communist party in Moldavia (now Moldova).
1952	Elected secretary of the Central Committee of the Communist party.
1960	Khrushchev appoints Brezhnev as president of the Soviet Union.
1964	Becomes first secretary (renamed general secretary in 1966) of the Communist party (October).
1968	"Brezhnev Doctrine" published (September 28). Soviet forces enter Czechoslovakia.
1979	Soviet intervention in Afghanistan.
1982	Brezhnev dies (November 10).

BIBLIOGRAPHY

Dornberg, J. *Brezhnev*. 1974.
Institute of Marxism–Leninism. *Leonid Ilyich Brezhnev*. 1977.

26

ANDROPOV

Yury Vladimirovich Andropov, June 15, 1914–February 9, 1984.

Secretary-General of the Communist Party 1982–1984 and Chairman of the Presidium of the Supreme Soviet 1983–1984.

Andropov was the son of a railway employee probably of Armenian origin. In 1933 he joined the Komsomol (Young Communist League), worked for a time as a Volga boatman, and in 1936 graduated from the Inland Waterways Transport College at Rybinsk on the upper Volga. He joined the Communist party in 1939 and the following year was appointed first secretary of the Komsomol organization in the Karelo-Finnish Autonomous Republic. By 1947 he became second secretary of the Communist party Central Committee in Karelia.

In 1953 Andropov moved to Moscow where he was assigned to diplomatic work. He was appointed ambassador to Hungary in 1954, where he was instrumental in the suppression of the 1956 national uprising while supporting Janos Kadar as leader of the Hungarian Communists. Recalled to Moscow in 1957, he became head of the Central Committee's department supervising the Communist parties in other republics. In May 1967 Leonid Brezhnev appointed Andropov head of the State Security Committee (KGB). A month later he was made candidate member and in April 1973 a full member of the Politburo. He relinquished his post as head of the KGB, and on May 24 was reelected to the Secretariat of the Central Committee. Two days after Brezhnev's death on November 10, 1982, the Central Committee unanimously elected Andropov as general secretary. Almost immediately after his election Andropov started fighting corruption, which under Brezhnev had been on the increase.

In December 1982 at a joint session of the Supreme Soviet and the Central Committee held to commemorate the sixtieth anniversary of the founding of the USSR Andropov spoke about the nationalities making up the Soviet Union: "It's not just a question of bringing nations together, but of fusing them." Andropov took some initiatives in foreign policy by adopting a conciliatory attitude toward China and by trying to create a division between Western Europe and the United States on trade and military issues. His only visit abroad as CPSU general secretary was to Prague in January 1983 for a meeting of the Political Consultative Committee of the Warsaw Treaty member states. At home he appealed for an efficient national economy through harder work and better social discipline, but with little result in the short duration of his leadership. After August 18, 1983, he was not seen in public and died February 9, 1984. He has been described as a "transitional" figure between the conservatism of Brezhnev and the radicalism of Gorbachev.

Yuri Andropov,
General Secretary
of the Communist
Party of the
USSR,
June 6, 1983.

CHRONOLOGY

1914 Andropov born (June 15).

1939 Joins the Communist party.

1954 Appointed ambassador to Hungary.

1967 Appointed head of the KGB (May).

1982 Becomes secretary general of the Communist party (November 12).

1983	Becomes chairman of the Presidium of the Supreme Soviet (June 16).
1984	Andropov dies (February 9).

BIBLIOGRAPHY

Medvedev, Z. *Andropov*. 1983.
Steele, J. and E. Abraham. *Andropov in Power*. 1983.

27

CHERNENKO

Konstantin Ustinovich Chernenko, September 24, 1911–March 10, 1985.

Secretary General of the Communist Party of the Soviet Union and President of the Presidium of the Supreme Soviet 1984–1985.

Chernenko, the son of peasants, joined the Communist party in 1931, becoming a party official in Krasnoyarsk region in 1933 and advancing to regional secretary in 1941. In 1948 he became head of the propaganda and agitation department in Moldavia, where he formed a close relationship with Leonid Brezhnev (first secretary of the Moldavian party, 1950–1952). Chernenko moved to Moscow when Brezhnev moved there in 1956. When Brezhnev became president of the Presidium of the USSR Supreme Soviet in 1960 he made Chernenko *chef de cabinet*. Later, in 1964, he became head of the general department of the party Central Committee; by then Brezhnev had become secretary general of the Communist party.

Chernenko had always had high expectations that he would be Brezhnev's successor as secretary general and Brezhnev would probably have handed over power to Chernenko, but Brezhnev died suddenly in November 1982. Chernenko was completely outmaneuvered by Yury Andropov. When Andropov died fifteen months later, Chernenko was unanimously elected secretary general of the Communist party of the Soviet Union and chairman of the presidium of the Supreme Soviet (titular chief of state). The other contender was Mikhail Gorbachev but the Politburo was suspicious of him and he was passed over.

Chernenko only had thirteen months in office before he died; the short periods of power for Andropov and Chernenko were a breathing space and marked the end of the Brezhnev era.

CHRONOLOGY

1911 Chernenko born (September 24).

1931 Joins the Communist party.

1941 Regional secretary of the Krasnoyarsk region.

1948 Head of the Propaganda and Agitation Department in Moldavia.

1960 Brezhnev appoints Chernenko as *chef de cabinet*.

1984 Elected unanimously secretary general of the Communist party (February 13).

Elected president of the Presidium of the Supreme Soviet (April 11).

1985 Chernenko dies (March 10).

BIBLIOGRAPHY

Shulman, S. *Kings of the Kremlin.* 2002.

28

GORBACHEV

Mikhail Sergeyevich Gorbachev, March 2, 1931–

General Secretary of the Communist Party, 1985, and
President of the Union of Soviet Socialist Republics 1988–1991.

Gorbachev was born in Privolnoye in southern Russia in 1931. He joined the Communist party in 1952 and graduated in law from Moscow State University in 1953. Gorbachev spent his whole working life in party affairs, first in Stavropol and then in Moscow. He was elected first secretary of the Stavropol city party committee in 1966, and progressed to first secretary of the Stavropol territory party committee in 1970. He was transferred to Moscow in 1978 to become Central Committee secretary for agriculture.

Under Yury Andropov (head of the Communist party, 1982–1983), he was second secretary. Andropov aimed for Gorbachev to be his successor, but Gorbachev was twice passed over as a candidate for the leadership. The old guard chose Konstantin Chernenko. However, in 1985, after Chernenko's death, he became party leader, sponsored by the then foreign minister, Andrei Gromyko. His rival, Viktor Grishkin, failed to get a seconder. At a Politburo meeting in July 1985, Gorbachev proposed that eighty-six-year-old Gromyko should be chairman of the Presidium of the USSR Supreme Soviet (effectively head of state), "a post as high as it was decorative."

Andrei Andreyevich Gromyko (1909–1989) was born in Belorussia. He became a member of the Communist party in 1931 and was elected to the Central Committee in 1956. He was ambassador to the United States (1943–1946) and served as Soviet representative to the United Nations Security Council from 1946 to 1948. Later he was ambassador to Britain from 1952 to 1953. He became foreign minister in 1957, and in 1983 was appointed first deputy premier. He was respected for his

ability as a negotiator and for his grasp of international affairs. He was president of the USSR (1985–1988).

Gorbachev's aim was to set Russia on a path that had been started in February 1917 and was thwarted by the October Revolution. To do this he believed in openness (*glasnost*) and restructuring (*perestroika*). Perestroika of society and the state was announced in 1985 by the Communist Party Central Committee of the USSR. The broad ideas of perestroika were then approved by the party Congress in 1986 and the decisions were recorded in a document, "Main Directions of the Economic and Social Development of the USSR in the Period 1986–1990 and the Prospects Up to the Year 2000." The social aspect of perestroika was encouraged when it was seen that progress depended on popular support. Decisions on economic reform came in 1987 following discussions in which 180,000 suggestions were put forward and the government submitted resolutions on planning, prices, finance and banking, supplies and technology, social and labor questions, and ministerial responsibilities in the Soviet Union and the republics. These were accepted as were the principles of self-financing and self-management. Gorbachev said "perestroika has a socialist character and nothing in common with bourgeois liberalization."

Mikhail Gorbachev during a break in the State of the World Forum in San Francisco, September 30, 1995.

In 1988 the Nineteenth Communist Party Conference, the first since 1941, was attended by about 5,000 delegates. It was convened by Gorbachev, to push through radical policies. The party was no longer in charge of economic management of the country, and it also lost its right to nominate candidates for state and soviet posts. Glasnost was also promoted through conference resolutions.

In January 1991 Gorbachev gave warnings that Lithuania should halt its drive toward independence and Soviet troops took control of

Vilnius, the capital. Fifteen were killed and more than 200 wounded during the takeover. The elected parliament remained in session behind barricades and thousands attended the funerals of those killed. There was also a march on the Kremlin by 100,000 Soviet sympathizers protesting against the killings. Gorbachev declared that a plebiscite on independence would be illegal, but Lithuanians overwhelmingly endorsed their declaration of independence made in 1990.

An attempted takeover of power was made by those opposed to the new political, economic, and social concepts. It became known as the August Putsch. On August 19, 1991, a group of hard-liners arrived in the Crimea at the *dacha* where the Gorbachevs were staying and demanded that the president declare a state of emergency and hand over power to the vice president. Gorbachev refused. A statement issued on August 19 and published by Tass said that "in keeping with the Constitution, presidential power had been transferred to Vice President Gennady Yanayev due to Mikhail Gorbachev's inability to perform his duties for health reasons," and that a state of emergency had been introduced in parts of the Soviet Union for six months to overcome "the profound crisis, political, ethnic, and civil strife, chaos and anarchy that threaten the lives and security of the Soviet Union's citizens."

On August 19, 1991, a group of hard-liners arrived in the Crimea at the dacha where the Gorbachevs were staying and demanded that the president declare a state of emergency and hand over power to the vice president.

The putsch lasted for three days. It became clear that the military and state security forces were not behind the coup, especially in the face of popular resistance, with the president of the Russian Federated Republic, Boris Yeltsin, setting himself at the head of the protestors apparently willing to fight for the new freedoms brought about by the reforms of perestroika. With the presence of tanks in the streets, he emerged from inside the barricaded Russian parliament building to denounce the hard-liners before an estimated 150,000 supporters. When troops failed to assault the building, it became clear that the coup was collapsing. St. Petersburg was a center of resistance to the putsch, led by the mayor in spite of a state of emergency declared by the military.

The coup's timing was linked to the proposed signing of an agreement to establish a union of sovereign states which would have devolved much of the Kremlin's powers to the republics. The putsch in fact achieved the opposite to what had been intended. Reform was given a powerful boost, the Communist party was fatally weakened, and Russia dominated the political scene with an agenda that favored an independent Russian state.

When Gorbachev returned to Moscow after the August Putsch, he found great hostility toward the Communist party, and although he made strong efforts to keep the union from breaking up, he failed. In November seven republics agreed on the formation of the Union of Sovereign States, which would leave Gorbachev only the duties of coordinating foreign policy and defense. Then, on December 8, Russia, Belarus, and Ukraine met to form the Commonwealth of Independent States, which would leave him no duties at all. The three republics agreed that each member of the commonwealth would be independent; a central authority, based in Minsk, would have clearly circumscribed powers; other republics of the old Soviet Union would be welcome as new members of the commonwealth; any republic would be free to leave the commonwealth after giving a one-year notice; the members of the commonwealth would work together to establish free-market economies; the commonwealth would observe all the international agreements previously signed by the USSR; and the old Soviet ruble would be the commonwealth's common currency.

In a meeting between Gorbachev and Yeltsin on December 17, it was decided that the USSR would dissolve on December 31, but even that deadline was advanced when, on December 21, eleven of the twelve republics joined the commonwealth and announced that the USSR no longer existed. On December 25, Gorbachev resigned as president of the USSR in a televised address saying, "I am leaving my post with apprehension, but also with hope . . . . I wish everyone the best."

CHRONOLOGY

1931   Gorbachev born (March 2).

1952   Joins Communist Party.

1955   Graduates in law at Moscow State University.

1985   General secretary of the Communist party (until 1991).

1990   President of the USSR.

1991   Resigns as president of the USSR (December 25).

BIBLIOGRAPHY

Brown, A. *The Gorbachev Factor.* 1996.

Davies, R. W. *Soviet History in the Gorbachev Revolution.* 1989.

Gorbachev, M. S. *Memoirs.* 1996.

Gorbachev, M. S. *Perestroika: New Thinking for Our Country and the World.* 1988.

Medvedev, Z. *Gorbachev.* 1986.

Miller, J. *Mikhail Gorbachev and the End of Soviet Power.* 1993.

Sakwa, R. *Gorbachev and His Reforms, 1985–1990.* 1990.

White, S. *Gorbachev in Power.* 1990.

Zemstov, I., and J. Farrar. *Gorbachev, the Man and the System.* 1989.

29

YELTSIN

Boris Nikolaievich Yeltsin, February 1, 1931–

President of the Russian Federation 1991–2000.

Yeltsin was born in Sverdlovsk oblast on February 1, 1931, and graduated as a construction engineer from the Urals Polytechnic Institute in 1955. A member of the Communist party from 1961 until 1990, he entered party work in 1968 in Sverdlovsk oblast and was elected first secretary of the Sverdlovsk oblast party committee in 1976. Transferred to Moscow as head of the construction department of the Central Committee Secretariat in April 1985, he quickly became first secretary of the Moscow city party committee but was dismissed after conflicts with more conservative elements in 1987. Subsequently he became the people's champion in Moscow, winning election to the USSR Congress of Peoples' Deputies in March 1989 with 89 percent of the vote and becoming chairman of the Russian parliament, against Mikhail Gorbachev's wishes, in 1990.

On June 12, 1991, Yeltsin was elected president of the Russian Soviet Federated Socialist Republic (RSFSR) in Russia's first democratic elections. He received 57.3 percent of the vote in a turnout of 74 percent. Zhirinovsky polled 8 percent. Gavriil Popov was elected mayor of Moscow with 65.3 percent of the vote. Yeltsin was sworn in on July 10 receiving the blessing of the Russian Orthodox Church. He used this position to urge greater democracy and greater speed for *perestroika*, as well as to champion ordinary peoples' rights.

On August 19, 1991, when the coup against Soviet Union President Gorbachev was being staged, Yeltsin went to the Russian parliament building in Moscow and proclaimed the plotters "criminals" and "traitors" and called on the population to resist. He was helped by elements of the army and the KGB who were opposed to the coup.

Boris Yeltsin

He rallied the people and called for the return of the president, but when Gorbachev did return, Yeltsin showed that he was in control. He acted independently of Gorbachev and signed decrees that were unconstitutional. For example, he proscribed the Communist party and seized all its property in Russia.

Following the attempted coup there was a struggle over economic reform among his advisers and between them and the economist Gregor Yavlinsky. This was resolved in October when Yeltsin sided with those who wanted Russia to go it alone and to decide its own pace of political, economic, and social reforms.

In Minsk, on December 8, Yeltsin joined with the presidents of Ukraine and Belarus (Belorussia) to proclaim a new commonwealth of independent states. The USSR or Soviet Union came to an end on December 8, 1991, and a new organization, the Commonwealth of Independent States (CIS), replaced it as a looser grouping creating a common trade area, a single command of strategic forces, and central control of nuclear weapons.

They also issued a statement: "The USSR, as a subject of international law and a geopolitical reality, ceases to exist." They stated that a new organization, the Commonwealth of Independent States (*Sodruzhestvo Nyezavisimikh Gosudarstv*), was established and invited all former republics of the USSR to join.

The USSR, as a subject of international law and a geopolitical reality, ceases to exist.

Kazakhstan, Kirgizstan, Tajikistan, Turkmenistan, and Uzbekistan discussed the Minsk Declaration at Askhabad in Turkmenistan on December 12 and, although initially wary of joining, decided to become members subject to being given the status of cofounders.

President Gorbachev described the Minsk Declaration as an "illegal and dangerous" constitutional coup.

On December 21 at Alma Ata, Kazakhstan, the leaders of all countries represented at the Minsk Declaration at Askhabad, plus Moldova, Azerbaijan, and Armenia, met to formalize the establishment of the CIS. The former Baltic states, Estonia, Latvia, and Lithuania, did not attend as they had become independent in September. Georgia sent observers.

Assurances were given at the meeting to the world community that single control would be maintained over the nuclear weapons on former Soviet territory and that the treaty obligations of the Soviet Union would be respected by the newly independent states. Russia took over many of the functions of the former Soviet Union.

With the resignation of Gorbachev as president of the USSR on 25 December 1991, Yeltsin assumed control over the armed forces in Russia, notified the UN that the Russian Federation would take over the Soviet Union's seat in the Security Council, and took possession of the launch codes for the Soviet nuclear arsenal.

From 1987, when he was dismissed as head of the Moscow Communist party, Yeltsin had suffered from heart trouble and had his first heart attack in 1995. Part of the cause was heavy drinking. Later that year he was absent from the Kremlin for two months and during the presidential elections in 1996 he suffered several further heart attacks. From 1997 to 1999 he had many periods in hospital and announced his retirement on December 31, 1999.

Margaret Thatcher, former British Prime Minister, said of Yeltsin, "His weaknesses were real enough. But they were more than matched by astonishing courage and large reserves of political wiliness. And had his bravery and cunning not also been accompanied by a typically Russian ruthless streak, he could never have scored victory after victory against the communists who wanted to drag Russia back to its Soviet past." Lord Hurd, a former British foreign secretary said of

Yeltsin, "What he lacked in intellectual subtlety he remedied in native political shrewdness. He could understand and respond to the problems of others."

CHRONOLOGY

1931   Yeltsin born (February 1).

1955   Graduated as a construction engineer.

1961   Joins Communist party.

1985   Called to Moscow by President Gorbachev.

1991   Elected president of the RSFSR (June 12).

Attempted coup against President Gorbachev by the Emergency Committee (August 18–21).

Yeltsin bans all activities of the CPSU and the Russian Communist party on the territory of the Russian Federation (November 6).

Gorbachev resigns as USSR President (December 25).

Soviet Union ceases to exist (December 31).

1999   Yeltsin announces retirement (December 31).

BIBLIOGRAPHY

Klepikova, E. *Boris Yeltsin: A Political Biography*. 1982.
Morrison, J. *Boris Yeltsin: From Bolshevik to Democrat*. 1991.
Yeltsin, B. *The View from the Kremlin*. 1994.

30

PUTIN

Vladimir Vladimirovich Putin, October 7, 1952–

*Prime Minister and Acting President in 1999 and President of the
Russian Federation from 2000–*

Vladimir Putin was born in Leningrad (now St. Petersburg), the son
of a factory foreman. He attended Leningrad State University and
studied law. His tutor was Anatoly Aleksandrovich Sobchak (1937–)
one of the leading reform politicians of the *perestroika* era. It has been
suggested that the Law School was a training ground for KGB oper-
atives. He later held important positions in the KGB.

In 1994 Putin became deputy mayor of St. Petersburg and in
1996 was appointed deputy chief administrator in the Kremlin under
Boris Yeltsin. Yeltsin made Putin prime minister in August 1999
having sacked five prime
ministers in seventeen
months. His public
approval rating soared

*Yeltsin made Putin prime minister in August 1999
having sacked five prime ministers in 17 months.*

when he launched a military operation against Chechnya. On September 30, 1999, federal troops entered Chechnya following terrorist attacks in several Russian cities. Because the military actions were
labeled "antiterrorist operations," no approval from the upper cham-
ber of the parliament, the Federation Council, or declaration of a
state of emergency in Chechnya was required. Thus the war was conducted outside the framework of legality.

On December 31, 1999, President Yeltsin announced his
retirement and so ended the rule of Russia's first president, which
began with the population hoping for a better future for Russia.
Yeltsin named Putin as acting president and he was confirmed in

Vladimir Putin at a Kremlin ceremony, April 2003.

office as president of the Russian Federation on March 26, 2000. The population looked for stability following Yeltsin's somewhat erratic behavior. "People don't want miracles, they want order, and Putin has given the impression that he can provide that," remarked one pollster.

Following the terrorist attacks on the United States on September 11, 2001, Russia became a U.S. ally in the antiterrorist campaign without asking for any reciprocity. Putin was the first foreign leader to offer President George W. Bush support. Thus Russia had offered unconditional support for the West.

Critics of Putin would claim that he has undermined the independence of democratic institutions in Russia and that the 1991 constitution that established the institutions has been destroyed. They would claim that he is responsible for war crimes and genocide in Chechnya, and that the explosions causing destruction to housing in Russia in 1999 when 249 civilians were killed was the work of Russian secret services and used as an excuse to justify the war in Chechnya. He is also accused of demonizing big business and for allocating 50 percent of the most important government posts to ex-KGB personnel.

Putin introduced a new type of political leadership that is pragmatic and rational. He restarted economic reform that had lapsed or stalled under Yeltsin. Margaret Thatcher, a former British Prime Minister said, "Vladimir Putin is clearly able to assess international events and to respond to them boldly, shrewdly, and effectively. It is not necessary to ascribe to him a tender conscience, nor the liberal instincts of a democrat, in order to appreciate his worth as a leader with whom the West can deal."

Russia in 2003 is divided among those who would like a return to the Communist system, those who aim for liberal-style reform, and those who are still trying to work out what is good for Russia after a decade of post-Soviet uncertainty.

CHRONOLOGY

1952 Putin born (October 7).

1975 Graduates in law from Leningrad State University.

1988 Director of the Federal Security Service (until 1999).

1999 Becomes prime minister (August 9).

Appointed acting president of the Russian Federation (December 31).

2000 Elected president of the Russian Federation (March 26).

2004 Elected president of the Russian Federation for second term (March 14).

BIBLIOGRAPHY

Lieven, A. and H. Bradner. *Chechnya: Tombstone of Russian Power.* 1999.
Putin, V. *First Person.* 2000.
Shevtsova, L. *Putin's Russia.* 2003.

GLOSSARY

ADRIANOPLE, TREATY OF. Treaty signed September 14, 1829, between Russia and Turkey concluding the war of 1828–1829. Russia obtained the right of unlimited transit of commercial ships through the Dardanelles, and of free trade without the Ottoman Empire. The European border of Turkey was established along the Prut and Danube Rivers. Turkey handed over to Russia the east coast of the Black Sea from the mouth of the Kuban River to the port of St. Nicholas and acknowledged the transfer to Russia of Georgia and other Transcaucasian lands. Autonomy was given to Serbia, and the independence of Greece was recognized. Moldavia and Walachia were to be occupied until Turkey paid an indemnity.

AGRARIAN REFORMS. The first major agrarian reform was the abolition of serfdom, an institution that had developed in the period of Kievan Russia and was consolidated in Muscovite Russia as a means of providing a bonded labor force to support the gentry in their obligation to defend the country. Serfs of private landowners were freed in 1861, royal serfs in 1863, and state serfs in 1866. In all cases the serf's homestead became his own property, hereditary within his family; other land was vested in the village as a whole. Serfs of private landowners were obliged to surrender part of their former allotments in return for freedom; royal serfs kept the maximum amount of allotment land permitted; state serfs kept all their land against cash rent; Cossacks kept two-thirds of their land against twenty years of army service, the land to be held in common. The system of holding land in common did not succeed; redemption cost was an excessive burden and the rules imposed by the villages were restrictive. Village allotment areas declined; the overall amount of land held by former serfs was still insufficient for their support. Stolypin's government enacted a second major agrarian reform in 1906; this was revised and extended in 1911. Peasants in communities that did not redistribute land periodically were given their current holdings outright; those in communities that did redistribute were given the right to apply for permanent ownership at the time of redistribution. The community was required to consolidate land into united holdings where it had been held in scattered strips. In 1911 such partitions into private holdings were extended from arable to grazing land, with the exclusion of traditional common lands. There was provision for the abolition of the nondistributing commune by majority vote, of the distributing commune by a two-thirds majority vote. The land held by the peasant household was vested in the head of the household.

In 1918 the Soviet government abolished all private ownership and made farming the sole basis of landholding but did not immediately proceed to collectivization. During the first Five-Year Plan (1928–1932) all land, whether formerly owned by peasants or gentry, was collectivized. In 1930 the central government conceded that enforced collectivization had been too severe and that peasants in collective farms were to be permitted small private holdings. In 1988 the law was changed to encourage sales from private plots or surpluses from collective farm output but it was not successful because of bureaucracy, poor transport facilities, and inertia. Another law of 1988 allowed fifty-year leases to peasants and in 1989 tenant farming was permitted.

AGROGOROD. Agricultural organization proposed by Nikita Khrushchev (1894–1971) under which farmers would live in flats and work on centrally-grouped private plots. A version was attempted in the Ukraine in the period 1959–1965.

AIX-LA-CHAPELLE, CONGRESS OF (1818). Meeting of the Quadruple Alliance (Great Britain, Austria, Prussia, and Russia) and France at Aix-la-Chapelle (now Aachen), attended by Tsar Alexander I. The alliance reaffirmed the political reorganization of Europe established by the Congress of Vienna (1814–1815) and restored France's status as an independent power. It withdrew its occupying forces and admitted France into what thus became the Quintuple Alliance.

ALL-RUSSIAN PERIOD. The reign of Peter I (the Great) (1682–1725), also known as the Imperial Age and the St. Petersburg Era.

APPARATCHIK. Full-time paid officials working in the Soviet Communist party *apparat* (party machine).

ARCHIMANDRITE. Highest rank for monastic superiors.

AUGUST BLOC. An organization of Russian socialist factions that met in Vienna in August 1912. Its desire was to keep the Russian Socialist Democratic Labor Party from being fragmented by Lenin and others. However, so many factions boycotted the August Bloc that any chance of success was virtually precluded from the outset. The dominant figure of the August Bloc was Leo Trotsky, who was supported by the Mensheviks and the Bundists. The August Bloc failed in its ostensible goal of unity and succeeded only in establishing several short-lived periodicals. By 1914 even Trotsky disowned the group and it faded into oblivion.

AUTOCRAT AND AUTOCRACY. Total power exercised by Russian tsars. Ivan III (the Great) modeled his court on that of the Byzantine emperors and used the titles tsar and autocrat (*samoderzhets*). The latter, as used in Moscow, originally referred to the complete independence of the Muscovite sovereign from any other ruler, but it came to mean an absolute monarch, particularly under Peter I (the Great). Even when the power of the tsar was limited by that of the state Duma and state council following the 1905 revolution, the title autocrat was retained in the constitution.

BALTIC GERMANS. The descendants of the Teutonic Knights and their followers who settled in the Baltic provinces. In the eighteenth century the provinces became part of Russia.

BALTIC STATES. Estonia, Latvia, and Lithuania, formerly part of the Soviet Union from 1940 to 1991. The Soviet Union had seized them in 1940 as part of the 1939 Nazi-Soviet Pact.

BARSHCHINA. Unpaid labor that serfs were obliged to render to a landlord. Under the barshchina system one part of an estate was divided into allotments and farmed by the peasants on their own account. The majority of the estate was managed directly by the owner and was cultivated by the labor of the same peasants. The peasants' obligations were discharged by work and no monetary payment was made, but the landlord paid the poll tax. Generally, three days a week were spent on the estate of the landlord. After the emancipation of 1861, this system survived in a modified form.

BELORUSSIANS. An east Slavic people living in Belorussia and surrounding areas, for 77 percent of whom Belorussian is the mother tongue. They first developed a national identity when the Lithuanians were outnumbered by Russians during the thirteenth and fourteenth centuries; this continued to grow, and by the late seventeenth century a Belorussian literature and press had appeared. There are Belorussian communities in Lithuania, Latvia, and the Bialystok district of Poland.

BLACK EARTH. *Chernozem,* or fertile black soil, that stretches from the Carpathians and the Black Sea to the Altay Mountains. Normally about one foot deep but in places over three feet. It is neutral chemically (neither alkaline nor acid) and has a calcareous layer under the humus. In this last respect it differs from similar soils in the United States.

BLACK TUESDAY. The day in Russia (11 October 1994) when the ruble lost over 20 percent of its value against the dollar. The crash caused panic in Moscow's financial institutions and led to the removal of the finance minister Sergei Dubinin and the governor of the Central Bank. It fell to even lower levels in January 1995 because of the Chechen conflict before stabilizing later.

BLOODY SUNDAY. Term used of the massacre in St. Petersburg on Sunday, January 22, 1905. A procession of workers and their families led by Father George Gapon was fired on by troops guarding the Winter Palace in St. Petersburg. Over one hundred people were killed and several hundred wounded, an event that helped to spark off the 1905 Russian revolution.

BOLSHEVIK. Militant majority under Lenin that emerged from a split in the Russian Social Democratic Party in 1903 (the Mensheviks made up the minority) and which seized power in October 1917.

BOYAR. A member of the Russian aristocracy in the sixteenth century, as distinguished from the *pomeshchik* (service noble). Boyars received their titles from the tsars, headed important offices, and participated in the deliberation of the *boyarskaya duma*. This was an advisory council to the Russian grand princes and tsars, consisting of important boyars, nobles, and high church dignitaries.

CALENDAR. Until 1700 Russia had its own national calendar that reckoned the years from an estimated beginning of the world and not from the birth of Christ. The year ran from September. In 1700 Peter I (the Great) adopted the Julian calendar, which had been or was about to be abandoned by Western Europe in favor of the Gregorian system. The Julian calendar was ten days behind the Gregorian calendar in the seventeenth century, eleven in the eighteenth, and twelve in the nineteenth, and by 1900 thirteen days behind. The Gregorian calendar was adopted by decree on January 26, 1918, fixing February 1, 1918, as February 14, 1918. The anniversary of the revolution of October 25 now became November 7 although it is still known as the "October" Revolution. Peter I (the Great) issued a decree on a new calendar on December 20, 1699.

All Greeks from whom we accepted our Orthodox faith number their years from eight days after the birth of Christ, that is from 1 January, and not from the creation of the world. There is a great difference in those two calendars. This year is 1699 since the birth of Christ, and on 1 January it will be 1700 as well as a new century. To celebrate this happy and opportune occasion, the Great Sovereign has ordered that henceforth all government administrative departments and fortresses in all their official business use the new calendar beginning 1 January 1700. To commemorate this happy beginning and the new century in the capital city of Moscow, after a solemn prayer in churches and private dwellings, all major streets, homes of important people, and homes of distinguished religious and civil servants should be decorated with trees, pine, and fir branches similar to the decoration of the Merchant Palace or the Pharmacy Building—or as best as one knows how to decorate his place and gates. Poor people should put up at least one tree, or a branch on their gates at the entrance of their homes. These decorations are to remain from 1 January to 7 January 1700.

CENTRAL EXECUTIVE COMMITTEE. From 1917 to 1936 the executive organ of the congresses of Soviets of workers' and soldiers' deputies. It was elected at the first congress of Soviets in July 1917. In 1922, following the formation of the USSR, there were all-union and also republic central executive committees. The chairmen of the committees acted as heads of state. As a result of the Stalin constitution of 1936, the role of the central executive committee was bestowed on the Supreme Soviet and its Presidium, now defunct.

CHEKA. Extraordinary Commission, organized as a network to combat counterrevolutionaries and saboteurs, established by the Bolsheviks on December 7, 1917.

CIVIL WAR (1917–1922). War following the October Revolution and the enforced dissolution of the constituent assembly, fought between the Reds, organized by Trotsky, and the White generals, who supported the provisional government or one of the former parties. In the winter of 1917–1918, the Bolsheviks overthrew General Kaledin's régime of Don Cossacks and fought anti-Bolshevik supporters in Orenburg and on the Manchurian frontier. The eastern and southern fronts were constituted in the summer of 1918. In March 1919 the Whites, under Admiral Kolchak, were nearing the Volga but were forced back until the capture of Kolchak in 1920. The northern front was liquidated in 1920 following the departure of Allied troops in 1919. The Baltic states and the German troops led by General von der Goltz complicated the position as did the intervention of Japan, Finland, Poland, Turkey, and Romania. The ultimate Red victory was due to the failure of the Whites to organize the peasants and unify their aspirations.

COLD WAR. Post-World War II tension between capitalist states—led by the United States—and Communist states—led by the USSR—which thawed following Gorbachev's emergence as Soviet leader in 1985 and appeared effectively over with East European Communism's collapse in 1989–1990.

COMINFORM. Communist Information Bureau formed in February 1947 to organize Communist activity in Europe, dissolved by Khrushchev in April 1956 as conciliatory gesture to the West.

COMINTERN. Communist International formed in March 1919 to coordinate international revolutionary Communist activity but which developed into an arm of Soviet foreign policy. Dissolved in May 1943 by Stalin to allay Western allies' fears.

COMMISSAR. Title of various high-ranking officials. Commissars were first appointed by the provisional government after the February 1917 revolution. Ministers were called commissars until 1946.

CONSTITUENT ASSEMBLY. Democratically elected assembly that met in Petrograd on January 18, 1918. It was dissolved by the Bolsheviks after one session.

CONSTITUENT REPUBLICS. The Union of Soviet Socialist Republics was formed by the union of the Russian Soviet Federated Socialist Republic, the Ukrainian Soviet Socialist Republic, the Belorussian Soviet Republic, and the Transcaucasian Soviet Socialist Republic. The Treaty of Union was adopted by the first Soviet congress of the USSR on December 30, 1922. In May 1925 the Uzbek and Turkmen Autonomous Soviet Socialist Republics, and in December 1929 the Tajik Autonomous Soviet Socialist Republic, were declared constituent members of the USSR, becoming union republics.

At the eighth congress of the Soviets on December 5, 1936, a new constitution of the USSR was adopted. The Transcaucasian Republic was split into the Armenian Soviet Socialist Republic, the Azerbaijan Soviet Socialist Republic, and the Georgian Soviet Socialist Republic, each of which became constituent republics of the union. At the same time the Kazakh Soviet Socialist Republic and the Kirghiz Soviet Socialist Republic, previously autonomous republics within the Russian Soviet Federated Socialist Republic, were proclaimed constituent republics of the USSR.

In September 1939 Soviet troops occupied eastern Poland as far as the Curzon line, which in 1919 had been drawn on ethnographic grounds as the eastern frontier of Poland, and incorporated it into the Ukrainian and Belorussian Soviet Socialist Republics. In February 1951 some districts of the Drogobych Region of Ukraine and the Lubin Voyevodship of Poland were exchanged. On March 31, 1940, territory ceded by Finland was joined to that of the autonomous Soviet Socialist

Republic of Karelia to form the Karelo-Finnish Soviet Socialist Republic, which was admitted into the union as the twelfth union republic. On July 16, 1956, the Supreme Soviet of the USSR adopted a law altering the status of the Karelo-Finnish Republic from that of a union (constituent) republic of the USSR to that of an autonomous (Karelian) republic within the Russian Soviet Federated Socialist Republic. On August 2, 1940, the Moldavian Soviet Socialist Republic was constituted as the thirteenth union republic. It comprised the former Moldavian Autonomous Soviet Socialist Republic and Bessarabia (17,095 sq mi/44,290 sq km, ceded by Romania on June 28, 1940), except for the districts of Khotin, Akerman, and Ismail, which, together with north Bukovina (4,029 sq mi/10,440 sq km), were incorporated in the Ukrainian Soviet Socialist Republic. The Soviet-Romanian frontier thus constituted was confirmed by the peace treaty with Romania, signed on February 10, 1947. On June 29, 1945, Ruthenia (Sub-Carpathian Russia, 4,903 sq mi/12,742 sq km) was, by treaty with Czechoslovakia, absorbed in the Ukrainian Soviet Socialist Republic.

On August 3, 1940, Estonia, Latvia, and Lithuania were incorporated in the Soviet Union as the fourteenth, fifteenth, and sixteenth union republics. The change in the status of the Karelo-Finnish Republic reduced the number of union republics to fifteen. After the defeat of Germany, it was agreed by the governments of Great Britain, the United States, and the USSR (by the Potsdam agreement), that part of eastern Prussia should be ceded to the USSR. The area, 4,498 square miles (11,655 sq km), which included the towns of Königsberg (renamed Kaliningrad), Tilsit (renamed Sovyetsk), and Insterburg (renamed Chernyakhovsk) was joined to the Russian Soviet Federated Socialist Republic by decree of April 7, 1946.

By the peace treaty with Finland, signed on February 10, 1947, the province of Petsamo (Pechenga), ceded to Finland on October 14, 1920, and March 12, 1946, was returned to the Soviet Union. On September 19, 1955, the Soviet Union renounced its treaty rights to the naval base of Porkkala-Udd and on January 26, 1956, completed the withdrawal of forces from Finnish territory. In 1945, after the defeat of Japan, the southern half of Sakhalin (13,896 sq mi/36,000 sq km) and the Kuril Islands (3,937 sq mi/10,200 sq km) were, by agreement with the Allies, incorporated in the USSR. Japan, however, asked for the return of the Etorofu and Kunashiri Islands as not belonging to the Kuril Islands proper. The Soviet government informed Japan on January 27, 1960, that the

Habomai Islands and Shikotan would be handed back to Japan on the withdrawal of American troops from Japan.

The USSR was formally dissolved by the Alma Ata Agreement of December 13, 1991, and replaced by the Commonwealth of Independent States on December 21, 1991.

CONTINENTAL SYSTEM. Method of economic warfare conducted by Napoleon in an attempt to bring down Great Britain during the Napoleonic Wars. In 1806 a decree sought to close continental ports to British trade, and in 1807 there was an attempt to extend the policy to neutral ships trading with Britain. In 1807 the policy was extended to Russian ports after the Treaties of Tilsit and to the Iberian Peninsula in 1808. It proved to be only partially effective because the British blockaded French trade and diverted trade elsewhere; moreover, there was widespread smuggling as well as noncompliance by many states.

COSSACKS. People of southern and southwestern Russia descended from independent Tatar groups and escaped serfs from Poland, Lithuania, and Muscovy. They established a number of independent self-governing communities, which were given special privileges by Russian or Polish rulers in return for military services. Known for their horsemanship each Cossack community provided a separate army. The Cossacks slowly lost their autonomy as Russia expanded in the seventeenth and eighteenth centuries; there were also occasional rebellions. Many fled Russia after the Revolution (1918–1921), and collectivization subsumed remaining Cossack communities. Originally frontiersmen; the name coming from a Turkic word (*kazak*) meaning "adventurer."

COUNCIL OF STATE. Advisory body formed in 1810 by Alexander I, whose members were appointed by the emperor. It was not a legislative body and the emperor was not obliged to follow its advice. In 1906 Count Witte redefined its role; only half of its members were to be appointed; the rest were to be elected.

CURZON LINE. Frontier between the former Soviet Union and Poland after 1945, originally proposed in negotiations in 1920 led by British foreign minister Lord Curzon. Although rejected by Poland when first suggested, the frontier was imposed by Germany and the Soviet Union following their 1939 attack on Poland and accepted at the end of World War II.

DANUBIAN PRINCIPALITIES. In 1812 Napoleon objected to Russian control of the Danubian principalities of Moldavia and Walachia as they were a threat to the growth of French influence in the Near East. By the Treaty of Adrianople (1829), Turkey recognized a Russian protectorate over the principalities, which were, however, to enjoy an autonomous existence. In 1848 Russia intervened to suppress a revolution by the Romanian national movement. Russian occupation of the Danubian Principalities in 1853, in an attempt to force the Turks to come to terms in the so-called Holy Land controversy, precipitated the Crimean War, which began in the same year. Moldavia and Walachia were occupied by Austria to separate the Russians from the Turks in the Balkans; eventually peace was established in 1856. Under the Treaty of Paris (1856), the Danubian Principalities were placed under the joint guarantee of the signatory powers.

DESTALINIZATION. Criticism of Stalin's policies and attempt at reform following his death in 1953. Khrushchev denounced his "cult of personality" and 1930s purges at the 20th Party Congress in 1956; Stalin's role was increasingly attacked in post-*glasnost* USSR.

DESYATOVSKIY'S REPORT. A. P. Zablotskiy-Desyatovskiy a government official under Alexander II, produced a report in 1841 on the condition of the serfs, mainly in central European Russia, which gave a horrifying account of the lives of peasant serfs and the callousness of the average landlord.

DIALECTICAL MATERIALISM. The philosophy of the world Communist movement, propounded by Marx and Engels, and later adopted by Lenin. Materialism stresses the priority of matter and the secondary importance of the mind, thus denying the possibility of a transcendental reality. Marx and Engels argued that materialism ceases to be mechanistic and becomes dialectical; chemical processes give rise to living processes, and living organisms develop consciousness. Thus everything is in a continual state of becoming; nothing is permanent, and all things contain contradictory aspects, the tension of which will transform them. The materialist conception of history states that environment conditions human development; man must therefore cooperate together to change the institutions of society, thus becoming in charge of his own condition. Hitherto, the state has been the instrument of the ruling class; the exploited must destroy it and create a workers' socialist state.

DISSIDENTS. Term formerly used particularly in the context of Russia, Communist Eastern Europe, and China to refer to those who refused to conform to the politics and beliefs of the society in which they lived. They have frequently been imprisoned and persecuted. Among the most famous were Alexander Solzhenitsyn, the Nobel Prize-winning novelist, expelled from Russia in 1974. In 1980 the most prominent Soviet dissident, Andrei Sakharov, was sentenced to internal exile in Gorky. The advent of Mikhail Gorbachev to the Soviet leadership produced rapid concessions on the treatment of dissidents. Notable dissidents in other Eastern bloc countries included members of the Charter '77 group in Czechoslovakia, including the playwright and politician Vaclav Havel.

DUAL ALLIANCE. Also known as the Dual Entente. An alliance between Russia and France that lasted from 1893 until the Bolshevik Revolution of October 1917.

DUAL ENTENTE. Alliance between Russia and France 1893–1917.

DUMA. Duma was the name of a Kievan political institution consisting of a council of boyars; but is better known as the elected legislative assemblies, which, with the State Council, comprised the Russian legislature from 1906 to 1917, and which were established in response to the 1905 revolution. The tsar could rule absolutely when the Duma was not in session and he could dissolve it at will. The first state Duma, elected by universal male suffrage but with limited power over financial and other matters, met for 73 days in 1906 and the second met in 1907 for 102 days. The first and second Dumas were unsuccessful in that—although it was expected that the representatives would be conservative—they were mainly liberal and socialist, and their demands for reform were totally unacceptable to the government. The franchise was then restricted, and the third Duma ran its full five-year term (1907–1912) and gave support to the government's agrarian reforms and military reorganization.

The fourth Duma sat from 1912 to 1917, but it gradually became opposed to the government's war policy and increasingly critical of the imperial régime and was suspended and finally abolished in 1917. It met in November 1916 to warn of the possibility of a revolution. On the abdication of Tsar Nicholas II, the provisional committee established by the Duma asked Prince Lvov to form a provisional government.

EASTERN BLOC. Pre-1990 Communist states of Eastern Europe: Bulgaria, Czechoslovakia, East Germany, Hungary, Poland, USSR, and which also included—despite their differences—Albania, Romania, and Yugoslavia.

EASTERN FRONT. Battle lines between Germany and Russia in World Wars I and II.

EASTERN QUESTION. Term describing the problem created by the instability of the Ottoman Empire in the nineteenth century. The whole area was a source of conflict among the Great Powers. At first only Austria, France, Great Britain, and Russia were involved, but from 1879 the German Empire became more concerned with Balkan affairs, as did Italy toward the end of the century. Russia was particularly anxious to gain access from the Black Sea to the Mediterranean Sea.

EDUCATION. The *Nestor Chronicle* mentions the establishment of schools in Kiev (988) and Novgorod (1028). Education was mainly confined to the clergy, but the first attempts at popular education came from the church. In the sixteenth and seventeenth centuries the Roman Catholic Church gave the lead and this was followed by the Orthodox Church, which opened a school at Lvov in 1586. In Muscovy the church and monastery schools taught reading, writing, and arithmetic in addition to religious subjects. The language of instruction was Church Slavonic, the counterpart in the Russian Orthodox Church to Latin in the West.

Peter I (the Great) was the great influence on education in the eighteenth century.

Moscow University was founded in 1755, because of the efforts of the scientist Mikhail Vasilyevich Lomonosov, for whom it is now named. The Smolny in Moscow and the Yekaterininsky in St. Petersburg, both boarding schools, were established for women in 1764. The School Act of 1786 established two types of national schools, with five- and two-year courses, respectively. By the beginning of the nineteenth century, there were 315 of these schools with 19,915 pupils, including 1,787 girls. The School Act of 1804 established four levels of schools: parish schools (1 year); country schools (2 years); secondary schools (4 years), extended to seven years in 1811; universities (4 years).

The universities were reformed in 1863, and in 1864 two acts were passed to improve elementary and secondary education. With the exception of the church schools, all the elementary schools were brought under the supervision of the Ministry of Education, and three types of secondary schools were created: classical, with Greek and Latin; classical, with Latin only; and modern. Education for women was made more available, and adult education saw the opening of 200 evening and Sunday schools. These liberal improvements were undermined by the minister of education, Count Dmitry Tolstoy when, in 1871, a decree made schools revert to classical curricula in order to distract students from the issues of the day. Thousands of students were excluded from the universities for political reasons. Emphasis on classicism was large abandoned in 1902 and a law providing for compulsory school attendance was enacted in 1908. By 1915 there were about 122,000 schools with 8,122,000 pupils. Under the Soviet system education was free and compulsory from ages seven to sixteen or seventeen. Coeducation was reintroduced in all schools on September 1, 1954. There were two types of general schools, with an eight-year or a ten-year curriculum; the minimum school-leaving age was seventeen. In 2001 in the Russian Federation there were 26,000,000 students, 2,009,000 teachers, and 71,078 schools of which 67,000 were primary schools for children aged six to thirteen.

EUROCOMMUNISM. West European Communist parties' attempt to distance themselves from the USSR and to seek power through parliamentary democracy within their own national traditions.

FABERGÉ, PETER CARL (1846–1920). Russian-born jeweler. He achieved fame through the ingenuity and extravagance of the jeweled objects he devised for the tsar and the Russian nobility in an age of ostentation that ended at the outbreak of World War I. He made the first imperial Easter Egg in 1885. The firm was founded by his father in 1842 in St. Petersburg. Later branches were opened in Moscow, Kiev, Odessa, and London.

FIELD OF MARS. An open space in St. Petersburg that was used for military parades, festivities, and fireworks, which was begun by Peter I (the Great). Its name is taken from the god of war. There was a Monument to Mars in the grounds of the home of the Russian leader, Count Suvorov. Originally known as the Field of Amusement, it was, in the eighteenth century, also known as the Tsarina's Meadow.

FINLAND STATION. Railway station in (Petrograd) St. Petersburg where Lenin arrived back in Russia from Switzerland in April 1917 in a sealed train.

FINLANDIZATION. Agreement under a 1948 treaty of friendship between the Soviet Union and Finland by which, effectively. in return for its independence, Finland pledged to defend the Soviet Union if any power attempted invasion through Finland. The term is thus applied to any neighbor of a major power that effectively becomes a client state.

GLASNOST. Soviet political and intellectual liberalization following appointment of Mikhail Gorbachev as Communist party secretary in 1985, encouraging a questioning or openness that ultimately weakened party authority. Glasnost caused increased nationalism, and elections in the communist countries favored nationalism and independence. The rise of Solidarity in Poland and the fall of the Berlin Wall in 1989 added to the pressures on Moscow.

GOSPLAN. Soviet State Planning Commission created centrally to control Stalin's economic programs from 1924 to 1953.

GREAT NORTHERN WAR. War, also known as the Second Northern War, fought by Russia, Denmark/Norway, and Saxony/Poland against Sweden. The Treaties of Stockholm (1719–1720) and the Treaty of Nystad (1721) established the peace and also made Russia a powerful state in the Baltic.

GREAT PATRIOTIC WAR. *See* WORLD WAR II.

GULAG. An acronym for the chief administration of corrective labor camps, which were publicly acknowledged in 1934–1960, but which, according to Alexandr Solzhenitsyn, have existed since 1918. Apart from the administration of these penal colonies, the gulag was also responsible for much economic production using forced labor. In 1940 the population of the gulags was 1,668,200 with 107,000 guards. From 1934 to 1947 there were 963,766 registered deaths.

HEMOPHILIA. The Tsarevich, Grand Duke Alexis Nicolayevich, the fifth child and only son of Tsar Nicholas II and Tsaritsa Alexandra Fyodorovna, suffered from hemophilia, a hereditary condition characterized by excessive bleeding, which usually affected only males; even a minor wound can result in fatal bleeding. The Tsaritsa was a granddaughter of Queen Victoria, several of whose descendants suffered from it. Rasputin's apparently successful treatment of Alexis gave Rasputin ascendancy over Alexandra.

IMPERIYA VSEROSSYSKAYA. Designation of the Russian state from an act passed by Peter I (the Great) in October 1721 until the abdication of Nicholas II in March 1917.

INTERNATIONAL, THE. The First International was formed in London by Karl Marx in 1864; its aim was to coordinate working-class movements in different countries and thereby to establish international socialism. There were disputes between the Marxist and anarchist members, culminating in the final separation between Marx and Bakunin (1872). The movement was dissolved in 1876. The Second International was formed in Paris in 1889, comprising the radical parties of Austria, Belgium, Denmark, Germany, Spain, Sweden, and Switzerland. A non-revolutionary movement, it collapsed with the outbreak of World War I. The Third International (Comintern) was formed in Moscow by Lenin and the Bolsheviks in 1917 and comprised the Communist elements excluded from the Second International. Its aim was world revolution. The Fourth International was formed by Trotsky in Mexico in the 1930s, and there was also a fifth international—the Situationist International—formed in 1954.

There have been two revivals of the Second—nonrevolutionary Socialist—International. The first (1923) ceased to operate in 1940 and the second in 1951.

IRON CURTAIN. Postwar dividing line through Central Europe between Communist and non-Communist states that collapsed in 1989–1990.

ISKRA **(THE SPARK).** Marxist newspaper founded by Lenin, published abroad after 1900, first in Germany, then London, and from 1903 in Switzerland. Also a satirical journal published in St. Petersburg (1859–1873).

JULY DAYS. Period from July 16 to 18, 1917, when servicemen and civilians, in sympathy with the Bolsheviks, tried to seize power from Kerensky's provisional government in Petrograd. Lenin considered their uprising inopportune; they received no significant support and the attempt failed. Bolshevik involvement was ascribed to pro-German sympathies and in general they were accused of treason. Lenin fled to Finland.

KADETS. Russian liberal party (Constitutional Democrats) formed after 1905 revolution that proposed a democratic republic after 1917 revolution; banned by the Bolsheviks in 1918.

KGB. Committee of State Security. Soviet secret police founded in March 1954 with responsibility for internal security, espionage, and counterespionage.

KOLKHOZ. Collective farms in the former Soviet Union. The term originated with the collectivization of agriculture in the USSR during the 1928–1933 Five-Year Plan when all individual farms and smallholdings were combined into the *kolkhoz* system. In theory a kolkhoz is a cooperative of a number of peasants who pool land and equipment and who are paid according to the amount of work done. In fact, kolkhozy were managed by the party, which appointed the chairman. Owing to the system of compulsory selling of produce to the state at prices fixed by the state, it was difficult for many kolkhozy to receive an adequate income. Also, the kolkhoz system offered few incentives for the workers to take an interest in the work. Membership of a kolkhoz was automatic for those born in it and was difficult to leave.

KOMSOMOL. Communist party of the Soviet Union's youth wing.

KREMLIN. The main fortress in a medieval Russian city, usually built on the high bank of a river, or rivers in the case of a confluence, and separated from the rest of the city by a wall with ramparts, a moat, and towers and battlements. The kremlin itself contained the palaces for the bishop and prince, their offices, a cathedral, and stores and weapons in case of siege. The best-known kremlin is the Moscow Kremlin, built according to a triangular design at the confluence of the Moskva and Neglinnaya Rivers. The rampart and red-brick towers were built by Italian architects in the days of Ivan III (the Great). The ornate spires were added in the seventeenth century. The Kremlin contains the Cathedral of the Dormition, the Cathedral of the Archangel Michael, and the Cathedral of the Annunciation, as well as the Palace of the Facets and Terem Palace.

The present Great Kremlin Palace was built in 1839–1840 by Konstantin Thon, in the Russo-Byzantine style.

KREMLINOLOGY. Name derived from the Moscow Kremlin, where the Supreme Soviet of the USSR held its sessions. Kremlinology is the study of the policies of the Soviet government. It also implies gleaning information or clues about the conduct of Soviet politics, which give an indication of what goes on behind the façade of monolithic unity among the leadership.

KULAK. Relatively prosperous peasants; millions were deported or murdered because of their opposition to Soviet agricultural collectivization between 1928 and 1932.

LUBLIN COMMITTEE. The Soviet-backed Polish Committee of National Liberation established in the city of Lublin on July 25, 1944 as the core of a Communist government for the country, recognized by the USSR in December 1944 as the provisional government. The committee joined with the London-based Polish government in exile to form a Polish Provisional Government of National Unity in July 1945.

MARXISM-LENINISM. Theories arising from the adaptation of nineteenth-century Marxism to twentieth-century facts, and in particular to the problems of governing Russia; it includes belief in "Socialism in one country" and peaceful coexistence with countries under different social systems.

MENSHEVIKS. Political party established in August 1917 at a congress of several Social Democratic groups. The Mensheviks proposed a proletarian party working with the liberals in order to replace the autocracy with a democratic constitution. Before 1917 "Menshevik" referred to the non-Leninist faction of the Russian Social Democratic Labor Party. Although the Mensheviks worked with the Bolsheviks during the 1905 revolution and reunited with them the following year, relations were strained. The Mensheviks themselves were divided into the "liquidationalists," the "party-minded Mensheviks" of the center, the followers of Pavel Axelrod, and the followers of Trotsky. In 1922 the Mensheviks were suppressed, and in 1931 a show trial took place in Moscow. In 1920 a group of Mensheviks left Russia and settled in the United States.

METROPOLITAN. Primate of the Orthodox Church. In the nineteenth century, a metropolitan resided in each of the historic capitals of the Russian Empire: Kiev, Moscow, and St. Petersburg.

MILITARY SETTLEMENTS (COLONIES). The first military settlement was established in 1810. Crown peasants were turned into hereditary soldiers, often bringing great hardship. Between 1812 and 1816 about 33 percent of the peacetime army was located in military settlements. There were several rebellions, notably at Chuguevin in the Ukraine (1819).

MIR. Rural assembly that administered an agricultural community. This did not always correspond to one village and generally it refers to the rural community and its inhabitants. After the emancipation in 1861, the *mir* was retained for administrative reasons but was abolished after the Stolypin reforms of 1906–1911.

MUSCOVY. State from the fourteenth to the eighteenth century. The grand princes of Vladimir were the first princes to rule Muscovy. As Moscow became more powerful it took over as capital of the grand principality. Ivan III (the Great) gained extra territory, including the republic of Novgorod in 1478. By the time of Ivan IV (the Terrible), Muscovy had extended its rule over Vyatka, Pskov, and Ryazan, as well as over the Tartar khanates of Kazan, Astrakhan, and part of Siberia. Under the house of Romanov the rest of Siberia and Ukraine were incorporated as well. The last tsar of Muscovy was Peter I (the Great), the first emperor of Russia.

NAMES. Before the October Revolution in 1917, first names were limited to saints' names. Name days of the saints were celebrated more commonly than birthdays. Other limitations on names were imposed, some relating to social status and occupation. Each person has at least three names: a first name, a patronymic, and a surname. The patronymic is formed by adding the endings -ovich, -evich, or –ich to the father's first name in the case of a man, or by adding –ovna, -evna, -inichna, or –ichna to the father's name in the case of a woman. In addition, a wide number of diminutive forms of the first name are also used, including Kolya for Nikolai, Masha for Mariya, Sasha for Alexander(a), Vanya for Ivan.

According to B. O. Unbegaun, in *Russian Surnames* (1972), the twelve most popular surnames in St. Petersburg in 1910 were: Ivanov, Vasilyev, Petrov, Smirnov, Mikhailov, Fedorov, Sokolov, Yakovlev, Popov, Andreyev, Alekseyev and Aleksandrov.

***NARODNAYA VOLYA* (PEOPLE'S FREEDOM OR WILL).** Revolutionary organization that came into being after the split of the *Zemlya* *i Volya* organization in 1879. It believed in the seizure of power, and in practice concentrated on the killing of high government officials. It was responsible for the assassination of Alexander II (1881). Led by Aleksandr Ulyanov, the St. Petersburg group attempted the assassination of Alexander III. Although some members later joined the Social Democrats and became Bolsheviks, by 1902 a large proportion had become members of the Socialist Revolutionary Party.

NEMETS. Literally, one who is dumb, unable to speak. Originally used to describe any foreigner, it became more specifically used to mean a German.

NERCHINSK, TREATY OF. A political and commercial agreement of 1689 between Russia and China that also established boundaries between the two countries. The agreement gave Russia Transbaikalia (east of Lake Baikal) and gave China the Amur valley, and it permitted Russian trade caravans to enter Peking (Beijing). The agreement was enlarged in 1727 and remained the basis of Russo-Chinese relations until the mid-nineteenth century.

NEW ECONOMIC POLICY. Economic policy practiced by the government in 1923–1928, replacing the policies of War Communism (1918–1921). It aimed at revitalizing the economy by allowing greater freedom in agriculture, industry, and trade. In this, the government was successful and raised the national income above that of 1913. The NEP was followed by the first Five-Year Plan.

NOBILITY. In Muscovite Russia, the government promoted the interests of the gentry by passing laws that limited the peasants' movements. From 1475 boyar families in state service were entered in a state genealogical book; many squabbles ensued as the boyars fought to maintain their rank. In 1722 Peter I (the Great) introduced compulsory state service, and with his Table of Ranks advancement was open to all. Titles of nobility were conferred on those who deserved it, regardless of social standing. In 1785, during what is considered the Golden Age of Nobles, Catherine II (the Great) issued a Charter to the Nobility; this recognized the gentry of each district and province as a legal body, headed by an elected district or regional marshal of nobility. Members of the gentry were also exempt from tax obligations and personal service. The position of the nobility began to decline considerably under Alexander I and Nicholas I. According to the 1877 census, the nobility owned 73,100,000 *desyatin* of land, but by 1911, it owned only 43,200,000 *desyatin*. (*Desyatin* equal to 2.7 acres or 1.092 hectares.)

OBROK. Annual payment by serfs to their masters. Most of the land of an estate was farmed by peasants on their own account and they paid the owner an annual amount known as *obrok*.

Sometimes payments were made in kind or by performing services. About 44 percent of peasants worked under this system in the eighteenth century and those working under obrok generally enjoyed greater freedom than those working under *barshchina*. Obrok is also a term used for the consolidation of taxes and for the owner being responsible for collecting taxes and delivering them to the authorities; thus the tenants were relieved of dealing directly with tax officials.

OCTOBER REVOLUTION. Bolshevik overthrow of Provisional Government and seizure of power on November 6–7, 1917, led by Vladimir Lenin (1870–1924). Under the Julian calendar then in operation in Russia, the month was October.

OGPU. Soviet counterrevolutionary security police formed in 1922 as GPU (State Political Administration), renamed OGPU (Unified State Political Administration) in 1923. Replaced by the NKVD in 1934.

OLD BELIEVERS. Patriarch Nikon introduced reforms into religious texts and rituals of the Orthodox Church to correct errors that had crept in since the translation from the original Greek. His reforms were opposed by a section of the church led by Archpriest Avvakum, Stephen Vonifatiev, and Ivan Neronov, who accused him of heresy (1653). Nikon was vindicated, and his opponents withdrew as a separate sect. They were persecuted severely, and some, believing the reforms to be an indication of the end of the world, committed self-immolation.

They rejected the sign of the cross made with three fingers (used in the Greek Church), the return to the pure Greek texts, the new spelling of "Jesus," and other small innovations. They had no theological basis for dissent, but simply refused to recognize any departure from Muscovite custom, regarding their own Muscovite culture as the true Russian tradition, to be copied by others and to be above compromise. The movement split during the eighteenth century into two sects. The *popovtsy* (priestly ones) continued to have priests, although they obtained them with difficulty. Some popovtsy eventually set up their own episcopate; others were reconciled to the Orthodox Church, keeping their own rites. The *bepopovtsy*, as their name indicates in Russian, had no priesthood, and developed a new religious life with no sacraments except baptism and confession.

They carried their conservatism into political life, denouncing the reforms of Peter I (the Great), whom they saw as the Antichrist. They suffered periodic persecution until an edict of toleration was passed in 1905. In 1971 the old rites were recognized as valid by the council of the Orthodox Church.

Some surviving groups, in Russia and abroad, maintain a seventeenth-century way of life. The group as a whole was always identified with the well-to-do peasant, shopkeeper, or small businessman who had plenty of commercial acumen and little sympathy for the landed gentry of the Orthodox establishment.

OLD CHURCH SLAVONIC. Slavic language based on Macedonian dialects spoken around Thessalonika. Its once relatively widespread usage is attributed to the fact that this is the language used by Saints Cyril and Methodius when translating the Bible and when preaching to the Moravian Slavs. The language as used after the twelfth century is referred to as Church Slavonic.

ORTHODOX CHURCH. The most important church in Russia and in the Soviet Union. In 1448 the Russian church became autocephalous, in that it was placed under the jurisdiction of an independent metropolitan in Moscow; it was thus no longer under the authority of Rome. In 1458, however, Rome appointed another "metropolitan of Kiev and all Russia." This metropolitanate, controlled by Roman Catholic Poland, accepted union with Rome in 1596. In 1686, however, the metropolitanate of Kiev was attached to the patriarchate of Moscow. Muscovite Russians came to regard themselves as the last true Orthodox believers, considering Moscow to be the "Third Rome." Patriarch Nikon's liturgical reforms resulted in a major schism in the Russian church. Millions of clergy and laity refused to accept a reformed Russian liturgy closely modeled on the Greek.

Peter I (the Great) rejected the Byzantine heritage and abolished the patriarchate in 1721, replacing it by a state department. Because of the church's reluctance to involve itself in social issues, the radicals of the nineteenth century grew increasingly disillusioned with it. On January 20, 1918, the Bolshevik government published a decree depriving the church of all legal rights. Following imprisonment for opposing the régime's religious policy, Patriarch Tikhon decided to conform with the state, and this tendency to conformism is still pursued. Savagely persecuted under Stalin and to a large extent suppressed under Khrushchev, the Orthodox Church in 2004 has more freedom. In August 2000, the Orthodox Church bestowed sainthood on Tsar Nicholas II, his wife and children, and more than 800 other twentieth-century martyrs.

PALE OF SETTLEMENT. Russian Jews were required to live in a defined area called the Pale of Settlement, and it was only in exceptional circumstances that a Jew could move out of the pale (pale meaning a fenced area).

PATRIARCH. Title conferred on the head of the Russian Orthodox Church from 1589 until the era of Peter I (the Great). It was reestablished in November 1917.

PAUPER'S ALLOTMENT. The pauper's allotment was an additional provision of the emancipation reform law of 1861. There were variants on the application of the land settlement in different areas of the country, but the basic plan was that the peasants would receive that part of the land that they had cultivated for themselves, which was roughly half of the total. They had to pay the landlords for the land they acquired, or, alternatively, they could take a quarter of their normal parcel of land, the pauper's allotment, without payment.

PERESTROIKA. Attempt at radical reform of Soviet economy introduced by Mikhail Gorbachev, Communist party leader from 1985, involving "restructuring" and increasing replacement of central control by market forces.

PETER AND PAUL FORTRESS. Built on Hare Island, St. Petersburg, in 1703 by Peter I (the Great), from 1718 onward the hexagonal fortress served as a prison for political offenders. It was built according to the designs of Lambert, a pupil of Vauban. Within the fortress is the Cathedral of St. Peter and St. Paul, by Domenico Andrea Trezzini (ca. 1670–1734), the golden spire of which is a focal point of St. Petersburg.

PETROGRAD SOVIET. Because Petrograd was the center of the February Revolution in 1917, the Petrograd soviet carried out the role of a national soviet for a few months but relinquished this in June to an all-Russian congress of soviets. After this, in theory at least, it became solely a local city soviet. Its voice and directorate was the executive committee that the delegates elected.

POGROM. Term meaning "destruction." Organized massacre in Russia, particularly involving attacks on Jews, the first of which was authorized by the tsarist authorities in 1881.

POLITBURO. Leading party committee in Communist-controlled states.

PROVISIONAL GOVERNMENT. Government of Russia between March and October 1917. Brought to power after the deposition of the monarchy, the provisional government was made up of the Duma but had to share power in Petrograd with the Workers' and Soldiers' Soviet.

QUADRUPLE ALLIANCE. Alliance first formed in 1813 between Russia, Austria, Great Britain, and Prussia and officially renewed in 1815. The four powers agreed to maintain the Second Peace of Paris (signed the same day) and to prevent the return of Napoleon Bonaparte. They also agreed to hold periodic conferences of sovereigns or chief ministers to maintain the stability of Europe and discuss matters of common interest. There were four such meetings: in Aix-la-Chapelle (Aachen; 1818), Troppau (1820), Laibach (1820–1821), and Verona (1822); by then, differences had emerged between Great Britain, which was opposed to direct intervention in the internal affairs of sovereign states, and the others, which were prepared to intervene directly to suppress revolution. Further differences emerged (between Russia and Austria) in 1825 and the system was abandoned. At the meeting in Aix-la-Chapelle in 1818, France was reacknowledged as one of the great powers of Europe and the Quadruple Alliance became the Quintuple Alliance.

QUINTUPLE ALLIANCE. Drawn up in 1818 on the admission of France to the former Quadruple Alliance of Russia, Great Britain, Austria, and Prussia, its purpose was to preserve the balance of power in Europe.

RAILWAYS. The first Russian railway line was opened from St. Petersburg to Tsarskoye-Selo in 1836. This was for horse traction because the locomotive had not arrived from England, and so exactly a year later it was opened with a locomotive. By order of the tsar a set of musical instruments, consisting of eleven trumpets and a trombone, were on the locomotive so that warning could be given of the approaching train. Locomotives were used only when forty or more passengers were to be carried; platform wagons were open for the transport of passengers seated in their own carriages. In 1851 the St. Petersburg-Moscow line was completed. However, it was in the 1860s–1870s that the basic network was constructed, and in 1891 work on the Trans-Siberian Railway was started. Expansion was rapid during World War I, during which 6,769 miles (10,900 km) of railway were built. Railways are still largely concentrated in European Russia, especially in the Moscow area, the Donets Basin, and western Ukraine. However, a number of new lines such as the Baikal-Amur mainline across eastern Siberia were constructed in the late twentieth century. Railways are constructed to a gauge of five feet (1,534 mm); thus coaches are more spacious than in the West.

The total length of USSR railways in January 1989 was 91,687 miles (146,700 km) (1913: 36,328 miles/58,500 km).

RED SQUARE (*KRASNAYA PLOSHCHAD*). Square in Moscow that lies along the northeastern wall and most of the Kremlin in front of the Kitay Gorod. It is linked to the Kremlin by three gates. It has existed since the fifteenth century as a market, and many main roads converged at this point. In 1812 the burning of Moscow destroyed much of Red Square. Osip Bovet replanned the square, and his buildings include the present department store GUM. It is the site of military parades and displays on public holidays. Lenin's mausoleum lies in front of the eastern walls.

REFUSENIKS. Predominantly Jewish Soviet citizens refused permission to emigrate from the USSR by the authorities.

REVISIONIST. Orthodox Marxists applied this to anyone who attempts to reassess the basic tenets of revolutionary socialism. Originating in Germany in the 1890s and 1900s, its chief exponents were Edouard Bernstein and Karl Knutsky. Regarded as heresy in the Soviet Union.

ROMANOVS. Last ruling dynasty of Russia (1613–1917), noted for their absolutism and for transforming Russia into a large empire. The first Romanov tsar was Michael, whose election ended the Time of Troubles. Peter I (the Great) was succeeded by his second wife, Catherine, the daughter of a Livonian peasant, and she by Peter II, the grandson of Peter, with whom the male line of the Romanovs terminated in the year 1730. The reign of the next three sovereigns of Russia—Anna, Ivan VI, and Elizabeth—of the female line of Romanovs, formed a transitional period, which came to an end with the accession of Peter III of the house of Holstein-Gottorp. All the subsequent emperors, without exception, connected themselves by marriage with German families. The wife and successor of Peter III, Catherine II (the Great), daughter of the prince of Anhalt-Zerbst, general in the Prussian army, left the crown to her only son, Paul, who became the father of two emperors, Alexander I and Nicholas I, and the grandfather of a third, Alexander II. All these sovereigns married German princesses, creating intimate family alliances with, among others, the reigning houses of Württemberg, Baden, and Prussia. The emperor was in possession of the revenue from the crown domains, consisting of more than one million square miles (2.6 million km) of cultivated land and forest, besides gold and other mines in Siberia, and producing a vast revenue, the actual amount of which was, however, unknown as no reference to the subject was made in the budgets or finance accounts, the crown domains being considered the private property of the imperial family.

In March 1917, during the Russian Revolution, Romanov rule ended with the abdication of Nicholas II. He and his immediate family were executed.

SAMIZDAT. Writings critical of the state written by dissidents in great secrecy, and circulated by hand from one person to another. Samizdat can be traced back to the 1820s to the poet Pushkin and it continued to flourish in the second half of the nineteenth century among revolutionary groups. The authorities strongly disapproved of circulating uncensored material and strict penalties were imposed on those who were caught.

SEALED TRAIN. Train that took Lenin, and thirty of his comrades, after years in exile, from Zurich, Switzerland, to the Finland Station, St. Petersburg, in April 1917. The journey through Germany, Sweden, and Finland was arranged by the German government with the aim of helping to bring to an end the fighting on the eastern front and so free a million troops to reinforce their armies in France.

SECOND ECONOMY. Term used in the Communist era for the "black economy" of the Soviet Union and Eastern Europe. It embraced not only black market transactions, but currency speculation, corruption, and independent enterprises condoned by the state.

SECOND FRONT. Allied invasion of Western Europe demanded by Stalin from 1941 to relieve German pressure on Soviet Union; opened with Anglo-American landings in Normandy on June 6, 1944.

SERFS. Peasants who could be bought, sold, and generally treated as chattels by the landowner. Although the 1649 code (*sobornoe ulozhenie*) forbade the owner to kill, wound, or mistreat his serfs, this code was frequently infringed, but the code also removed the time limit for reclaiming runaway peasants. Tax had to be paid on a serf, and he spent half his working day on the landowner's estate. At times peasant rebellions occurred, such as the uprising led by Stenka Razin in 1670. Various schemes for the emancipation of the serfs were considered from the time of Catherine II (the Great), but serfdom was finally abolished only in 1861.

SEVEN YEARS' WAR (1756–1763). Properly named the Austro-Prussian War of 1756–1763. Russia fought Prussia until the beginning of 1762, when the two countries made a separate peace. Prussia had been allied with Great Britain against Austria, France, Russia, Sweden, and Saxony. The treaty of Hubertusburg (Hubertsburg) between Austria, Prussia, and Saxony was signed in 1763. Russia succeeded in eliminating French influence from Poland.

SIDE-BURNITES. In 1837 Nicholas I issued a decree forbidding the wearing of beards and whiskers by civil servants and this was later extended to include students.

SINGING REVOLUTION. Estonian demands for independence from the soviet Union. It was a revolution in which no shots were fired and no blood was shed. The protests began in June 1988 with demands for the release of two political prisoners, Mart Niklus and Enn Tarto.

SOVIET. Term derived from the Russian word meaning council. There were soviets at every level of the party apparatus, ranging from the Supreme Soviet to the republican, provincial, and local soviets. Membership was by election. The function of soviets was summed up in Stalin's description of soviets as "transmission belts from the party to the masses." They emerged in the 1905 and 1917 revolutions.

SOVKHOZ. State-owned farm in the USSR.

STALINISM. Name given to Stalin's political theorizing and rule of the USSR, the Eastern Bloc Countries, and the World Communist movement. Based on Marxism, Leninism, and national Bolshevism, Stalin, with the help of Molotov, Zhdanov, and Vyshinsky, added such doctrines and ideas as the existence of the state under full communism, Socialist Realism in the arts, the concept of building socialism in one country, the people's great love for the Communist party, their unanimous support of Stalin, and the security organs to eliminate "misguided" dissenters. Concentration camps were much in use, especially during Stalin's Great Purge. Some aspects of Stalinism became obsolete, particularly after Khrushchev's secret report to the Twentieth Party Congress; others, such as the role of the Communist party, remained until the breakup of the USSR.

STATE CAPITALISM. Term used by Lenin to describe the combination of central economic control and compromise with private financial interests in 1918 to preserve Bolshevik rule. More latterly a description of pre-1990 East European régimes.

STRELTSY. The *Streltsy* were Russian infantrymen, the first to carry firearms, established by Ivan IV in 1550. They formed a large proportion of the Russian army for a century and also provided the tsar's bodyguard. At the end of the seventeenth century, they started to exercise political influence, having become discontented by their conditions of service. They became involved in the struggle for succession to the Russian throne begun in 1682, between the half-brothers Peter I and Ivan V. Supporting Ivan, in 1682 they staged a revolt against Peter's mother's family, the Naryshkins. They named both Ivan and Peter tsars and made Ivan's sister Sophia Alekseyevna the regent. In 1698, then 50,000 strong, they were unsuccessful in an attempt to unseat Peter I and restore Sophia. Peter I was on his Western European expedition, but the revolt had been rigorously dealt with before he reached Moscow. However this did not stop him launching bloody reprisals against the Streltsy in which he took an active personal part. The Streltsy were then disbanded.

TRIPLE ENTENTE. Agreement between Britain, France, and Russia to resolve their outstanding colonial differences; it became a military alliance in 1914.

TROTSKYIST. Follower of Leo Trotsky (1879–1940) who believed Stalin had betrayed the Russian Revolution and called for renewed socialist world revolution; briefly fashionable among student activists in the 1960s and 1970s.

TSAR. Title of the Russian rulers first used by Ivan IV in 1547. Peter I (the Great) adopted the title of Emperor of All Russia. It remained in popular usage until the abdication and execution of Tsar Nicholas II in 1918. The tsar's wife was known as tsarina or tsaritsa and his eldest son as the tsarevich.

UNION OF SOVIET SOCIALIST REPUBLICS (USSR). The union was declared "no longer in existence" in December 1991, and the Commonwealth of Independent States was formed.

In 1917 when the revolution broke out, a provisional government was appointed, and in a few months a republic was proclaimed. Late in 1917 power was transferred to the second All-Russian Congress of Soviets. This elected a new government, the Council of People's Commissars, headed by Lenin. Early in 1918 the third All-Russian Congress of Soviets issued a Declaration of Rights of the Toiling and Exploited Masses, which proclaimed Russia a republic of Soviet workers', soldiers', and peasants' deputies; and in the middle of 1918 the fifth congress adopted a constitution for the Russian Soviet Federated Socialist Republic. In the course of the civil war other Soviet republics were set up in Ukraine, Belorussia, and Transcaucasia. These first entered into treaty relations with the Russian Soviet Federated Socialist Republic and then, in 1922, joined with it in a closely integrated union. The total area was 8.65 million square miles (22.4 million sq km). The capital was Moscow. Population in 1991 was 291 million.

VIENNA, CONGRESS OF. The assembly (1814–1815) that reorganized Europe after the defeat of Napoleon Bonaparte. It was attended by the four countries mainly responsible for the overthrow of Napoleon: Austria, Great Britain, Prussia, and Russia. Although Castlereagh (British foreign secretary) was anxious to oppose Russian expansionism, Russia gained the Duchy of Warsaw, thereafter called the Kingdom of Poland.

WAR COMMUNISM. Name given to the Bolshevik government's social and economic policies of 1918–1921. In order to support the Bolsheviks in the Civil War fully and to build communism in general, War Communism was characterized by the nationalization of industry and trade, wages in kind for workers, and enforced labor service. These measures were unpopular, and in 1921 there occurred several uprisings. War Communism was replaced by the New Economic Policy in 1921.

WARSAW PACT, THE. The Warsaw Treaty of Friendship, Cooperation, and Mutual Assistance was established in May 1955; its unified military command was dissolved in March 1991 and the residual political organization in July 1991. Its members were Bulgaria, Czechoslovakia, East Germany, Hungary, Poland, Romania, and the USSR; Albania withdrew its membership in 1968. It was prompted by the inclusion of West Germany in the Western Alliance. In theory, the Warsaw Pact was to provide resources, men, and money to be used for defense purposes; in practice, the available forces were controlled by the USSR, which benefited from it, since it provided a buffer zone between East and West and reduced Soviet military expenditure. Its close work with Comecon had encouraged the rapid growth of arms factories in Eastern Europe. The organization prevented any one non-Soviet army from becoming too powerful. No Eastern European officer could command national forces without Soviet approval. Many Eastern European officers were trained at the Frunze Military Academy in the Soviet Union.

WHITE RUSSIANS. Anti-Bolshevik monarchist forces in the 1917–1921 Russian civil war, many of whom went into exile following the Red Army victory.

WORLD WAR I. War broke out in July 1914 between Austria and Serbia. Nicholas II believed that Russians would support a stand in the Balkans. Russia mobilized to support Serbia. This action made a crisis in the Balkans a European crisis. Germany declared war on Russia on August 1. The Russian government hoped that a war would unite the Russian people in common purpose. Patriotism and enthusiasm, as well as support for Nicholas II, waned when, after some early victories against Austria, Russia sustained great losses in fighting Germany and the western provinces were lost.

Communications broke down, and there were widespread shortages of food and ammunition. To make matters worse, the Nicholas dismissed the Duma and took personal charge of the war, leaving internal government in the incapable hands of Tsaritsa Alexandra and Rasputin, the monk. The February Revolution (1917) was the outcome of widespread misery and bitterness, and Nicholas II abdicated. In the spring of 1918 the Bolsheviks made peace with the Germans at Brest-Litovsk, at which Russia accepted Germany's harsh demands. Great Britain and France, alarmed at losing their ally and fearing that the Germans might discover large consignments of arms sent to Russia, marched into Russia, together with the Americans and Japanese.

WORLD WAR II. In order to concentrate Hitler's attentions on the West, in 1939 Stalin secretly arranged with Hitler to allow German armies to enter Poland, and as a result, Russia gained eastern Poland and the Baltic states. Following the invasion, Great Britain and France declared war, but Russia remained neutral and secured eastern Poland and the Baltic states. Later that year Russia invaded Poland (September) and Finland (November). In 1941 Hitler ordered the invasion of Russia, which began on June 22. The Nazis advanced, overpowering Russian resistance with great barbarity and violence. By the summer of 1941 Leningrad (St. Petersburg) was besieged and defeat seemed imminent, but the Russians put up determined resistance and stymied the Germans. The bitter winter of 1941–1942 killed thousands of German soldiers, while in the east the Red Army prepared to counterattack. In the spring the German advance began for a second time, and in September they reached Stalingrad, the scene of an extremely fierce battle. In November the Red Army launched a counterattack, surrounded the Germans, and forced them to surrender in February 1943. The Russians then began driving westward. The following year, the British and Americans landed in France, and the Germans, attacked from east and west, were defeated.

In 1945 Stalin, Churchill, and Roosevelt met at Yalta to discuss the surrender and occupation of Germany, the war against Japan, and the establishment of the United Nations. The war was known in Russia as the Great Patriotic War and resulted in twenty million dead (7.5 million in the armed forces). U.S. losses were 292,000 and British and Commonwealth forces 398,000.

ZEMSKY SOBOR. Occasional gatherings of the estates of the realm, including boyars, clergy, gentry, and sometimes burghers and peasants, called by Muscovite tsars to consider matters of special importance. First called by Ivan IV (the Terrible) in 1549, they met five or six times before 1613, when an assembly convened to elect a new tsar, Michael Romanov. It met continually as an influential advisory body until 1622. It continued to be important until about 1660. It was abandoned by Peter I (the Great).

FURTHER READING

Many of the titles in the following bibliographies have been consulted to produce this reference book. It is not an exhaustive bibliography and only includes books from original English sources or translations.

Encyclopedias and Who's Who

Brown, A., et al. *The Cambridge Encyclopedia of Russia and the Soviet Union.* 1982.

Florinsky, M. T. *McGraw-Hill Encyclopedia of Russia and the Soviet Union.* 1961.

McCauley, M. *Who's Who in Russia since 1900.* 1997.

Paxton, J. *Encyclopedia of Russian History: From the Christianization of Kiev to the Break-Up of the USSR.* 1993.

Shaw, W., and D. Pryce. *Encyclopedia of the USSR: 1905 to the Present.* 1990.

Utechin, S. V. *Everyman's Concise Encyclopaedia of Russia.* 1961.

Atlases

The Times Atlas of World History. 1989.

Channon, J. *The Penguin Historical Atlas of Russia.* 1995.

    One-volume handbook for students and interested lay readers alike with over sixty full color maps.

Gilbert, M. *The Routledge Atlas of Russian History.* 2002.

    This atlas of 169 maps covers not simply the wars and expansion of Russia, but a wealth of less conspicuous details of Russian history from famine and anarchism to the growth of naval strength, as well as war and conflict, politics, industry, economics, transport, trade, and culture.

Milner-Gulland, R. *Atlas of Russia and the Soviet Union.* 1989.

    A valuable atlas although it was published before the break-up of the Soviet Union, giving a graphic description of the development of Russian culture and society. Unfamiliar terms are explained in the reference section.

Value of the book is enhanced by the inclusion of a chronological table, a table of rulers of Russia, a bibliography, a gazetteer and an index.

Chronologies

Conte, F. *Great Dates in Russian and Soviet History.* 1994.
> This publication provides comprehensive and quick access to the chronological history of this major world power.

Paxton, J., and E. W. Knappman. *Calendar of World History.* 1999.

General Histories

Auty, R. and D. Obolensky. *An Introduction to Russian History.* 1976.
> Very good on Russian geography and contains an excellent bibliography.

Chapman, T. *Imperial Russia, 1801–1905.* 2001.
> This work traces the development of the Russian Empire from the murder of Tsar Paul to the reforms of the 1890s that were an attempt to modernize the autocratic state.

Chubarov, A. *Russia's Bitter Path to Modernity.* 2003.
> A history of Soviet and post-Soviet Eras.

Crankshaw, E. *The Shadow of the Winter Palace: The Drift to Revolution, 1825–1917.* 1976.
> A thorough and penetrating work, showing how conditions in nineteenth-century Russia led to the Revolution and to the Soviet period.

Grey, I. *The Romanovs: The Rise and Fall of a Russian Dynasty.* 1971.
> Portrays each ruler as a person, and describes his or her policies and achievements (1613–1917), illuminating the contrasts between the strong and the weak rulers, and between their autocratic power and their deep belief in the Orthodox Church, with its precept of humility.

Hosking, G. *A History of the Soviet Union.* 1985.
———. *Russia: People and Empire, 1552–1917.* 1997.
> A companion to Hosking's excellent *History of the Soviet Union.*

Lincoln, W. B. *The Romanovs.* 1981.
Platonov, S. F. *The Time of Troubles.* 1970.
Riasanovsky, N. *History of Russia.* 1993.
> Standard textbook.

Roberts, G. *The Soviet Union in World Politics*. 1998.
> Coexistence, revolution and cold war, 1945–1991.

Rogger, H. *Russia in the Age of Modernisation and Revolution 1881-1917*. 1983.
> Excellent textbook dealing with the reigns of the last two tsars.

Sakwa, R. *The Rise and Fall of the Soviet Union*. 1999.
> A comprehensive overview of the rise and fall of the Soviet system. Using eyewitness accounts, official documents and newly available material, Sakwa places the Soviet experience in comparative and historical context.

Saunders, D. *Russia in the Age of Reaction and Reform 1801–1881*. 1992.
> Excellent textbook covering the political, diplomatic, intellectual, social, and economic history of nineteenth-century Russia.

Service, R. *The Russian Revolution, 1900–1927*. 1991.
Seton-Watson, H. *The Russian Empire 1801–1917*. 1967.
> Good on political and diplomatic matters.

_____. *The Decline of Imperial Russia, 1855–1914*. 1956.
> A thorough, authoritative, and readable outline of the history from the Crimean War to World War I.

Vernadsky, G., and R. T. Fisher. *A Source Book for Russian History from Early Times to 1917*. 3 vols. 1972.
> Best collection of prerevolutionary documents.

Warnes, D. *Chronicle of the Russian Tsars*. 1999.
> A beautifully illustrated reign-by-reign record of the rulers of imperial Russia with many quotations.

Yakovlev, A. A. *A Century of Russian Violence in Soviet Russia*. 2003.

Leaders

From Michael to Peter I (the Great) 1613–1725

Anderson, M. S. *Peter the Great*. 1978.
> Good on the contradictory aspects of the character of Peter I (the Great).

Anisimov, E. V. *The Reforms of Peter the Great*. 1993.
Fuhrmann, J. *Tsar Alexis, His Reign and His Russia* 1981.
Hughes, L. *Russia in the Age of Peter the Great*. 1998.

Although not a biography of Peter I (the Great), he dominates the text and it is probably the best account of Petrine Russia.

Hughes, L. *Sophia: Regent of Russia 1657–1704.* 1990.
de Jonge, A. *Fire and Water: A Life of Peter the Great.* 1979.
    A biography of distinction.

Lentin, A. *Russia in the Eighteenth Century: From Peter the Great to Catherine the Great, 1696–1796.* 1973.
    A concise history of a formative period of westernization, reform, and the rise of Russia as a great power. A good introduction to the period.

Longworth, O. *Alexis Tsar of All the Russias.* 1984.
Massie, R. K. *Peter the Great: His Life and World.* 1981.
    Best on the Petrine wars.

O'Brien, C. B. *Russia under Two Tsars—The Regency of Sophia.* 1952.
Raeff, M., ed. *Peter the Great Changes Russia.* 1972.
    The first edition published in 1963 was entitled *Peter the Great, Reformer or Revolutionary.* Contains descriptions, short histories and historical assessments by various prominent authoritative contributors.

Soloviev, S. M. *History of Russia: Tsar Alexis, A Reign Ends.* Vol. 23. 1998.
Troyat, H. *Peter the Great.* 1988.

From Catherine I to Catherine II (the Great) 1725–1796

Alexander, J. T. *Catherine the Great: Life and Legend.* 1989.
Anisimov, E. V. *Empress Elizabeth: Her Reign and Her Russia.* 1995.
Brennan, J. *Enlightened Despotism in Russia: The Reign of Elizabeth 1741–1762.* 1987.
Cronin, V. *Catherine: Empress of All the Russias.* 1978.
Curtiss, M. *A Forgotten Empress: Anna Ivanovna and Her Era.* 1974.
Dukes, P. *Catherine the Great and the Russian Nobility.* 1967.
    A study based on the materials of the Legislative Commission of 1767.

Dukes, P. *Russia under Catherine the Great.* 2 vols. 1977–1978.
Empress Catherine II. *Memoirs.* 1955.
Gleason, W. J. *Moral Idealists, Bureaucracy, and Catherine the Great.* 1981.
Haslip, J. *Catherine the Great.* 1977.
Lentin, A. *Voltaire and Catherine the Great: Selected Correspondence.* 1974.
Leonard, C. S. *Reform and Regicide: The Reign of Peter III of Russia.* 1993.
Longworth, P. *The Three Empresses.* 1982.

Madariaga, I. de. *Catherine the Great: A Short History.* 1990.

————. *Russia in the Age of Catherine the Great.* 1981.

Raeff, M. *Catherine the Great: A Profile.* 1972.

Sebag Montefiore, S. *Prince of Princes: The Life of Potemkin.* 2000.

> Catherine II (the Great) called him her "twin soul," "darling husband," "one of the greatest, strongest and wittiest eccentrics" and her "hero" and "master" in politics.

Soloviev, S. M. *Empress Anna.* 1984.

Talbot Rice, T. *Elizabeth Empress of Russia.* 1970.

From Paul to Nicholas II 1796–1917

Almedingen, E. M. *So Dark a Stream: A Study of the Emperor Paul I of Russia, 1754–1801.* 1959.

> A very readable short biography.

————. *The Emperor Alexander II: A Study.* 1962.

> The author wrote this original biography of the "Tsar liberator" (Tsar from 1855 to 1881) with understanding and erudition, with an excellent chapter on the successes and errors of the emancipation of the serfs.

————. *The Emperor Alexander I,* 1964.

> The lucid style of the author and her account of the early influences of Alexander's grandmother, Catherine II, and of F. C. de La Harpe, the Swiss humanist tutor chosen by her, make this an excellent introduction to the reign.

Gibbes, C. S. *Tutor to the Tsarevich.* 1975.

Harcave, S., ed. *The Memoirs of Count Witte.* 1990.

Hartley, J. *Alexander I.* 1994.

de Jonge, A. *The Life and Times of Grigorii Rasputin.* 1982.

> Clearly written history of one of Russia's most extravagant yet influential figures whose religious, political, and personal life has always been surrounded by myth.

Kochan, M. *The Last Days of Imperial Russia.* 1976.

Lane, T. H. von. *Sergei Witte and the Industrialization of Russia.* 1963.

Lieven, D. *Nicholas II: Emperor of All the Russias.* 1993.

Lincoln, W. B. *Nicholas I Emperor and Autocrat of All the Russias.* 1978.

McConnell, A. *Tsar Alexander I.* 1970.

McGrew, E. R. *Paul I of Russia.* 1992.

Mosse, W. E. *Alexander II and the Modernization of Russia*. 1958.

Palmer, A. *Alexander I: Tsar of War and Peace*. 1974.

The author shows how Alexander I was caught in two conflicting worlds, his loyalties divided between Catherine II (the Great) and the Enlightenment and the militaristic régime of his father, Paul.

Presniakov, A. E. *Emperor Nicholas I of Russia: The Apogee of Autocracy, 1825–1855*. 1974.

Raeff, M. *Speransky: Statesman of Imperial Russia, 1772–1839*. 1957.

Deals with one of the most important figures of the period.

Ragsdale, H. *Tsar Paul and the Question of Madness*. 1988.

Riasanovsky, N.V. *Nicholas I and Official Nationality in Russia, 1825–1855*. 1959.

Thompson, J. M. *Count Witte and the Tsarist Government in the 1905 Revolution*. 1971.

Verner, A. M. *The Crisis of Russian Autocracy: Nicholas II and the 1905 Revolution*. 1990.

From Kerensky to Stalin 1917–1953

Alliluyeva, S. I. *Twenty Letters to a Friend*. 1967.

Applebaum, A. *Gulag: A History of the Soviet Camps*. 2003.

Explains how the Soviet Union's economy became heavily reliant on gulag prisoners' labor by the time of the World War II.

Bolt, R. *State of Revolution*, 1977. A play.

Boobbyer, P. *The Stalin Era*. 2000.

Drawing upon a great range of primary sources, this book is an account of Stalinist thought and policy, and their effects.

Bullock, A. *Hitler and Stalin: Parallel Lives*. 1991.

Deutscher, I. *The Prophet Armed*. 1954.

Deutscher, I. *The Prophet Unarmed*. 1959.

Eastman, M. *L. Trotsky, the Portrait of a Youth*. 1926.

Fitzpatrick, S. *Stalinism*. 1999.

Sheila Fitzpatrick has collected together not only the classics of the revisionist period, including Moshe Lewin, but also new work by young Russian, American and European scholars, in an attempt to reassess this contentious and deeply politicized subject.

Knight, A. *Beria Stalin's First Lieutenant*. 1993.

Lee, S. J. *Lenin and Revolutionary Russia*. 2002.

Examines the background to and the course of the Russian Revolution of 1917 and Lenin's régime. It explores all the key aspects such as the development of the Bolsheviks as a revolutionary party, the 1905 revolution, the collapse of the tsarist regime, the Russian civil war, as well as historical interpretations of Lenin's legacy in Russian history.

Lee, S. J. *Stalin and the Soviet Union.* 1999.

This book examines the Soviet leader's domestic and foreign policy, covering core topics such as his rise to power, the economy, society, culture, and the cold war.

Leggatt, G. *The Cheka: Lenin's Political Police.* 1981.

Pearson, M. *The Sealed Train.* 1975.

Based on careful research, this is the story of Lenin's journey through enemy Germany to Petrograd (St. Petersburg), and of the events before and after, with an especially vivid of the October Revolution. Glossary of political parties and institutions in Petrograd in 1917.

Radzinsky, E. *Stalin.* 1996.

Rappaport, H. *Joseph Stalin: A Biographical Companion.* 1999.

Reese, R .R. *The Soviet Military Experience.* 1999.

History of the Soviet Army, 1917–1991.

Rogovin, V. Z. *1937: Stalin's Year of Terror.* 1998.

Schapiro, L. B. *The Origin of the Communist Autocracy.* 1955.

Sebag Montefiore, S. *Stalin: The Court of the Red Tsar.* 2002.

Stalin files from the Presidium archive have been released and this, together with many interviews with children and survivors and children of Stalin's inner circle, has allowed Sebag Montefiore to write this well-rounded picture of Stalin.

Seagal, R. The Tragedy of Leon Trotsky. 1979.

Traitor, hero, or prophet? A reassessment.

Service, R. *Lenin: A Political Life,* 3 vols. 1985–1995.

Shub, D. *Lenin: A Biography.* 1966.

A single-volume biography of the founder of world Communism.

Shukman, H. *Stalin.* 1999.

Smith, E. E. *The Young Stalin.* 1968.

Trotsky, L. *The Real Situation in Russia.* 1928.

Includes Lenin's "Last Testament."

Trotsky, L. *Stalin: An Appraisal of the Man and His Influence,* edited and translated by C. Malamuth. 1941.

Ulam, A. B. *Stalin: The Man and His Era.* 1973.

Volkogonov, D. *Lenin: Life and Legacy.* 1984.

Volkogonov, D. *Stalin.* 1994.

Watson, D. *Molotov: A Biography.* 2003.

Wolfe, B. *Three Who Made a Revolution.* 1948.

From Malenkov to Chernenko 1953–1985

Beschloss, M. *The Crisis Years: Kennedy and Khrushchev.* 1991.

Breslauer, G. *Khrushchev and Brezhnev as Leaders: Building Authority in Soviet Politics.* 1982.

Burlatsky, F. *Khrushchev and the First Russian Spring,* translated by D. Skillen. 1991.

Crankshaw, E. *Khrushchev: A Biography.* 1966.

Ebon, M. *Malenkov, Stalin's Successor.* 1953.

> A short, rather sketchy biography, with English translations of some of his speeches.

Filzer, D. *The Khrushchev Era—De-Stalinisation and the Limits of Reform in the USSR, 1953–1964.* 1993.

Frankland, M. *Khrushchev.* 1966.

Hanak, H. *Soviet Foreign Policy Since the Death of Stalin.* 1972.

Institute of Marxism-Leninism. *Leonid Ilyich Brezhnev: A Short Biography.* 1977.

> An official biography, with a foreword by Brezhnev, including the new constitution of the USSR.

Johnson, P. *Khrushchev and the Arts: The Politics of Soviet Culture, 1962–1964.* 1965.

Khrushchev, N. S. *Khrushchev Remembers,* 1971.

> Reminiscences by Khrushchev, who probably never intended them to be published. The first memoir of its kind to come from any Soviet leader.

Khrushchev, N. S. *Khrushchev Remembers: The Glasnost Tapes.* 1990.

———. *Khrushchev Remembers: The Last Testament.* 1974.

> This second volume was mainly dictated since publication of the first and deals with his years in power, 1954–1964. Discusses the U-2 affair, the Cuban missile crisis, the Suez crisis, the Vietnam war, and so on. He also describes his agricultural policy, dealings with dissidents and the creation of the vast submarine fleet. He denounces the invasion of Czechoslovakia in 1968 and expresses his hope for peaceful coexistence with the West.

Khruschev, S. N. *Khrushchev on Khrushchev: An Inside Account of the Man and His Era.* 1992.

Linden, C. *Khrushchev and the Soviet Leadership: With an Epilogue on Gorbachev.* 1990.

McCauley, M. *Khrushchev and the Development of Soviet Agriculture: The Virgin Lands Programme, 1953–1964.* 1976.

McCauley, M., ed. *Khrushchev and Khrushchevism.* 1987.

McCauley, M., ed. *The Khrushchev Era 1953–1964.* 1995.

Medvedev, R., and Zh. Medvedev. *Khrushchev: The Years in Power.* 1977.

Medvedev, Z. *Andropov.* 1983.

Paloczi-Horvath, G. *Khrushchev: The Road to Power.* 1960.

Pistrak, L. *The Grand Tactician: Khrushchev's Rise to Power.* 1961.

Serov, A., ed. *Nikita Khrushchev: Life and Destiny.* 1989.

Steele, J. and E. Abraham. *Andropov in Power.* 1983.

Taubman, W. *Khrushchev: The Man and his Era.* 2003.

Tompson, W. J. *Khrushchev: A Political Life.* 1995.

From Gorbachev to Putin 1988–

Ali, T. *Revolution from Above: Where is the Soviet Union Going?* 1988.

Aron, L. *Yeltsin: A Revolutionary Life.* 2000.

Aslund, A. *Gorbachev's Struggle for Economic Reform.* 1989.

Berliner, J. S. *Soviet Industry from Stalin to Gorbachev: Essays on Management and Innovation.* 1988.

Bialer, S., ed. *Politics, Society and Nationality Inside Gorbachev's Russia.* 1989.

Bleaney, M. *Do Socialist Economies Work?* 1988.

Breslauer, G. *Gorbachev and Yeltsin as Leaders.* 2002.

Brown, A. *The Gorbachev Factor.* 1996.

> The *perestroika* era, well described.

Crouch, M. *Revolution and Evolution: Gorbachev and Soviet Politics.* 1989.

D'Agostino, A. *Soviet Succession Struggles: Kremlinology and the Russian Question from Lenin to Gorbachev.* 1988.

Davies, R. W. *Soviet History in the Gorbachev Revolution.* 1989.

> What glasnost did to Soviet history.

Gorbachev, M. S. *Memoirs* 1996.

———. *Perestroika: New Thinking for our Country and the World.* 1988.

Graham, T. E. *Russia's Decline and Uncertain Recovery.* 2002.

Gunlicks, A. B., and J. B. Treadway, eds. *The Soviet Union Under Gorbachev: Assessing the First Year.* 1988.

Hazan, B. A. *From Brezhnev to Gorbachev: Infighting in the Kremlin.* 1987.

Hill, R. J., and J. A. Dellenbrant, eds. *Gorbachev and Perestroika: Towards a New Socialism.* 1989.

Hoffman, D. E. *The Oligarchs: Wealth and Power in the New Russia.* 2003.

Hosking, G. *The Awakening of the Soviet Union.* 1990.

Jack, A. *Inside Putin's Russia.* 2004.

Kagarlitsky, B. *Dialectic of Change.* 1989.

Klebnikov, P. *Godfather of the Kremlin: Boris Berezovsky and the Looting of Russia.* 2000.

Klepikova, E. *Boris Yeltsin: A Political Biography.* 1982.

McFaul, M. *Russia's Unfinished Revolution.* 2000.

Medvedev, Z. *Gorbachev.* 1986.

Meier, A. *Black Earth: A Journey through Russia after the Fall.* 2004.

> The author laments the years lost, by President Yeltsin, to rebuild Russia.

Merridale, C., and C. Ward, eds. *The Historical Perspective: Perestroika.* 1991.

Miller, J. *Mikhail Gorbachev and the End of Soviet Power.* 1993.

Miller, R. F., J. H. Miller, and T. H. Rigby. *Gorbachev at the Helm: A New Era in Soviet Politics.* 1987.

Morrison, J. *Boris Yeltsin: From Bolshevik to Democrat.* 1991.

Niiseki, K. *The Soviet Union in Transition,* 1987.

Pravda, A. *Soviet Foreign Policy Priorities under Gorbachev.* 1988.

Reddaway, P., and D. Glinsky. *The Tragedy of Russian Reforms.* 2001.

Sakwa, R. *Gorbachev and his Reforms, 1985–1990.* 1990.

> This publication brings together in a single volume an analysis of the personalities, policies, and politics involved in the changes that took place under President Gorbachev.

Sakwa, R. *Russian Politics and Society.* 2002.

> This revised edition consolidates the reputation of *Russian Politics and Society* as the single most comprehensive standard textbook on post-Soviet Russia.

Schmidt-Haüer, C. *Gorbachev: The Path to Power.* 1986.

Shevtsova, L. *Putin's Russia.* 2003.

———. *Yeltsin: Myths and Reality.* 1999.

Sixsmith, M. *Moscow Coup: The Death of the Soviet System.* 1991.

Thom, F. *The Gorbachev Phenomenon: A History of Perestroika.* 1989.

Truscott, P. *Putin's Progress.* 2004.

Tucker, R. C. *Political Culture and Leadership in Soviet Russia: From Lenin to Gorbachev.* 1987.

Veen, H.-J. *From Brezhnev to Gorbachev: Domestic Affairs and Soviet Foreign Policy.* 1987.

White, S. *After Gorbachev.* 1993.

White, S. *Gorbachev in Power.* 1990.

Wilson, A. and N. Bachkatov. *Living with Glasnost: Youth and Society in a Changing Russia.* 1988.

Yeltsin, B. *The View from the Kremlin.* 1994.

Zemstov, I., and J. Farrar. *Gorbachev, the Man and the System.* 1989.

Nobility

Becker, S. *Nobility and Privilege in Late Imperial Russia.* 1985.

Dukes, P. *Catherine the Great and the Russian Nobility: A Study Based on the Materials of the Legislative Commission of 1767.* 1967.

>Describes the nobility up to 1767, the measure enacted by the commission, and Catherine's ambitions and achievements.

Jones, R. E. *The Emancipation of the Russian Nobility 1762–1785.* 1973.

Pipes, R. *Russia Under the Old Regime.* 1974.

Religion

Bordeaux, M. *Opium of the People.* 1965.

>Bordeaux begins with an outline of the religious history of tsarist and then of Soviet Russia. This is followed by a wide ranging survey of developments in recent years.

Bordeaux, M. *Religious Ferment in Russia.* 1968.

Bushkovitch, P. *Religion and Society in Russia: The Sixteenth and Seventeenth Centuries.* 1992.

Cracraft, J. *The Church Reform of Peter the Great.* 1971.

>The church reform of Peter I (the Great) is an event of outstanding importance in modern Russian history; indeed it contributed to the modernization of Russia.

Crummey, R. *The Old Believers and the World of Antichrist.* 1970.

Curtiss, J. S. *The Russian Church and the Soviet State 1917–1950.* 1953.

Ellis, J. *The Russian Orthodox Church: A Contemporary History.* 1986.

Freeze, G. *The Parish Clergy in Nineteenth-Century Russia.* 1983.

———. *The Russian Levites: Parish Clergy in the Eighteenth Century.* 1977.

Hackel, S. *The Orthodox Church.* 1971.

Hosking, G. A. *Church, Nation and State in Russia and Ukraine.* 1991.

Marshall, R. H. *Aspects of Religion in the Soviet Union.* 1971.

Serfdom

Bartlett, T. *Land Commune and Peasant Community in Russia.* 1990.

Blum, J. *Lord and Peasant in Russia from the Ninth to the Nineteenth Century.* 1961. Best history of serfdom and the problems of rural Russia.

Eklof, B., and S. Frank. *The World of the Russian Peasant.* 1990.

Emmons, T. *The Russian Landed Gentry and the Peasant Emancipation.* 1968. Collection of essays.

Field, D. *The End of Serfdom: Nobility and Bureaucracy in Russia, 1851–1861.* 1976.

Gill, G. *Peasants and Government in the Russian Revolution.* 1979.

Hoch, S. *Serfdom and Social Control in Russia: Petrovskoe a Village in Tambov.* 1986.

Kolchin, P. *Unfree Labor: American Slavery and Russian Serfdom.* 1987.

Koslow, J. *The Despised and the Damned: The Russian Peasant Through the Ages.* 1972.

Laird, R. D. *Collective Farming in Russia.* 1958.

Lewin, M. *Russian Peasants and Soviet Power.* 1968.

Moon, D. *Russian Peasants and Tsarist Legislation on the Eve of Reform.* 1992.

Pavlovsky, G. A. *Agricultural Russia on the Eve of the Revolution.* 1930.

Robinson, G. T. *Rural Russia under the Old Régime.* 2d ed. 1967.

Semenova-Tian-Shanskaia, O. *Life in the Russian Village.* 1993.

Shanin, T. *The Awkward Class.* 1970.

Smith, R. E. F. *The Enserfment of the Russian Peasantry.* 1968.

Volin, L. *A Century of Russian Agriculture: From Alexander II to Khrushchev.* 1970.

Vucinich, W. S. *The Peasant in Nineteenth-Century Russia.* 1968.

Worobec, C. D. *Peasant Russia: Family and Community in the Post-Emancipation Period.* 1991.

Zaionchkovsky, P. *The Abolition of Serfdom in Russia.* 1978.

Women

Engel, B. *Between the Fields and the City: Women, Work and Family in Russia, 1861–1914.* 1994.

Engel, B. *Mothers and Daughters: Woman of the Intelligentsia in Nineteenth Century Russia.* 1983.

Farnsworth, B., and I. Viola. *Russian Peasant Women.* 1992.

Glickman, R. *Russian Factory Women.* 1984.

Ransel, D. *The Family in Imperial Russia.* 1978.

Stites, R. *The Women's Liberation Movement in Russia.* 1978.

Law, Crime, and Punishment

Orlovsky, D. *The Limits of Reform: The Ministry of Internal Affairs in Imperial Russia, 1802–1881.* 1981.

Orlovsky examines the structure and personnel of this most prominent of government institutions.

Satter, D. *Darkness and Dawn: The Rise of the Russian Criminal State.* 2003.
Squire, P. *The Third Department.* 1968.
Wortman, R. *The Development of a Russian Legal Consciousness.* 1976.

Revolutions and Rebellions

Acton, E. *Rethinking the Russian Revolution.* 1990.
Alexander, J. *Autocratic Politics in a National Crisis: The Imperial Russian Government and Pugachev's Revolt 1773–1775.* 1969.
Avrich, P. *Russian Rebels 1600–1800.* 1972.
Barratt, G. *The Rebel on the Bridge: A Life of the Decembrist Baron Andrey Rozen 1800–84.* 1975.
Bradley, J. F. N. *Civil War in Russia 1917–1920.* 1975.

A scholarly attempt at a balanced interpretation, after consulting newly opened sources: the Trotsky Archive; Smolensk Archive; personal papers and diaries of the White leaders, especially of Denikin and Wrangel; the archives of the Western Allies, and so on. Separate chapters are devoted to the war in Siberia, in south Russia, and in northwestern Russia.

Bunyan, J., and H. H. Fisher. *The Bolshevik Revolution, 1917–18: Documents and Materials.* 1934.
Chamberlain, W. H. *The Russian Revolution, 1917–1921.* 1935.

The best general history of the revolution and its aftermath by an American journalist.

Hough, R. A. *The Potemkin Mutiny.* 1961.

The story of the mutiny on the battleship *Potemkin* at Odessa, which was one of the centers of the 1905 revolution.

Kochan, M. *The Last Days of Imperial Russia.* 1976.

A first chapter on the 1905 revolution is followed by the author's "attempt to depict objectively life and society during the last months of Imperial Russia's glory...," including a chapter on "The Dispossessed" (the workers), and another on "The World of Art."

Mazour, A. G. *The First Russian Revolution 1825: The Decembrist Movement, its Origins, Development, and Significance.* 1966.

First published in 1937, this remains the best account in English.

Mehlinger, H. D., and J. M. Thompson. *Count Witte and the Tsarist Government in the 1905 Revolution.* 1971.

Miller, M. A. *Kropotkin.* 1976.

Politkovskaya, A. *A Small Corner of Hell: Dispatches from Chechnya.* 2003.

Explains that a negotiated settlement of the war was not in sight in 2002 while the status quo was so lucrative.

Raeff, M. *The Decembrist Movement.* 1966.

Reed, J. *Ten Days that Shook the World.* 1926.

A classic account of the Bolshevik Revolution by an American journalist strongly sympathetic to the Bolsheviks.

Seddon, J. H. *The Petrashevsky: A Study of Russian Revolutionaries of 1848.* 1985.

Venturi, F. *Roots of Revolution.* 1960.

Expansion of Russia and Foreign Policy

Anderson, M. S. *The Eastern Question 1774–1923: A Study in International Relations.* 1966.

———. *The Great Powers and the Near East 1774–1923.* 1970.

Atkin, M. *Russia and Iran, 1780–1828.* 1980.

Baumgart, W. *The Peace of Paris 1856: Studies in War, Diplomacy, and Peacemaking.* 1981.

Curtiss, J. S. *Russia's Crimean War.* 1979.

Geyer, D. *Russian Imperialism: The Interaction of Domestic and Foreign Policy 1860–1914.* 1987.

Gillard, D. *The Struggle for Asia 1828–1914.* 1977.

Grimsted, P. K. *The Foreign Ministers of Alexander I: Political Attitudes and the Conduct of Russian Diplomacy, 1801–1825.* 1969.

Ingle, H. N. *Nesselrode and the Russian Rapprochement with Britain, 1836–1844.* 1976.

Jelavich, B. *Russia and the Formation of the Romanian National State 1821–1878.* 1984.

Kannan, G. F. *The Decline of Bismarck's European Order: Franco-Russian Relations, 1875–1890.* 1979.

Katz, Z. *Handbook of Major Soviet Nationalities.* 1975.

Kazemzadeh, F. *Russia and Britain in Persia 1864–1914.* 1967.

MacKenzie, D. *The Serbs and Russian Pan-Slavism 1875–1878.* 1967.

Morgan, G. *Anglo-Russian Rivalry in Central Asia 1810–1895.* 1981.

Mosse, W. E. *The Rise and Fall of the Crimean System 1855–71.* 1963.

Petrovich, M. B. *The Emergence of Russian Panslavism 1856–1870.* 1956.

Puryear, V. J. *England, Russia, and the Straits Question 1844–1856.* 1931.

Rich, N. *Why the Crimean War? A Cautionary Tale.* 1985.

Roberts, I. W. *Nicholas I and the Russian Intervention in Hungary.* 1991.

Rupp, G. H. *A Wavering Friendship: Russia and Austria 1876–1878.* 1976.

Saab, A. P. *The Origins of the Crimean Alliance.* 1977.

Saul, N. E. *Distant Friends: The United States and Russia, 1763–1867.* 1991.

Saul, N. E. *Russia and the Mediterranean 1797–1807.* 1970.

Schroeder, P. *Austria, Great Britain, and the Crimean War.* 1972.

Sumner, B. H. *Russia and the Balkans, 1870–1880.* 1937.

Thomson, G. S. *Catherine the Great and the Expansion of Russia.* 1947.

Wandycz, P. S. *The Lands of Partitional Poland, 1793–1910.* 1974.

Wetzel, D. *The Crimean War: A Diplomatic History.* 1980.

Wood, A. *The History of Siberia: From Russian Conquest to Revolution.* 1991.

War and Military

Chew, A. F. *The White Death: The Epic of the Soviet-Finnish War.* 1971.

Daria, O. *The Burning of Moscow 1812.* 1966.

Englund, P. *The Battle of Poltava: The Birth of the Russian Empire.* 1992.

> A vivid account of three violent days.

Josselson, M. *The Commander: A Life of Barclay de Tolly, Alexander I's Minister of War 1810–1813.* 1980.

Solzhenitsyn, A. *August 1914.* 1972.

> The story of the defeat of the Russian armies by the Germans at Tannenberg (August 26–30)—especially of General Samsonov's Second Army—regarded as a turning point of Russian history. The theme of personal responsibility is central to this book, which has been compared with Tolstoy's *War and Peace.*

Zhukov, G. K. *The Memoirs of Marshal Zhukov.* 1971.

> Memoirs of his life from his birth in Kaluga Province, joining the army in 1915, his part in the civil war, his vital role as successful commander in the war of 1941–1945, up to the defeat of Germany.

Culture and Education

Alston, P. L. *Education and the State in Tsarist Russia*. 1969.

Belmuth, D. *Censorship in Russia 1865–1905*. 1979.

Brooks, J. *When Russia Learned to Read: Literacy and Popular Literature, 1861–1917*. 1985.

Brower, D. *Training the Nihilists: Education and Radicalism in Tsarist Russia*. 1975.

Carr, E. H. *The Romantic Exiles: A 19th Century Portrait Gallery*. 1968.

> Pen portraits of Herzen and others who left Russia in the nineteenth century. Covers the period 1825–1855.

Eklof, B. *Russian Peasant Schools: Officialdom, Village Culture, and Popular Pedagogy, 1861–1914*. 1986.

Flynn, J. *The University Reform of Alexander I*. 1988.

Grant, N. *Soviet Education*. 1972.

Gray, C. *The Russian Experiment in Art, 1863–1922*. 1971.

> Examines the vitally significant Russian contribution to the modern movement in art and architecture.

Jacoby, S. *Inside Soviet Schools*. 1974.

Marker, G. *Publishing, Printing, and the Origins of Intellectual Life in Russia, 1700–1800*. 1985.

Nahirny, V. *The Russian Intelligentsia*. 1983.

Seregny, S. *Russian Teachers and Peasant Revolution: The Politics of Education in 1905*. 1989.

Sinel, A. *The Classroom and the Chancellery: State Educational Reform in Russia under Count Dmitry Tolstoy*. 1973.

Struve, G. *Russian Literature under Lenin and Stalin*. 1972.

Talbot Rice, T. *A Concise History of Russian Art*. 1963.

> An expert survey giving a complete picture of the remarkable variety and wealth of the many forms in which art has expressed itself in Russia.

Walker, G. P. M. *Soviet Book Publishing Policy*. 1978.

GENERAL CHRONOLOGY

Time of Troubles (1584–1613)

1584	Ivan IV (the Terrible) dies.
1584–1598	Rule of Tsar Fyodor I.
1587–1598	Boris Godunov acts as regent.
1589	Formation of the office of patriarch in Moscow. Metropolitan is raised to rank of patriarch.
1591	Death of Prince Dmitri at Uglich; Boris Godunov is accused of having him assassinated.
1594	Boris Godunov is named regent. Census taken of all cultivated land and registration of all peasant laborers is undertaken.
1597	Death of Fyodor I and end of Rurik dynasty (December 27).
1598	Boris Godunov is elected tsar by the *zemsky sobor*, and is crowned (February 8).
1605	Death of Boris Godunov and beginning of a period of unrest (April 1). Russia threatened with Polish and Swedish conquest. Accession of Fyodor II April 13, murdered June 10.
1605–1606	Rule of False Dmitri I.
1606–1610	Rule of Tsar Vasily Shuisky; he promises to govern with the Duma and the zemsky sobor.
1610–1612	Poles occupy Moscow.
1610–1613	Interregnum.
1610	Russians offer throne to Polish Prince Władysław. The second False Dmitri is murdered by Tatars (December 1).
1611	Formation of popular militia to the north and east of Moscow.
1611–1612	National uprising against Poles.

1611–1617	Swedes occupy Novgorod.
1612	Militia relieves Moscow and drives out Poles.

Michael (1613–1645)

1596	Michael born (July 12).
1613	The zemsky sobor elect Michael Romanov as tsar and he is crowned by Metropolitan Cyril in Moscow (February 11).
	Russian delegation is sent to Poland, but Sigismund III ignores its overtures.
	Philaret, father of the tsar is taken prisoner.
	Poland attacks Mozhaisk, Kaluga and Tula.
1614	Siege of Tula by Swedes.
1615	New zemsky sobor is elected.
	Gustavus Adolphus, king of Sweden, is defeated at Pskov. The German emperor Matthias offers to mediate the Russo-Swedish conflict.
1615–1616	The Duma and the zemsky sobor vote for an emergency tax (20 percent on property, and one hundred rubles per estate). The Stroganovs loan the state 56,000 rubles.
1617	Russia and Sweden sign the Peace of Stolbovo. The Swedes return Novgorod but keep Ingria (Ingermanland) and Livonia, as well as fortifications along the border. Free trade is established between Sweden and Russia.
1618	Philaret Romanov, father of the tsar, is freed by the Poles and is elected patriarch and shares power with his son. Under Philaret's influence, from 1622 to 1633, the role of the zemsky sobor is gradually reduced.
	Poland and Russia sign a fourteen-year truce at Deulino. Russian prisoners are released and Russia abandons Smolensk without obtaining Władysław renunciation of the Russian throne.
1619	The zemsky sobor makes an inventory of taxable land taken; peasants who had fled their land are encouraged to return; a special department is set up to deal with official abuses of power; a project to reform provincial administration, giving priority to elected assemblies, is put through and a national budget is established.

1621	The zemsky sobor issues a circular that encourages rural districts to resist the efforts of local officials to exact illegal taxes and corvées (unpaid labor).
1623	A French delegation comes to Moscow seeking an alliance against Poland and the Hapsburg Empire.
1624	Marriage of Michael to the princess Maria Vladimirovna Dolgorukaya, who dies in 1625.
1625	Michael marries Evdokia Lukianovna Streshneva, who dies in 1645.
1626	Gustavus Adolphus seeks to ally himself with Russia against Poland.
1626–1633	Military reforms are instituted: 5,000 foot soldiers, as well as cannon makers and instructors, are recruited from abroad, and arms are purchased from Holland and Germany.
1627	The powers and responsibilities of the magistrates and local tribunals are strengthened, usurping the prerogatives of the provincial governors (*voevoda*).
1628	Punishments are made more humane; a limitation is placed on the infliction of corporal punishment to recover debts.
1632	The tsar declares war on Poland following the death of Sigismund III.
1633	Philaret dies. Michael Romanov restores power to the zemsky sobor convoking it during crises.
1634	The Russians capitulate to the Poles. A permanent peace between Russia and Poland is established on the basis of the territorial status quo.
1637	The Don Cossacks seize Azov.
1645	Michael dies, and his eldest son, Alexis, succeeds him. The accession to the throne is confirmed by a vote of the zemsky sobor (July 13).

Alexis (1645–1676)

1629	Alexis born in Moscow (March 9).
1645	Boris Morozov, Alexis's former tutor, exercises a *de facto* regency.

1646	Russian delegation travels to Poland and the tsar proposes that the Dnieper Cossacks and the Don Cossacks be combined, and that Russian and Polish troops join forces to invade the Crimea.
	Gradual elimination of the boyar Duma, in favor of a Privy Council of boyars formed by the close advisers of the tsar.
	Department of Secret Affairs established. Initially a secret police and secret tribunal. Census of households is conducted. Tax rates are increased, and a tax on salt is established.
1647	Code of military law is promulgated. A Russian-Polish alliance begins military action against the Turks.
1649	The zemsky sobor publishes a new legal code (*Ulozhenie*).
1651	Khmelnitsky suffers defeat at the hands of the Poles, and he signs the Treaty of Belaia Tserkov.
1652	First confrontation between Russians and Chinese on the Amur River takes place following the expedition of Khabarov (1649–51).
1653	Alexis ceases to convoke the zemsky sobor on a regular basis. With the intercession of Patriarch Nikon, Khmelnitsky asks for the assistance of the tsar. Despite the treaty signed with Poland, the zemsky sobor accepts the idea of an intervention on the side of the Cossacks.
1656	With imperial mediation, the Treaty of Vilna is signed. Alexis will be offered the Polish throne on the death of Jan Casimir; in return, Alexis must abandon his conquests in Lithuania and Ukraine and ally himself with Poland against Sweden.
	Russia enters into its first negotiations with China.
1658	Russian troops invade Ukraine and provoke an uprising against Vygovsky.
	Three-year truce is signed by Sweden and Russia. Under its terms, Russian conquests in Livonia are guaranteed.
1661	Permanent peace is signed by Russia and Sweden.
	Alexis renounces his conquests in Livonia.
1669	After the Peace of Andrusovo (1667), the Department of Foreign Affairs (directed by Afanasi Ordyn-Nashchokin) ceases to be responsible to the Duma and becomes autonomous.

1670–1671	Uprising of Stenka Razin who together with fugitive serfs and others savage Ukraine and southern Russia.
1671	Tsar Alexis marries Natalia Naryshkina. Execution of Stenka Razin.
1672	Russians establish embassies to all major European states. Birth of Peter I (the Great) (May 30).
1674	Tsarevich Alexis dies. His younger brother Fyodor becomes the new heir to the throne.
1675	Using Jesuit intermediaries, Russia enters into new negotiations with China in Peking.
1676–1681	War with the Ottoman Empire and in the Crimea; confirming Russian possession of Ukrainian territories.

Fyodor III (1676–1682)

1661	Fyodor born (May 30).
1676	Fyodor III accedes to the throne.
	Actual power is exercised first by Artamon Matveyev (until he is exiled to Siberia in July), and then by the clan of the tsar's late mother, Maria Miloslavskya (who dies in 1669).
1678	An accord is reached between Poland and Russia, renewing the armistice of Andrusovo.
1679–1682	The penal code is revised and maiming is prohibited.
1681	Fyodor III convokes the zemsky sobor to consult with him on the reorganization of the army.
	The Peace of Bakhchisarai ends the Russo-Turkish conflict. Under its terms, all the lands between the Don and the Dniester Rivers are to remain unoccupied, and no towns are to be established in the territory between Kiev and the lower Dnieper.
1682	Fyodor III abolishes the *mestnichestvo*, the system of aristocratic precedence in the civil and military services. Death of Fyodor III (April 27).

Ivan V (1682–1696)

1666   Ivan V born.

1682   Ivan declared first tsar. Peter second tsar, and Sophia regent. Both Ivan and Peter crowned (June 25).

1696   Ivan dies (January 29).

Sophia (1682–1689)

1657   Sophia born (September 17).

1682   Becomes regent to Ivan and Peter (May 29).

1686   Concludes "The Eternal Peace" with Poland.

1689   Agrees to the Treaty of Nerchinsk with China. Sophia overthrown as regent by supporters of Peter I (the Great) and exiled.

1698   Sophia forced to take the veil under the name of Susanna following unsuccessful attempt to restore her as regent (October).

1704   Sophia dies (July 14).

Peter I (the Great) (1682–1725)

1672   Peter I (the Great) born (May 30).

1682   After *streltsy* attack on the Kremlin, Ivan V and Peter I are established as co-tsars at a double coronation.

            Beginning of the regency of Sophia with Prince Vasily Golitsyn as foreign minister. Execution of Archpriest Avvakum.

1682–1689   Sophia regent, with Peter I (the Great) as co-ruler and then as tsar.

1684   Institution of formal persecution of Old Believers.

1686   Russia enters the Holy League with the Holy Roman Emperor, Venice, and Poland.

1687   Slavo-Greek-Latin Academy in Moscow begins to function.

            Unsuccessful campaign against the Crimean Tatars.

1688   Peter I (the Great) marries Evdokia Lopukhina. Unsuccessful campaign against the Crimean Tatars.

1689   Sophia's regency overthrown, with Ivan's consent.

1690	Peter I (the Great) creates the first regiments of Preobrazhensky and Semenosky Guards.
1693	Peter I (the Great) visits Archangel and founds a shipyard.
1694	Natalia Naryshkina, the regent, dies.
1695–1697	Russia's conquest of Kamchatka.
1696	Death of Ivan V.
	Peter I (the Great) becomes sole tsar.
	Capture of Azov, after an unsuccessful attack in the previous year.
	Building of a naval squadron begins there.
1697–1698	"Great Embassy" to Western Europe.
	Peter I (the Great) visits the Netherlands, England, and Austria. He lives near a shipbuilding works at Zaandam where he works as an ordinary laborer. In London (1698) he meets William III and visits the Observatory and the Mint.
1698	Streltsy revolt breaks out and is savagely suppressed. Peter returns to Moscow. More than 200 are condemned to death. Sophia, the ex-regent, is sent into exile to the Cloister of the Intercession in Suzdal.
	A permanent army is established.
	Peter I (the Great) orders the shaving of beards and the wearing of Western clothes. François Lefort, adviser to Peter I (the Great) dies.
1700	Peace is made with the Ottoman Empire. Outbreak of war with Sweden (Great Northern War) and Russian defeat at Narva. Patriarch Adrian dies but no successor is appointed and he is replaced by acting head of church.
	Julian calendar adopted.
1701	Foundation of navigation school at Moscow.
	Monasteries required to turn over revenues to state.
1703	St. Petersburg is founded.
	Vedmosti, Russia's first newspaper, published in Moscow.
1704	Sophia, the ex-regent, dies and is buried in the Novodevichy Convent (July 14).
	Reform of alphabet.

1705	The first systematic conscription for the armed forces in Europe is established.
	Beard tax introduced.
1705–1708	Outbreak of uprisings in Astrakhan, Bashkiria and the Don region against the tsar's policies.
1707	Great advance of Charles XII against Russia begins.
	Outbreak of Cossack rising in the Don area until 1708.
1708	Local administration by the creation of eight (later ten) *gubernii* (administrative provinces) and their subdivisions.
	The Swedes are defeated at the battle of Lesnaya but are joined by Mazepa.
1709	Decisive Russian victory over Sweden at Poltava, forcing Charles XII to take refuge in Turkey.
1710	Russians take Livonia and Estonia.
	Edict issued making official a simplified Cyrillic alphabet. Old Slavonic alphabet is retained only by the Church.
	Census of population.
1711	Outbreak of war with the Ottoman Empire and Russian defeat on the Prut, and loses the former Ottoman fortress of Azov (regained in 1739). Peter I (the Great) abolishes most trading monopolies and establishes monetary reform. Tsar's Council (Boyar Duma) replaced by the Senate to supervise the administration.
1712	St. Petersburg replaces Moscow as capital of Russia.
1713	Peace treaty with the Ottoman Empire.
1714	Decree forbids subdivision of estates among the heirs when the holder dies.
	Kormaleniya (method of payment in kind paid by local population to administraiton, established in the fourteenth century) abolished and civil servants placed on a salary.
1715	Royal Naval Academy established at St. Petersburg.
1716	Flight of the Tsarevich Alexis to Vienna and Naples.
	Russian occupation of Mecklenburg provokes the hostility of Britain and Emperor Charles VI.
	Ustav voinsky (Military Code) issued.

1716–1717	The second journey to Western Europe by Peter I (the Great). He visits the Netherlands and Paris.
	Alexis returns to Russia.
1718	Death of Alexis (June 18).
	Creation of the administrative colleges.
	Unsuccessful peace negotiations with Sweden in the Åland islands begin.
	Beginning of first "soul" census.
	Colleges replace *prekazy* (Moscow government departments).
1719	Abolition of most state monopolies, excepting salt.
	Ladoga canal construction begins (completed 1731).
1720	*Morskoy ustav* (Naval Code) and *Generalny reglament* (General Regulation) issued; increasing efforts being made to systematize the machinery of government.
1721	War with Sweden is ended by the treaty of Nystad.
	Dukhovny reglament (Spiritual Regulation) issued and the patriarchate abolished, replaced with Holy Synod.
	Merchants allowed to purchase villages in order to attach laboring force to industrial and mining enterprises.
	Senate proclaims Peter I (the Great), emperor.
	Peter I (the Great) acquires the right to nominate his own successor and assumes title of "Emperor of all the Russias."
1721–1723	Russo-Persian war.
1722	Table of Ranks promulgated (January 13).
1724	Catherine, the second wife of Peter I (the Great), married privately in 1707, is crowned as empress.
	Poll (Soul) tax introduced.
	First comprehensive protective tariff.
	Establishment of the Academy of Sciences in St. Petersburg, later known as the Imperial Academy of Science.
1725	Death of Peter I (the Great) without having designated a successor (January 28).

Catherine I (1725–1727)

1683   Catherine I born (April 5).

1725   Accession to the throne (January 28).

             Succession supported by Imperial Guards and most ministers.

             Vitus Bering's first expedition.

1726   Seven-member Supreme Privy Council, presided over by the empress, established.

1727   Death of Catherine and accession of Peter II, grandson of Peter I (the Great) and son of Tsarevich Alexis (May 6).

Peter II (1727–1730)

1715   Peter II born (October 12).

1727   Accession to the throne (May 6).

             Government by Supreme Privy Council during tsar's minority.

             Council dominated by Prince Aleksandr Menshikov.

1730   Death of Peter II from smallpox (January 19).

Anna (1730–1740)

1693   Anna born (January 28).

1730   Anna elected to the throne by the Supreme Privy Council.

             Unsuccessful attempt by Supreme Privy Council to impose conditions on Anna.

             Supreme Privy Council abolished and Senate restored (April 28).

             Inheritance law of 1714 repealed.

1731   Establishment of Noble Cadet Corps and reestablishment of secret police, abolished by Peter I (the Great).

1733–1735 War of Polish Succession.

1735–1743 Bering's second expedition. He dies in Alaska.

1735   War with Turkey; Azov regained.

1736	Compulsory state service by nobles limited to twenty-five years and may begin at age twenty, but one son of each family may remain home to manage estates.
	Professional serfs attached in perpetuity to factories and mines.
1737	Serfs denied right to buy land.
ca. 1740	Imperial Ballet School established at the Winter Palace.
1740	Death of Empress Anna (October 17).

Ivan VI (1740–1741)

1740	Ivan VI born (August 12).
	Ivan VI succeeds as nominal emperor.
1741	Ivan VI and his family deposed and imprisoned (November 25).
1764	Ivan VI stabbed to death by his jailers (July 5).

Elizabeth (1741–1761)

1709	Elizabeth born (December 18).
1741	Accession to the throne.
1741–1743	War with Sweden.
1742	Elizabeth issues manifesto designating her nephew, the duke of Holstein, as her successor.
1743	Treaty of Åbo gives Russia a portion of Finland.
1744	Death penalty abolished.
1745	Marriage of Peter, duke of Holstein, nephew of Empress Elizabeth and heir to Russian throne, to Princess Sophie Augusta (later Catherine) von Anhalt-Zerbst.
1747–1782	Winter Palace, Smolny Convent and Peterhof Palace built by Rastrelli.
1749	First Russian oilfield discovered.
1753	Internal tariffs and tolls in Russian Empire abolished, and establishment of State Nobility Bank.

1754	University of Moscow founded and establishment of Commercial Bank in St. Petersburg.
1756	First permanent theater opens in Russia.
	Academy of Fine Arts opens in St. Petersburg.
1756–1762	Russia involved in Seven Years' War.
1761	Death of Empress Elizabeth (December 25 OS–January 5, 1762 NS).

Peter III (1728–1762)

1728	Peter III born.
1761	Peter III becomes tsar (January 5, 1762).
	"Manifesto of *Dvoryanstvo* Liberty" exempting the nobility (*dvoryanye*) from compulsory state service, allowing them to travel freely and to enter the service of foreign states.
	Secret police abolished and torture banned.
	Church and monastic properties sequestered; law effective in 1764.
1762	Peter III abdicates (June 29).
	Peter III murdered in mysterious circumstances (July 6).

Catherine II (the Great) (1762–1796)

1729	Catherine born in Stettin (*now* Szczecin), Poland (May 2).
1745	Marries Peter Feodorovich, heir to the Russian throne (August 21).
1762	Catherine, wife of Peter III, gains throne by coup d'état (June 28).
	Peter III abdicates (June 29).
	Peter III murdered in mysterious circumstances (July 6).
	Senate ratifies coup d'état (August).
	Catherine II (the Great) crowned in Moscow (September 13).
1763	Senate divided into six departments, each with a procurator general in charge.
1764	Automatic promotion for certain categories of civil servants.

Ivan VI murdered.

Church lands managed by the Economic College.

Most commercial and manufacturing monopolies abolished.

Abolition of office of Hetman in Ukraine.

First Hermitage is begun in St. Petersburg.

Election of Stanislaw Poniatowski, former lover of Catherine II (the Great), as king of Poland, following Poland's occupation by Russian troops.

Russo-Prussian alliance and secret convention on Poland.

Regulation on the education of children is issued and the establishment of a school for young noble girls (the future Smolny Institute).

Diderot, the French encyclopedist, sells his library to Catherine II (the Great). She allows him to use it and also gives him a yearly pension of £1,000.

1765	Landowners allowed to punish serfs by sending them to penal servitude in Siberia.
	Free Economic Society founded in St. Petersburg.
1766	Annexation of the Aleutian Islands.
1767	Automatic promotion rules for civil servants extended.
	Legislative Commission established to draft new code of laws. It met until December 1768 but failed to complete the work. It consisted of 564 deputies: 30 percent nobles, 39 percent city dwellers, 14 percent state peasants, 12 percent national minorities, 5 percent state administration. One deputy was an ecclesiastic and serfs were not represented.
1768	War with Turkey.
1769	Advisory Council to Catherine II (the Great) formed.
	Russia's first satirical journals, *Vsyakaya vsyachina* and *Truten*, published.
1772	First partition of Poland.
1773	Institute of Mines created.
1773–1775	Peasant and Cossack uprising under Yemelyan Pugachev. He declares himself Peter III and promises to liberate the serfs.
1774	Peace with Turkey concluded at Kuchuk-Kainardji.

1775	Provincial reform, increasing the number of provinces and making local government responsible to the Senate.
	Manufacturing activity open to all.
1781–1786	Ukraine and the Crimea incorporated into the empire.
1782	Pugachev executed in Moscow.
	The equestrian statue of Peter I (the Great) by Falconet is unveiled.
1782–1785	Hermitage built by Quarenghi.
1783	The nobility, dvoryanye, allowed to operate private printing presses.
	Count Grigory Orlov dies, Catherine II's lover who helped to put her on the throne.
1783–1784	Taurida Palace built by Starov.
1785	Charter of the Nobility (Dvoryanstvo) expands aristocratic privilege by confirming nobles in hereditary tenure of estates and freedom from compulsory state service and sets up local and regional corporations of nobles which choose officials subject to crown approval.
	Charter to the Towns, which divides urban population into six groups, each of which elects representatives to town assembly; actual business of urban government carried out by executive board of six, one from each group, but police powers left to officials appointed by crown.
1787–1791	War with the Ottoman Empire.
1788	War with Sweden, until 1790.
1790	Publication of Radishchev's *Journey from St. Petersburg to Moscow*, a violent critique of autocracy and serfdom. He was arrested and condemned to death but sent into exile in Siberia.
	Treaty of Verala with Sweden.
1791	Catherine II (the Great) decrees Pale of Settlement, twenty-five western provinces where Jews are permitted permanent residence.
1792	Russia and Turkey sign Treaty of Jassy.
1793	Second partition of Poland by Russia and Prussia.
1794	Catherine II (the Great) declares her intention to prevent Grand Duke Paul from succeeding to the throne.

| 1795 | Third partition of Poland by Russia, Prussia and Austria. |
| 1796 | Catherine II (the Great) dies (November 6). |

Paul (1796–1801)

1754	Paul born (September 20).
1796	Accession to the throne (November 6).
	All people detained by the Secret Chancellery freed and a general amnesty declared for all officials facing prosecution.
	Treasury Ministry established.
	Article 15 of the Charter of 1785 is abolished. This exempts the nobility from corporal punishment.
	Forces sent to Persia by Catherine II (the Great) recalled.
1797	All unauthorized printing presses closed.
	Coronation of Tsar Paul.
	Decree issued on freedom of religion.
	Law on succession to the throne according to genealogical seniority.
1798	Russia joins second coalition against France.
	Importing of French books prohibited.
1799	Department of Appanages established, endowed with sufficient lands to provide for the needs of the imperial family.
	Russian-American Company chartered.
	Campaign in northern Italy and Switzerland under Suvorov.
1800	Ministry of Commerce established.
	Importing of all foreign books prohibited.
	Paul forms alliance with Napoleon against England.
1801	Tsar Paul strangled (March 12).
	Georgia annexed by Russia.

Alexander I (1801–1825)

1777	Alexander I born (December 12).
1801	Alexander I ascends throne (March 12).
	Reform measures announced. Political prisoners are released and an amnesty declared. Foreign books again freely imported. Charter of Nobility reaffirmed.

Secret (or Unofficial) Committee meets.

A twelve-member permanent council established to study and prepare laws.

Georgia is annexed to Russia (September).

1802   Senate becomes the supreme institution of administration and justice.

Eight ministries established: War, Navy, Foreign Affairs, Justice, Interior, Finance, Education, and Commerce.

1803   Education is reorganized and Russia is divided into six educational districts.

1804   Kharkov and Kazan Universities founded.

Statute on Jews.

Mild censorship law introduced.

Report shows the superiority of paid over forced labor.

Jews guaranteed freedom of religion as long as they reside in the Pale of Settlement.

1805   Russia joins the third coalition against France.

1806   War with Turkey following Russia's occupation of the Danubian principalities.

Reconstruction of the Admiralty and the construction of the Institute of Mines and the Smolny Institute begin.

1807   Treaty of Tilsit with Napoleon Bonaparte (June 25).

Russia joins the Continental System.

Serfdom abolished in the Grand Duchy of Warsaw.

1807–1811   Speransky reforms.

1808   Plan to codify laws.

Sale of serfs at markets and fairs is forbidden.

1809   Abortive attempt to introduce civil service examinations.

Abolition of owners' rights to deport serfs to Siberia.

Conquest of Finland (September).

1810   State Council established to replace Permanent Council (1801) following the completion of Plan for State Reform (1809), which aimed at a move toward constitutional monarchy.

1811   Ninth ministry (of Police) created.

Completion of the Marinsky and Tikhivin Canal Systems, connecting the Baltic to the Volga.

1812   French invade Russia (June 12).

Smolensk lost (August 6).

Russians defeated at the Battle of Borodino (August 26).

French enter Moscow (September 2).

Grand Army retreat begins (October 7).

1813   Grand Alliance against France.

1814   Paris taken and Alexander enters at the head of his troops (March 18–19).

1815   Congress of Vienna. Russia gains the Grand Duchy of Warsaw (May 28).

Formation of kingdom of Poland under Russian control.

Its constitutional charter provides for an elected Diet (or *Sejm*, a legislative assembly), a government, and an army.

First steamship in Russia constructed in St. Petersburg.

Peasant unrest in Poltava, Kursk, and Orenburg.

Holy Alliance and Quadruple Alliance formed.

1816   Establishment of Union of Salvation, first secret organization of the future Decembrists.

Serfdom abolished in the Baltic provinces.

1817   State monopoly on alcohol.

1819   Ministry of Police combined with Ministry of Interior.

University of St. Petersburg founded.

1820   Jesuits expelled from Russia.

Peasant uprising in the Don region.

1821   Union of Salvation dissolved and replaced by the Southern Society in Ukraine and the Northern Society in St. Petersburg.

Patriotic Society founded in Warsaw.

1822   Right to deport serfs to Siberia reinstated.

1825   Death of Alexander I at Taganrog, and he is buried in the Cathedral of the St. Peter and St. Paul Fortress in St. Petersburg.

Decembrist revolt.

Pushkin's *Boris Godunov.*

Moscow Telegraph and *Northern Bee* founded.

Nicholas I (1825–1855)

1796	Nicholas I born (June 25).
1825	Accession to the throne (December 14).
	Grand Duke Constantine, considered by most to be the heir presumptive, swears allegiance to Nicholas I.
1826	Execution of five Decembrist conspirators and over 100 deportations to Siberia.
	Second Section established with the task of codification of laws.
	Third Section established, secret police, which had been abolished by Alexander I.
	Censorship Code introduced.
1826–1828	War with Persia.
	Treaty of Turkmanchai and annexation of Armenia.
1827	State monopoly on alcohol abolished.
	To encourage religious conversion, Nicholas I orders that Jews serve in army for 25 years.
1828	Fourth Section responsible for women's education and public assistance established.
1828–1829	War with Turkey.
	Treaty of Adrianople.
1830	Forty-five volume *Complete Collection of Laws of the Russian Empire* published.
	Cholera riots.
	Literary Gazette founded.
1830–1831	Suppression of Polish revolt.
	Polish constitution abrogated.
1832	Polish constitution replaced by organic law and Poland integrated into Russian Empire.
1832–1833	Treaty of Unkiar-Skelessi.
1833	Fifteen-volume *Code of Laws* published.

It is made illegal to sell serfs without land at auction and also illegal to separate families.

Münchengratz agreement.

1834   Aleksandr Herzen banished to Vyatka.

University of Kiev founded.

1835   Reform of university statutes reduces autonomy of universities.

1836   Fifth Section responsible for administration of state peasants established.

Paul A. Chaaday declared insane by Nicholas I for critique of Russian backwardness in his "First Philosophical Letter" published in *Telescope*.

First performance of Gogol's *Government Inspector* and Glinka's *A Life for the Tsar*.

1837   Pushkin killed in a duel.

Ministry of State Domains established, replacing Fifth Section.

First passenger railway–from St. Petersburg to Tsarkoe Selo.

1840   Bakunin leaves Russia for Germany.

1841   Lermontov killed in a duel.

Auction of serfs forbidden.

1842   Construction started on Moscow–St. Petersburg Railway (completed in 1851).

Gogol's *Dead Souls* appears.

1843   Sixth Section responsible for the administration of the Caucasus.

1845   Hereditary dvoryanstvo restricted to top five ranks.

Revised version of Criminal Code.

Petrashevsky Circle meets in St. Petersburg.

Russian Geographic Society founded.

1846   Dostoyevsky publishes *Poor Folk* and *The Double*.

Aleksandr Herzen's *Who is to blame?* is published.

1847   Turgenev publishes *A Sportsman's Sketches*.

Aleksandr Herzen leaves Russia.

1848   Revolution in France, Austria, Italy, and Germany.

Publication of Karl Marx's *Communist Manifesto*.

1849	Nicholas I intervenes to help Austria put down Hungarian revolt.
	Petrashevsky Circle members arrested.
	Dostoyevsky and others sentenced to death but reprieved on scaffold and then deported to forced labor in Siberia.
1851	Opening of Moscow-St. Petersburg Railway.
1852	Leo Tolstoy publishes *Childhood*.
	Death of Gogol.
1853–1856	Crimean War.
1855	Death of Nicholas I (February 18).

Alexander II (1855–1881)

1818	Alexander II born (April 29).
1855	Alexander II ascends the throne (February 19).
1856	Treaty of Paris ends Crimean War.
	Hereditary nobility (dvoryanstvo) restricted to top four of the Table of Ranks.
	Alexander II advocates abolition of serfdom and appoints Select Committee. "Better to begin to abolish serfdom from above than to wait until it begins to abolish itself from below."
1857	Aleksandr Herzen founds *Kolokol* (*The Bell*) in London.
	Introduction of protective tariffs.
1858–1860	Russian penetration in northeast Asia.
	Acquisition of Amur and Maritime provinces from China under terms of the Treaty of Aigun.
1858	Peasants working on the domains of the Imperial family are emancipated.
1859	Conquest of Caucasus complete except for Circassia (1864).
1860	Treaty of Peking.
	Foundation of city of Vladivostok.
	Rural courts introduced.
	State bank established.
1860–1873	First railway boom.

1861	Emancipation of serfs.
	Zemlia i Volia (Land and Freedom), a revolutionary secret society, is established in St. Petersburg.
	Army ceases to be used as punishment for criminals.
	Turgenev publishes *Fathers and Sons*.
	St. Petersburg Conservatory of Music founded.
	Reestablishment of local government in Polish provinces.
1863	Polish rebellion.
1863–1864	Reforms of law, education, and local government (*zemstva*).
1864	Legal reform.
	Introduction of zemstva and city self-government.
1864–1868	Conquest of Central Asia.
1864–1880	Russia conquers Turkestan.
1865	Odessa University founded.
	Censorship relaxed.
1866	Prussia defeats Austria at Königgrätz.
	Attempt on Tsar Alexander II's life by D. V. Karakozov.
	Moscow Conservatory founded.
	Dostoyevsky's *Crime and Punishment* published.
1867	Sale of Alaska and the Aleutian Islands to United States.
1868	Tolstoy's *War and Peace* finished (begun 1863).
1870	Lenin born in Simbirsk (April 22).
	Formation of the Russian section of the First International.
	Compulsory military service introduced.
	Municipal dumas reorganized.
	First major strike in Russian history at the Neva Cotton-spinning Mill, St. Petersburg.
	Repudiation of Black Sea claims of the 1856 Treaty of Paris.
1871–1872	Education changes brought about by Dmitri Tolstoy, minister of education, strengthens teaching of classical languages.
1871	London Convention on the Straits.
	Bakunin's *Dieu et l'état*.
1872	Translation of Karl Marx's *Das Kapital* published in Russia.

1873	Three Emperors' League.
	Attempt on Alexander II's life.
1873–1874	First "Going to the People" movement.
	"Land and Liberty" secret society founded.
1874	Compulsory military service introduced.
1876	*Swan Lake* ballet by Tchaikovsky.
	Translation of Bible into modern Russian.
1877–1878	Russo-Turkish war ends with the Treaty of San Stefano.
	Mass trials of radicals, populists, and revolutionaries (50 tried in March 1877 and 193 in January 1878).
1878	Bismarck presides over the Congress of Berlin.
	Vera Zasulich shoots St. Petersburg police chief but is acquitted by the jury.
	Terrorist assassinates chief of gendarmes (August).
	Temporary laws introducing courts-martial for terrorists.
	Secret circular authorizing arrest and exile of persons suspected of seditious intent.
	Northern Union of Russian Workers formed in St. Petersburg.
	Mass strikes in St. Petersburg.
1878–1881	Development of terrorist activity.
	Dynamiting of Winter Palace; wrecking of imperial trains.
1879	Electric lighting installed in St. Petersburg.
	"Land and Freedom" split into "People's Will" and "Black Partition."
	Stalin born.
	Two attempts on life of Alexander II.
	"Temporary Governors General" created.
	Tchaikovsky's *Eugene Onegin*.
1880	Assassination attempt on life of Alexander II.
	Third Section abolishes former duties undertaken by Interior Ministry.
1881	Alexander II assassinated in St. Petersburg by the National Freedom Group on the day he agrees to discuss political change.

Alexander III (1881–1894)

1845	Alexander III born (February 26).
1881	Accession to the throne (March 1).
	Establishment of the Okhrana, Department for Safeguarding Public Security and Public Order.
	Institution of Emergency Powers, the tsar reaffirms his commitment to autocracy.
	Ascendancy of Konstantin Pobedonostsev.
	Major edict concerning "Temporary Laws," that is, rule of martial law.
	Pogroms against Jews occur in Elizavetgrad, Kiev and Odessa.
1882	*Communist Manifesto* by Marx and Engels is translated into Russian.
	Peasant Bank founded.
	Reduction of peasant redemption payments.
	Factory inspections established.
1883	Transcaucasus Railway from Baku to Batum completed.
1884	*The Annals of the Fatherland* is suppressed.
	Holy Synod is given control over all primary schools.
	Universities lose their autonomy.
1885	Anglo-Russian crisis over Afghanistan.
	Land Bank for the nobility founded.
	New edition of Criminal Code.
	Night work banned for women and children in textile mills.
1885–1887	Bulgarian crisis.
1886	Law requiring state peasants to buy out their land allotment.
	Abolition of soul tax (except in Siberia).
	Special rules governing forced labor.
1887	Poll tax abolished, the last remnant of serfdom (January).
	"Reinsurance Treaty" between Russia and Germany.
	Execution of Lenin's brother, and four others, for participating in attempt on the life of Alexander III.

1888	University of Tomsk opens.
1889	Restrictions on internal migrations are enacted.
1891	Construction of Trans-Siberian Railway begins (completed in 1904).
	Secret Franco-Russian military convention against the Triple Alliance concluded.
	Many Jews evicted from Moscow and lose rights gained under Alexander II.
1891–1893	Severe famine in twenty-one provinces of European Russia.
1892	Count Sergei de Witte (1849–1915) appointed Minister of Finance and Commerce. He revolutionizes industry, commerce, and transport.
1894	Death of Alexander III at Livadia in the Crimea (October 20).

Nicholas II (1894–1917)

1868	Nicholas II born (May 6).
1894	Accession to the throne (October 29).
1895	Lenin founds the Union of Struggle for the Liberation of the Working Class in St. Petersburg (November).
	Majority of members of the union are arrested, including Lenin and Martov. Lenin's sentence was fifteen months in prison and exile to Siberia for three years (December).
	Nicholas II condemns the "insane dreams" of elected assemblies.
1896	Expansion into Manchuria.
	Construction of the Chinese Eastern Railway is agreed, which will provide direct connection between Chita and Vladivostok through Manchuria. Russia has an eighty-year lease.
	Several thousands of people die in a stampede among crowds attending the coronation festivities of Nicholas II in Moscow.
	Tsar makes official visit to France.
1897	Foundation of Moscow Art Theater.

First census in Russia; total population 129,000,000 of which 13 percent is urban.

1898   Port Arthur leased by China.

Foundation of Marxist Russian Social-Democratic Labor Party. Manifesto drafted by Pyotr Struve. Sergei Diaghilev publishes first edition of *Mir Isskustva* (The World of Art); continues until 1904.

1899   Student demonstrations and strikes occur at universities throughout the empire.

Hague Convention.

1900   The newspaper *Iskra* (Spark) published in Leipzig and sold clandestinely in Russia.

Lenin leaves Russia to live abroad.

Russian is made the official language of Finland.

1901   Leo Tolstoy excommunicated from the Orthodox Church.

1902   Trans-Siberian Railway opens. Journey from Moscow to Vladivostok takes fourteen days.

Foundation of Socialist Revolutionary Party.

Lenin's *What is to be done?* is published.

1903   The Social-Democratic Labor Party, meeting at its second congress in Brussels and later in London, splits into Bolshevik (led by Lenin) and Menshevik (led by Martov) wings; the Bund withdraws, having been refused autonomy within the party.

General strike in Baku; disturbances throughout Russia together with strikes.

1904–1905   Russo-Japanese war.

1904   Tsarevich Alexis is born (August).

Assassination of Vyacheslav Plehve, minister of interior, who had carried on a systematic policy of repression.

Zemstvo Conference demands a constitution and wider range of liberal reforms. An imperial ukase promises limited reforms.

Dogger Bank incident.

1905   Surrender of Port Arthur (January).

Bloody Sunday (January).

Battle of Mukden (February–March).

Destruction of Russian fleet at Tsushima by Japanese (May).

Mutiny on the battleship *Potemkin* (June).

Draft law on the establishment of a Consultative State Duma published (August).

Treaty of Portsmouth, New Hampshire, ends Russo-Japanese conflict. Russia cedes to Japan Port Arthur, the southern portion of the Manchurian railway, and the southern half of Sakhalin Island (September).

Assassination of Grand Duke Sergei.

Abortive revolution and general strike.

Establishment of Soviets of Workers' Deputies.

Tsar issues manifesto promising a constitution and an elected parliament with genuine legislative power. The tsar also grants freedom of the press, free speech, and religious toleration (October).

The Constitutional Democratic party (Kadets) is formed (October).

Redemption payments are abolished for former serfs.

1906 Tsar issues Fundamental Law of the Empire by which the tsar retains most of his autocratic power.

Legislative power is to be divided between the Duma and the upper house, half the members of which are to be appointed by the tsar. When the Duma is not in session the government may legislate by decree (May).

First Duma assembles; votes on confidence in the government (May).

Pyotr Stolypin becomes prime minister.

Deadlock over the constitutional issue leads to the dissolution of the Duma (July).

New legislation enabling peasants to consolidate holdings and leave communes (November).

1907 The Second Duma meets; also known as the "Red Duma" and "Duma of Extremes" (March).

The Third Duma meets; also known as "The Duma of the Lords."

Hague Convention.

Lenin emigrates and will not return to Russia for ten years.

1909	Women's access to universities is restricted and Jews are restricted by quotas.
	State Council refuses to let Old Believers form congregations.
1910	Death of Leo Tolstoy.
1911	Assassination of Pyotr Stolypin by a double agent.
1912	Massacre of 270 mine workers in Lena goldfields after brutal repression.
	First issue of *Pravda* (Truth), the Bolshevik daily newspaper. Vyacheslav Molotov heads the editorial board and Joseph Stalin is also a member (May).
	Term of Third Duma ends (June).
	Elections to the Fourth Duma (November).
1914	General strike in St, Petersburg (August).
	Germany declares war on Russia (August).
	Russia defeated at Battle of Tannenberg (August).
	St. Petersburg renamed Petrograd (August).
	Russians force Austrians from Galicia (September).
	Russia suffers severe losses at Battle of the Masurian Lakes (September).
	Sale of alcohol forbidden for the duration of the war.
1915	Austro-German offensive in Galicia defeats Russians (May).
	Further Austro-German offensive leads by the autumn to over a million Russian casualties (July).
	Duma meets to consider the way the war is being conducted (August).
	Six parties in the Duma form the Progressive Bloc and demand a responsible ministry (August).
	Tsar assumes supreme command of the armed forces (September).
	Tsar rejects offer of resignation by his ministers to make way for a more popular administration (September).
	Tsar prorogues Duma (September).
	The number of strikes increases throughout the year.
1916	Duma meets (February).

Goremykin replaced as prime minister by Stürmer (February).

There are over three million refugees in Russia because of military retreats (May).

Brusilov offensive gains some territory but fails to achieve decisive victory and costs over a million casualties (June–October).

Strikes and sporadic mutinies of soldiers at the front (September–October).

Rasputin murdered (December).

1917 Duma meets (February).

About 80,000 workers go on strike in Petrograd and there is a demonstration to commemorate the event of Bloody Sunday (February).

Tsar leaves Petrograd for army General Headquarters (March).

Izvestiya calls on people to take power (February 28).

Large-scale demonstrations in Petrograd (March).

Queues at bakers' shops and crowds continue to demonstrate against the régime (March).

Police fire on crowds (March).

Strikes break out and soldiers join with the people; the tsar orders suppression of the trouble (March).

Police fire at demonstrators, but more soldiers join the protesters (March).

Tsar prorogues Duma (March).

Formation of Committee of State Duma to replace tsarist government (March).

"Army Order No. 1" (*prikaz*) issued by Petrograd Soviet puts armed forces under its authority and urges rank and file to elect representatives to the soviet (March 1).

Tsar Nicholas II, in Pskov, abdicates for himself and for his son, in favor of his brother, Grand Duke Michael, at the same time confirming the new ministry and asking the country to support it. Grand Duke Michael chooses not to accept the throne unless he is asked by the Assembly (March 2).

The Provisional Government forbids the use of force against rioting peasants (March).

Constituent Assembly meets; abdication of Grand Duke Michael (March).

Crown properties transferred to state (March).

Lenin arrives back in Petrograd in the "Sealed Train" (April 7).

"April Theses" published in *Pravda* having been read by Lenin on April 17.

Kornilov resigns command of forces in Petrograd, and Milyukov and Guchkov resign from the government (May).

Kerensky helps to reorganize provisional government (May).

Start of renewed offensive on southern front (June).

Soldiers at front refuse to obey orders.

Kornilov insists on offensive being called off and is appointed commander-in-chief (June).

Start of northern offensive backed by Kerensky.

Germans and Austrians drive Russians back after early successes (July).

Provisional government restores capital punishment and courts martial (July).

Bolsheviks organize demonstrations by sailors and Red Guards but the unrest is put down by loyal troops—the "July Days."

Fearing arrest, Lenin flees to Finland (July).

Lvov and Kadet ministers resign (July).

Kerensky (1917)

Formation of new government with Kerensky as prime minister (July 9).

Kornilov appointed commander-in-chief (August).

Kerensky resigns. Party leaders give him a free hand to form new government (August).

Kerensky holds Moscow State Conference to settle differences with Kornilov but fails to reach agreement (August).

Riga falls to Germans (September).

Troops begin to move against Petrograd, and Kerensky denounces Kornilov "plot" against the government. Collapse of movement followed by arrest of Kornilov and fellow generals (September).

Kerensky proclaims a republic (September).

Bolshevik majority in Moscow soviet (September).

Trotsky becomes chairman of Petrograd soviet (October).

Lenin secretly returns to Petrograd from Finland (October).

Decision by Bolshevik Central Committee to organize an armed rising (October).

Formation of Military Revolutionary Committee by Bolsheviks (October).

Parliament refuses to give Kerensky powers to suppress the Bolsheviks (November).

Bolsheviks organize headquarters in St. Peter and St. Paul Fortress and move on strategic points. Lenin takes command (November).

Bolsheviks seize power in Petrograd, taking key installations and services; the "October Revolution" (November).

The Winter Palace cut off and ministers of provisional government arrested.

Lenin (1917–1922)

1917

Kerensky flees. Lenin announces the transfer of power to the Military Revolutionary Committee and the victory of the socialist revolution (November).

Lenin makes the Decree on Peace, an appeal for a just peace without annexations and indemnities, and the Decree on Land, affirming that all land is the property of the people (November).

Bolshevik government is formed (November).

Counter-offensive by Kerensky against Petrograd fails (November).

Bolsheviks establish power in Moscow (November).

Metropolitan Tikhon elected patriarch in Moscow (November).

Left-wing social revolutionaries enter government after agreement with Bolsheviks (December).

Escape of Kornilov and fellow generals from prison in Bykhov (December).

Bolsheviks occupy Supreme Headquarters at Mogilev (December).

Finland declares itself independent from Russia (December).

Russia and Germany agree to a ceasefire and start negotiations for a peace treaty in Brest-Litovsk (December 22).

Establishment of the *Cheka* (the All-Russian Extraordinary Commission for the Struggle against Counterrevolution, Sabotage and Speculation) headed by Felix Dzerzhinsky (December).

Banks are nationalized (December).

1918   Opening of Constituent Assembly (January).

Constituent Assembly dispersed (January).

Introduction of the Gregorian calendar (February 1–14). (All dates are now given in the "new style," in common with the rest of the Western world.)

Central Council of Ukraine concludes separate peace with Central Powers, having declared its independence (February).

Brest-Litovsk negotiations broken off after German ultimatum (February).

Treaty of Brest-Litovsk between Russia and the Central Powers (the German and Austrian Empires) is signed. Russia cedes Poland and territory on the Baltic, and allows independence for Finland and Ukraine. There are supplements to the treaty signed with Bulgaria, Romania, and Turkey. Russia surrenders to Turkey: Kars, Ardahan, and Batum. The treaty is later invalidated after the 1918 Allied victory (March 3).

German troops continue to advance into central Russia and the Crimea (March).

Soviet government moves the capital from Petrograd to Moscow (March).

Allied ships and troops arrive in Murmansk (April).

Execution of imperial family at Ekaterinberg (July 17).

Anton Ivanovich Denikin (1872–1947) advances towards the Volga River and besieges Tsaritsyn, where Stalin is sent as the party's representative. Denikin successfully withstands the siege (August 6–7).

British forces land at Baku, ostensibly to defend the area against the Turks, but also to protect the oilfields (August 14).

Japanese, with British and Americans, land at Vladivostok; some 20,000 troops involved (August 14).

Denikin occupies the Black Sea port of Novorossiisk, where the imperial fleet has already been scuttled (August 26).

Trotsky's Red Army recaptures Kazan (September 10).

Soviet government, following the armistice between Germany and the Allies, denounces the Brest-Litovsk Treaty (November).

1919   The Red Army takes Riga in Latvia, where Baltic Germans have been in power, and Kharkov in Ukraine (January 3).

An agreement is alleged to have been signed between the Bolsheviks and the German communist Karl Liebknecht to assist with "Russian Gold," the establishment of a German Soviet Republic. Karl Radek is in Berlin with the hope of raising the German revolutionaries and is arrested. During this month German soldiers murder Liebknecht and Rosa Luxemburg after an attempted rising in Berlin (January 5).

The "Russian Political Conference" is held in Paris, consisting of senior imperial Russians abroad at the time, including ambassadors. Prince Lvov is designated chairman. It is hoped that this body will coordinate the governments in Russia: Southern (Denikin), Siberian (Kolchak), and Northern (Chaikovsky). Unity is never achieved nor is recognition of the conference by the Western Allies achieved.

Communist International holds first congress in Moscow. The Comintern is formed in expectation of the revolution spreading throughout the world (2–7 March).

The withdrawal of Allied troops from Russia is decided (March 21).

The People's Commissariat for Internal Affairs (NKVD) officially institutes labor camps run by the Cheka (April 15).

Beginning of the Russo-Polish War. The Poles destroy Bolshevik rule in Lithuania (April 24).

Mensheviks and the Socialist Revolutionaries are expelled from the Central Executive Committee of the Soviets. The Mensheviks (who are the Russian Social Democratic Labor party) have maintained their ideals and gained popular strength but have no political power, newspapers nor armed force. They continue to gain seats on soviets throughout the country and to hold, individually, senior posts, especially in trade unions until 1921 (June 14).

Allied troops evacuate Archangel (September 19).

Kharkov taken by Red Army (December 12).

Kiev taken by Red Army and a reorganized Bolshevik régime takes power in Ukraine (December 16).

An armistice is signed in Estonia with the Bolshevik government (December 31).

1920 The soviets gain control of most of eastern Siberia (January-February).

Kolchak resigns as "supreme ruler" of all Russia, abdicating in favor of Denikin, and appoints Semenov commander of the White forces in the Far East (January 4).

Wrangel takes over from Denikin and starts reorganizing the civil administration in the Crimea (April 4).

Poles take Kiev (May 6).

Kiev retaken by Red Army (June 12).

Russo-Polish peace treaty (October 12).

Finland and Russia sign a peace treaty at Tartu. While the Arctic port of Petsamo is given to Finland, along with the Karelian Isthmus as a boundary, part of Karelia is included as an autonomous republic in the Russian Soviet Federated

Socialist Republic (RSFSR). Finnish fortifications are also to be demolished (October 14).

Baron Pyotr Wrangel (1878–1928) is expelled from Crimea, ending Russian counterrevolution (November 16).

The Ukrainian Soviet Socialist Republic signs a Treaty of Alliance with the Soviet Union (December 20).

1921   The last appearance of the anarchists in Russia as their survivors are released from prison for the day of Prince Kropotkin's funeral (February 13).

Gosplan, the State Planning Commission, is established (February 22).

The sailors of the battleship *Petropavlovsk* at Kronstadt call for free elections of new soviets, freedom of speech, the liberation of all socialist political prisoners, equal rations for all, and full rights for land-holding peasants and small industrialists who are not employers (February 28).

Kalinin, the nominal head of state, goes to Kronstadt to appeal to the sailors, and to warn them. The outcome is a mass meeting that elects a non-Bolshevik revolutionary committee. There are 16,000 sailors, soldiers, and workers in revolt. They send delegates to Petrograd (March 1).

A trade agreement is signed with Great Britain, having been negotiated since May 1920. This marks a change in the Soviet state's status, for it is de facto recognition by a major international power. Other states follow to share any advantage of the new trade area (March 16).

Pravda reports that 25 million people in Russia are starving (June 26).

1922   Eleventh Party Congress. It defines the limits of the New Economic Policy (NEP), the state retaining control of large-scale industry, national transport, and foreign trade, about which Lenin later showed great optimism (March–April).

Arrest of Patriarch Tikhon and the dissolution of the Orthodox Church Holy Synod (April 3).

Lenin suffers a stroke, losing his power of speech. Stalin becomes the principal link between Lenin and the Politburo (May 26).

The Treaty of Rapallo is signed by the Soviet Union and Germany, mutually renouncing reparations for war damage and establishing diplomatic and economic relations (November 12).

Lenin has further strokes, but he continues working and dictates his *Letter to Congress*, also known as his *Testament*, with the often-quoted adverse comment on Stalin, his praise of Trotsky, and the ambiguous remarks on Zinoviev and Kamenev (December 13–23).

The Union of Soviet Socialist Republics (USSR) is formed by the federation of the republics of Russia, Ukraine, Belorussia, Transcaucasia, Khorezm, Bokhara, and the Far Eastern Republic (December 30).

1923   Lenin dictates a codicil to his *Letter*, warning of Stalin's ambition and proposing his removal from the general secretary post (January 4).

Lenin's third stroke. It renders him permanently without speech (March 9).

Stalin (1923–1953)

1924   Death of Lenin. The three who had been leading the party during his illness (Stalin, Zinoviev, and Kamenev) block Trotsky's gaining a majority in the Politburo (January 21).

USSR recognized by Great Britain as "the *de jure* rulers of those territories of the Old Russian Empire" (February 1).

The "Zinoviev letter" published in Britain. It purported to be a secret directive from the Comintern to the British Communist party and was confirmed as such by British intelligence. There are anxious reactions arising from a fear and misunderstanding of international Bolshevism. The letter leads to the crushing of Britain's socialist Labor party at the next election and years of mistrust of the USSR (October 24).

1927   Trotsky is expelled from the Politburo (January 17).

Trotsky and Zinoviev expelled from the Central Committee (October).

1928   Collectivization starts (January 27).

1929	Trotsky is expelled from the USSR and is exiled to Turkey (January).
1930	Unemployment is stated not to exist any more in the USSR (October).
1932	Writers' Union Organizing Committee starts, with the new creed of "socialist realism" (May). Abolished during the revolution, internal passports are reintroduced in the Soviet Union (December 27).
1933	The Communist party orders a purge of its members, mainly to weed out undesirables who have joined since 1929. A new central Purge Commission is formed. By the end of 1933 one-third of the party (1,149,000) have been examined, of whom one in six is expelled. This purge is similar in its methods to earlier party purges (January).
	Metro-Vickers trials: the accused are Russian technical experts and five British engineers who are charged with being agents of foreign capitalism (April).
	The United States of America and USSR establish diplomatic relations (November).
1934	The "Law on the Betrayal of the Motherland" is issued, making the death penalty obligatory for those found guilty and making members of a family collectively responsible for violations of the law (June 8).
	USSR is admitted to the League of Nations (September 18).
	Sergei Mironovich Kirov is murdered in Leningrad by Nikolayev. Arrests are made of suspects and supposed accomplices accused of being Zinoviev supporters. This begins a new terror (December 1).
1935	The coal miner Alexei Stakhanov is reputed to have hewed 102 tons of coal in a day, overfulfilling his quota by 1,400 percent. The Stakhanovite program is announced, urging workers to achieve such over-production and be rewarded with honor and money (August 31).
1936	New Soviet constitution is adopted (December 5).
1937	Eight Russian army chiefs are executed.
	During the following months, Stalin executes most of the Soviet army's top leadership and 35,000 of 80,000 other officers (June 11).

1939	Germany attacks Poland (September 1).
	France and Britain issue ultimatums, which expire and bring these nations to war with Germany (September 3).
	Russian troops cross the Polish eastern border (September 17).
	Boundary and friendship treaty with Germany, including secret protocols on the resettlement of Ukrainians and Belorussians, signed by Stalin and Ribbentrop (September 28).
	After declaring that Finland was threatening it, the Soviet Union bombs Helsinki and invades Finland (November 30).
	The USSR is expelled from the League of Nations without any nation voting in its support (December 14).
1940	The Red Army launches an attack on the Finnish "Mannerheim Line" (January 15).
	Finland stops fighting against the Soviet Union (March 12).
	Over 4,000 Polish officers are shot by the NKVD (*Narody Komitet Vnutrennih Del*—People's Commissariat of Internal Affairs) in Katyn Forest, near Smolensk. The discovery is made in 1943 and blamed on the Germans. Later examination proves the contrary (March–May).
	Newly elected governments in Estonia, Latvia and Lithuania, supposedly with over 99 percent support, are formed and all ask to be incorporated into the USSR (July 21).
	Trotsky is assassinated in Mexico (August 20).
	Hitler issues the orders for "Barbarossa," the invasion of Russia (December 18).
1941	"Barbarossa," the German invasion plan, is put into operation (June 22).
	At 3.30 a.m. Minsk military district tells Zhukov that Ukrainian towns are being bombed and the Baltic military district reports raids on Lithuania. Zhukov reaches Stalin's office and is ordered to assemble the Politburo (June 22).
	The British prime minister Winston Churchill sends a personal message to Stalin, offering assistance (July 7).
	A military pact is signed in Moscow between Britain and the Soviet Union (July 12).

The German offensive on Moscow begins (September 30).

German tanks are at Moscow's second defense line, sixty miles (95 km) from the city (October 18).

A state of siege is declared in Moscow (October 19).

1942   Churchill meets Stalin in Moscow and discusses the war, particularly the possibility of an Anglo-American second front being opened in Europe (August 12–16).

1943   The siege of Leningrad is lifted south of Lake Ladoga after more than a year's isolation (January 12).

Roosevelt and Churchill hold a conference at Casablanca in North Africa, to which Stalin is invited but does not go, given the pressure of the war and his belief that all his allies should do is to attack in the west. The outline plans produced at Casablanca mean that the USSR will continue to bear the brunt of the fighting until the next year, 1944 (January 12).

The German von Paulus is promoted to field marshal, but despite this encouragement, he surrenders at Stalingrad with 91,000 soldiers and 24 generals—16,700 had already surrendered and 70,000 had died (January 31).

The largest tank battle in the history of warfare takes place in and around Kursk where, on July 10, the German offensive is halted by Rokossovsky's artillery and effective antitank weapons, with the demoralizing use of antitank rockets from aircraft. More than 6,000 tanks on each side were engaged in the battle (July 5–August 23).

Orthodox ecclesiastical administration and church seminaries are allowed to be reestablished. Metropolitan Sergius is elected patriarch and is officially received by Stalin (September 8).

Allied conference at Teheran, without China on Stalin's insistence. Stalin demands a second front by the Anglo-Americans in 1944 and tells Roosevelt and Churchill that Russia will join the war against Japan, but only after the defeat of Germany. Postwar Europe is discussed. The Soviet Union demands and gets the promise that its borders will be at least those of June 1941 and that part of East Prussia will be included. Poland will not have any part of Ukraine or Belorussia. The Soviet Union claims those parts of

Poland east of the "Curzon Line" and Poland is allowed to move its borders westward to the Oder River. It is agreed that Finland will maintain its national identity. On the question of the Far East, Stalin requires an ice-free port and Dairen is suggested with Soviet use of the Manchurian railway (November 28–December 1).

Roosevelt proposes to Stalin a postwar international organization of about forty nations with the United States and the Soviet Union, Britain, China, and a few other nations serving as an executive committee. This is the beginning of the idea of the United Nations (November 28–December 1).

1944 Leningrad is relieved after 870 days of siege (January 27).

Churchill and Eden, the British foreign secretary, in Moscow. With Harriman, the U.S. ambassador, they ask Stalin how long it will be before the Soviet Union declares war on Japan (October 9).

1945 The heads of the Allied governments, the Great Powers, including Stalin, Roosevelt, and Churchill meet at Yalta in the Crimea. Stalin agrees to end the Russo-Japanese Neutrality Pact of 1941 and declare war on Japan two or three months after Germany's surrender, provided "The Mongolian People's Republic is maintained; the 1904 gains by Japan against Tsarist Russia are returned, including Sakhalin, Dairen to be internationalized; the Soviet Union to have a naval base at Port Arthur and the railways to be brought back to Sino-Russian control, the Kurile Islands to be given to the Soviet Union" (February 4–11).

As Soviet troops reach the center of Berlin, Hitler kills himself in his bunker headquarters (April 30).

Unconditional surrender is signed by the Germans with the Anglo-Americans (May 7).

The Potsdam Conference is attended by Stalin, Truman, the U.S. president, and Churchill (whose place is taken by Attlee after the British elections) (July 17–August 2).

The first atomic bomb is dropped on Japan at Hiroshima. The Soviet Union is not consulted (August 6).

Soviet Union declares war against Japan (August 8).

The Japanese surrender ceremony is held on the U.S. battleship *Missouri* with the Soviet general K. N. Derevyanko present (September 2).

1946   Churchill's "Iron Curtain" speech at Fulton, Missouri (March 5).

Stalin tells the U.S. ambassador that he demands a base in the Turkish Dardanelles (March 5).

1947   Aid is offered to all Europe under the "Marshall Plan" of the U.S. secretary of state; Stalin refuses it. The Czechoslovak coalition government (with its Communist premier Gottwald) decides to accept it (June).

Currency reform is announced in the USSR, rendering all existing banknotes useless but exchangeable, ten for one new ruble in cash, with varying exchanges for amounts held, legally, in banks. The aim is to wipe out the profits of wartime speculators (December 16).

1948   Travel restrictions are imposed by Russians between their zone and the Allied zones of West Germany (April).

The Soviets refuse further collaboration with the Berlin four-power control council (June).

Berlin blockade: Berlin, lying within the Soviet occupation zone of Germany and divided into four sectors, each controlled by one of the Allies, is seen as an obstruction to Soviet control of their zone. They try to isolate the city by land, closing the roads and railways from the western zones, which means that food and fuel supplies are cut off. The Western Allies respond with a massive airlift of fuel, food, and other supplies. The blockade and the airlift last nearly a year (June).

1949   Comecon set up in Moscow (January 25).

The Berlin blockade lifted (May 12).

1950   The death penalty is reinstated for espionage, treason, and sabotage (January 12).

Tass, the Russian news agency, announces the testing of the first Soviet atomic bomb (September 25).

1952   Soviet Union sends a diplomatic note to the United States, proposing a peace treaty with Germany, with all Germany becoming a neutral area. The United States does not accept this (March 10).

1953   The "Doctors' Plot": nine Kremlin doctors, seven of whom are Jewish, are arrested, accused of espionage for a U.S. Jewish organization and of murdering party leaders, including Zhdanov. Confessions are obtained (although two of the doctors die during the investigation) (January 13).

Malenkov (1953)

Joseph Stalin dies (March 5).

A conference of Politburo members and the Council of Ministers is held. Malenkov takes over his posts as its chairman, or premier, and party secretary; Beria retains control of the security services and Bulganin takes over the armed forces. A week later Khrushchev is moved from the party secretaryship for Moscow and appointed to the party secretariat (March 5).

Khrushchev (1953–1964)

The arrest of the doctors is condemned in the press as having been irregular and unlawful. *Pravda* attacks MGB (Ministerstvo Gosudarstvennoi Bezopasnoski—Ministry of State Security 1946–1953) men who had caused dissension among "people of different nationalities." This is the end of the anti-Semitic campaign of Stalin's last years (April).

Khrushchev is elected first secretary of the Communist Party Central Committee (September 12).

Execution of Beria and other leading MVD (*Ministerstvo Vnutrennykki Del*—Ministry of External Affairs) officers announced publicly (December 23).

1954   At a Four Powers conference in Berlin of Britain, France, the United States, and the USSR, Molotov proposes a peace treaty with Germany with both states, East and West, signing as equals (thus ensuring the recognition of two Germanys). The conference ends without a decision (January 25–February 18).

In contrast to Malenkov's consumerism, Khrushchev proposes to the Presidium to improve the economy through the Virgin Lands campaign, using fallow land for increased grain production (January 22).

The first nuclear power station is put in operation at Obninsk, near Moscow (June 27).

1955 Malenkov is dismissed as premier on charges of mismanagement of industry and agriculture; replaced by Bulganin (February 8).

The Warsaw Pact, a military alliance between the USSR, Bulgaria, Czechoslovakia, East Germany, Hungary, Poland, and Romania, is signed. It is a response to the inclusion of West Germany in the North Atlantic Treaty Organization (May 14).

1956 Twentieth Party Congress. The most important session excludes the press and features Khrushchev's speech attacking Stalin and the "Cult of Personality" and revealing for the first time details of the purges (February 14–25).

Riots in Budapest, the capital of Hungary, against the Communist régime (October 23).

Khrushchev sends in Russian tank forces to crush the Hungarian revolt. Imre Nagy (1895–1958) the Hungarian prime minister is later shot, in 1958, without an open trial. He is publicly rehabilitated in 1989 (November 4).

1957 The USSR launches *Sputnik I*, the world's first artificial satellite. This causes considerable consternation in the West; the first American satellite is not launched until 1958 (October 4).

Boris Pasternak's novel *Dr. Zhivago* is published abroad, first in Italy, having been rejected by Soviet publishing houses (October 4).

1958 Khrushchev is appointed chairman of the Council of Ministers (March 26).

The Pasternak affair: he is awarded the Nobel Prize for Literature for his novel *Dr. Zhivago*; in the Soviet Union he is attacked by the Writers' Union and the Komsomol (October 23).

1959 Russian rocket *Lunik II* lands on the moon (September).

Formal charter establishing the Council for Mutual Economic Assistance (COMECON) is ratified.

The Chinese express anger at the Russian failure to support them in their claim for Indian territory (September).

Khrushchev visits the United States, staying with President Eisenhower. He holds a press conference, visits farms in Iowa, and steel works in Pittsburgh (September).

1960   The American U2 reconnaissance aircraft piloted by Gary Powers is shot down near Sverdlovsk (May 1).

1961   The Berlin Wall is erected, cutting off West Berlin (August 13).

The Soviet Union resumes nuclear testing (August 13).

Albania breaks off relations with Russia (August 13).

Stalin's body is removed from the Lenin Mausoleum in Red Square. All cities and other places named after Stalin are changed (October 30).

1962   The Cuban missile crisis. Soviet guided anti-aircraft missiles are sent to Cuba, but U.S. President Kennedy warns that he will not tolerate any such weapons in Cuba (September).

Kennedy orders a blockade of Cuba and puts the U.S. forces on alert. Soviet troops are equally placed on alert. Soviet ships are halted outside the blockaded area. After messages between the two leaders, the weapons are returned to Russia.

1963   Brezhnev becomes secretary of the Central Committee (June).

1964   While Khrushchev is on holiday at the Black Sea, meetings of the Politburo, Presidium and Central Committee agree to dismiss him. He is retired quietly with a pension (October 13–14).

Brezhnev (1964–1982)

Khrushchev is replaced by Brezhnev as first secretary and Kosygin as chairman (premier) of the Council of Ministers (October 13–14).

1966	Twenty-third Party Congress. The Politburo is reintroduced, replacing the Central Committee Presidium and bringing in younger men (March–April).
1968	The Soviet Union and Warsaw Pact allies invade Czechoslovakia. Alexander Dubcek (1921–1992), first secretary of the Czechoslovakian Communist party, and the Central Committee are replaced with hardliners led by Gustav Husák (August 21).
1969	The first space station is put into orbit by the USSR (January 16).
1972	Visit of U.S. President Nixon, signing the first SALT anti-ballistic missile treaty, interim agreement on offensive missiles (May 22).
1974	Solzhenitsyn expelled from USSR after publication of *The Gulag Archipelago* (February 13).
	Nixon's second visit to the USSR; agreements on nuclear arms control signed (July).
1975	The Nobel Peace Prize is awarded to the Soviet scientist Sakharov (December).
1977	Brezhnev made chairman of the Presidium of the Supreme Soviet, nominal head of state (June 16).
1979	SALT II (the Soviet-American Treaty on the Limitation of Strategic Arms) is signed by Brezhnev and U.S. President Carter in Vienna (July 18).
	USSR invades Afghanistan. By 1988 Soviet casualties will be 13,000 dead and 35,000 wounded (December 24).
1980	Kosygin resigns, and dies shortly afterward (October–December).

Andropov (1982–1984)

1982	The death of Leonid Brezhnev (November 10).
	Andropov is elected General Secretary of the Central Committee of the CPSU (Communist Party of the Soviet Union) (November 12).
1983	A South Korean airliner, having strayed off course, is shot down by Soviet fighters, killing 269 people (September 1).

Chernenko (1984–1985)

1984   Yuri Andropov dies (February 9).

Konstantin Chernenko is elected secretary general and president of the Presidium (February 13).

1985   Chernenko dies (March 10).

Gorbachev (1985–1991)

Mikhail Gorbachev is elected general secretary of the Central Committee of the Communist party (April).

Gromyko is elected chairman of the Presidium of the Supreme Soviet, head of state (July 2).

The Soviet Union announces a unilateral moratorium on all nuclear explosions (August 6).

1986   Twenty-seventh Party Congress. Mikhail Gorbachev stresses the need for radical change after the stagnation of the Brezhnev years. He calls for a restructuring (*perestroika*) of Soviet society. The party adopts his line and follows his call for a greater openness (*glasnost*) in public dealings (February 24–April 6).

Chernobyl: the atomic power station explodes (April 26).

The remaining Chernobyl atomic reactor is buried under a security mound of metal and concrete (October 2).

1988   The withdrawal of Soviet troops from Afghanistan begins (April 15).

The 1,000th anniversary of Christianity in Russia celebrated (June 5–17).

1989   Vaclav Havel, the Czech dissident playwright, is sentenced to nine months imprisonment for subversion. The sentence is later reduced and he is released in May (February 21).

Soviet security forces suppress pro-independence demonstrations in Tbilisi, capital of Georgia (April 9).

Gorbachev is elected chairman of the Supreme Soviet of the USSR (May 25).

The Berlin Wall opens and thousands flock through (November 9).

Summit meeting between U.S. President George Bush and Gorbachev is held off Malta (December 2–3).

Alexander Dubček becomes Chairman of the Federal Assembly and Vaclav Havel, of Civic Forum, is elected president of Czechoslovakia (December 28).

1990   Central Committee of the Communist party ends the one-party monopoly in the Soviet Union.

The Georgian parliament declares its sovereignty (March 9).

Mikhail Gorbachev is sworn in as first (and last) president of the Soviet Union (March 15).

Gorbachev orders a show of military strength in Lithuania (March 22).

Estonian Communist party votes for independence from the Soviet Union (March 25).

Soviet troops occupy Communist government buildings in Lithuania (30 March).

The Soviet Union starts a blockade of all imports of fuel and power to Lithuania (April 19).

Latvia declares independence from the Soviet Union (May 4).

At the annual May Day parade Gorbachev and the Politburo are booed off the rostrum by demonstrators (May 5).

Estonia declares independence from the Soviet Union (May 8).

Boris Yeltsin is elected president of the Russian Soviet Federal Socialist Republic and declares Russian law has priority over Soviet Union law (May 29).

Presidents Bush and Gorbachev agree to reduce the number of long-range nuclear missiles and to destroy half of their chemical weapons (May 31–June 3).

The Warsaw Pact decides to become a mainly political body. Hungary declares it wishes to leave the pact (June 8).

The Central Committee announces over 130,000 resignations from the Communist party in the previous six months (June 13).

The Russian republic declares itself a sovereign state
(June 20).

Boris Yeltsin offers Lithuania a treaty of cooperation with
Russia (July 8).

Miners strike in the Donbas and Kuzbass, calling for the
government's resignation and the removal of the party from
industry, the army, education, and all other bodies (July 11).

Gorbachev is reelected as general secretary by a two-thirds
majority. He rejects conservative suggestions of slowing
down perestroika (July 11).

Boris Yeltsin resigns from the Soviet Communist party
(July 12).

The Ukrainian parliament declares sovereignty, claiming the
right to its own armed forces, banking system, its own foreign policy, and the primacy of its laws (July 16).

West German Chancellor Helmut Kohl and President
Gorbachev agree on terms for German reunification with
safeguards for Soviet security interests. It is agreed that East
Germany shall be included in NATO (July 16).

President Gorbachev is awarded the Nobel Peace Prize
(October 15).

1991   The Soviet Union sends troops into two insurgent Baltic
republics. Soldiers fire on crowd in Vilnius, Lithuania, killing
15 (January 7–13).

Between 100,000 and 300,000 people demonstrate in
Moscow against the Baltic crackdown (January 20).

Lithuanians vote to secede from the Soviet Union
(February 9).

President Boris Yeltsin, the Russian leader, calls on President
Gorbachev to resign (February 19).

Estonians and Latvians vote to break away from the Soviet
Union (March 3).

Georgia becomes the fifth Soviet republic to secede (April 9).

Taking 60 percent of the vote, Yeltsin becomes the first
democratically elected president of Russia (June 12).

Last Soviet troops leave Hungary and Czechoslovakia
(June 19–21).

Soviet officials' attempt to overthrow President Gorbachev fails, weakening central government. The failed coup results in the suppression of the Communist party and the collapse of the Soviet Union.

Ukraine declares independence from the Soviet Union (August 24).

Leaders of three former Soviet republics, Russia, Ukraine, and Belarus, agree to form the Commonwealth of Independent States.

Yeltsin (1991–1999)

Gorbachev resigns as president of the Soviet Union (December 25).

Soviet Union officially ceases to exist (December 31).

1992 Cold war relegated to history–Presidents Bush and Yeltsin sign statement of general principles (February 1).

The International Monetary Fund (IMF) approves Russia's plan for reform (March 31).

Russia's thirteen-member Constitutional Court backs Boris Yeltsin's ban of official Soviet and Russian Communist parties in 1991 (November 30).

1993 United States and Russia sign START II arms treaty (January 3).

Last 6,000 Russian troops leave Poland.

Russian military forces have been stationed there since the end of World War II (August 7).

Russian troops leave Lithuania (August 31).

Russian President Boris Yeltsin announces presidential elections for June 1994 (September 23).

Russians narrowly approve Yeltsin's proposed draft constitution (December 12).

1994 U.S. President Bill Clinton, Russian President Boris Yeltsin, and Ukraine President Leonid Kravchuk sign a treaty under which Ukraine agrees to give up its nuclear arsenal (January 14).

Russian troops leave Estonia and Latvia (August 31).

Russian military forces invade the Republic of Chechnya, which had declared itself independent in 1991 (December 11).

1995 Russian parliament urges President Boris Yeltsin to seek a political settlement in Chechnya (January 13).

Agreement is reached by Ukraine and Russia on the future of the Black Sea fleet (June 9).

Negotiated truce ends the fighting in Chechnya. Its status in the Russian republic to be determined later (July 30).

In Russian elections, Communists record parliamentary gains, taking 22 percent of the vote and 157 of 450 seats in the Duma; they had held only 45 seats (December 17).

1996 Boris Yeltsin wins a runoff election with 54 percent of the vote to retain the presidency of Russia (July 3).

Greek co-owners of *Pravda* suspend publication when the owner is denied access to *Pravda* offices (July 24).

1997 The U.S. space shuttle *Atlantis*, with a crew of six, docks with the Russian space station *Mir*, which has a crew of two (January 14).

A Communist attempt in parliament to oust Russian President Boris Yeltsin fails (January 22).

The Russian republic of Chechnya holds presidential and parliamentary elections; Aslan Maskhadov is elected president (January 27).

U.S. President Bill Clinton and Russian President Boris Yeltsin, meeting in Helsinki in a two-day summit, reach an agreement regarding NATO's expansion into Eastern Europe (March 21).

Leaders of NATO nations and President Yeltsin of Russia, meeting in Paris, sign the Founding Act on Mutual Relations, Cooperation, and Security, an agreement that establishes a new basis for the relationship between the former adversaries (May 27).

The Russian Duma approves a bill that severely limits the activities of religious groups that have not practiced in the country for at least fifty years (June 23).

Russian President Boris Yeltsin signs a decree reducing the Russian armed forces by nearly one-third, to 1.2 million (July 16).

Russian and Chinese leaders sign an agreement regulating the 4,300-kilometer (2,580-mi) border between the two countries (November 10).

1998 Russian Duma confirms Sergei Kiriyenko as Russian prime minister (April).

Russian Duma confirms Yevgeny Primakov as Russian prime minister (September 11).

Latvia votes to ease regulations for ethnic Russians to acquire Latvian citizenship; the existing laws are criticized as unduly harsh (October 3).

Russia admits that it cannot pay its foreign debts and plans to renegotiate its international loans (November 4).

Russia fails to pay $362 million due on a loan from a group of commercial banks (December 29).

1999 Prime Minister Yevgeny Primakov is dismissed by President Yeltsin who appoints Sergey Stepashin in his place (May 12).

Stepashin is dismissed as prime minister. Vladimir Putin is appointed prime minister (August 9).

President Yeltsin announces his retirement. Vladimir Putin is appointed acting president of Russia (December 31).

Putin (1999–)

2000 Russia issues a new national security strategy, replacing one adopted in 1997; the document criticizes the United States and Western Europe for expansionism and it allows for the use of nuclear weapons in war if other methods of resolution have been exhausted (January 14).

Acting Russian President Vladimir Putin announces that Russian troops have taken Grozny, the capital of the secessionist republic of Chechnya. The Chechen insurgents retreat to the mountainous southern regions of the republic (February 6).

Vladimir Putin is elected president of Russia with about 53 percent of the vote; having served as acting president since 1999 (March 26).

The Russian Federation Council, the upper house of Russia's parliament, votes to ratify the START-II treaty; the Duma (lower house) had approved the treaty, which called on Russia to halve its strategic arsenal, on April 14.

Vladimir Putin is sworn in as President of Russia (May 7).

At Katyn, Russia, a memorial is dedicated to the 4,000 Polish officers who were massacred there by Soviet secret police in 1940 (July 28).

The Russian nuclear submarine *Kursk* sinks in the Barents Sea; rescuers reach it on August 21 to find the vessel flooded and all 118 crew members dead (August 12).

In the course of a four-day meeting in Moscow, the Jubilee Bishops' Council of the Russian Orthodox Church votes to canonize Tsar Nicholas II, the last of the Romanov dynasty to have ruled Russia, and his family (August 14).

The Russian parliament votes to restore the old Soviet national anthem with new lyrics (December 8).

The Chernobyl nuclear power station is officially closed (December 15).

2001   The Russian space station *Mir*, after 5,511 days in space and 86,330 orbits of Earth, splashes down in the South Pacific Ocean (March 23).

Russian President Putin and Chinese President Jiang Zemin sign a mutual friendship treaty, the first between the two countries in more than fifty years (July 16).

A special train arrives in Vladivostok, Russia, from Moscow as part of a celebration of the centenary of the 9,267-kilometer (5,728-mi)-long Trans-Siberian Railroad (July 18).

President Putin promises to channel arms supplies and military equipment to the Northern Alliance, the Taliban's opposition in Afghanistan (September 24).

Russia praises a UN Security Council resolution to combat terrorism (September 29).

President Putin and European Union leaders pledge "joint action" in the fight against terrorism at a summit in Brussels (October 3).

A Russian court closes the last major independent television station in Russia, TV-6 (November 26).

2002   The Roman Catholic Church creates four new dioceses within Russia (February 11).

NATO proposes to Russia the creation of a NATO-Russia Council to serve as a parallel organization to NATO's North Atlantic Council; this was officially agreed in May (February 14).

Presidents Putin and Bush sign an arms control treaty agreeing to reduce their respective strategic nuclear warheads by two-thirds over the next ten years (May).

The United States formally withdraws from the Anti-Ballistic Missile Treaty, signed in 1972 by U.S. President Richard M. Nixon and Soviet leader Leonid Brezhnev; the following day Russia announces that it is abandoning the 1993 START-II accord (June 13).

Belarus rejects the plan put forward by Russian President Putin for a union of Belarus and Russia in which Belarus would essentially be absorbed by Russia (August 14).

President Putin and Azerbaijani President Heydar Aliyev sign an agreement establishing the two countries' borders in the Caspian Sea and thus divide energy resources in the sea (September 23).

A siege of a theater in Moscow, in which 750 people were held hostage by Chechen rebels for three days, ends when Russian troops storm the building. An anesthetic gas, used to combat the rebels, also kills at least 127 hostages (October 26).

Russia and Iran agree to speed up completion of a nuclear power plant; this is opposed by the United States fearing that Iran will use the plant to develop nuclear weapons (December 25).

2003   Over 50 people killed in a suicide bombing of a Cheechen government building in the north of the republic (May 12)

Yukos oil company chief and millionaire, Mikhail Khodorkovsky, is arrested and detained in connection with investigations into fraud and tax evasion. Khodorkovsky gave his support to the liberal opposition to President Putin (October 25)

Elections for the State Duma (450 seats) resulted in United Russia winning 222 seats with 37.6 percent of the votes and the Communist Party of the Russian Federation winning 51 seats with 12.6 percent of the vote. Presidnet Putin, who endorses the United Russia, gained almost total control of the Duma. Turnout was 55.8 percent (December 7)

2004   Vladimir Putin reelected President of the Russian Federation for a four-year term, obtaining 71.2 percent of the vote (March 14)

INDEX